The Sibling Relationship

The Sibling Relationship

A Force for Growth and Conflict

Joyce Edward, M.S.S.A., BCD

JASON ARONSON
Lanham • Boulder • New York • Toronto • Plymouth, UK

Published by Jason Aronson
An imprint of Rowman & Littlefield Publishers, Inc.
A wholly owned subsidary of The Rowman & Littlefield Publishing Group, Inc.
4501 Forbes Boulevard, Suite 200, Lanham, Maryland 20706
http://www.rowmanlittlefield.com

Estover Road, Plymouth PL6 7PY, United Kingdom

British Library Cataloguing in Publication Information Available

Library of Congress Cataloging-in-Publication Data

The hardback edition of this book was previously cataloged by the Library of Congress
as follows:

Edward, Joyce.
  The sibling relationship : a force for growth and conflict / Joyce Edward.
    p. cm.
  Includes bibliographical references and index.
  1. Brothers and sisters—Psychological aspects. I. Title.
  BF723.S43E39 2011
  155.9'24—dc22   2010043840

ISBN: 978-0-7657-0732-1 (cloth : alk. paper)
ISBN: 978-0-7657-0733-8 (pbk. : alk. paper)
ISBN: 978-0-7657-0734-5 (electronic)

Printed in the United States of America

This book is dedicated to my beloved husband,
Jess Edward (1921–2010).

Contents

Acknowledgments

I am deeply indebted to all of those who have encouraged, supported, and facilitated the writing of this book. To Patsy Turrini, Bea Weinstein, Cecily Weintraub, and Diana Siskind, friends and colleagues, my warmest thanks for reviewing each chapter and giving me the benefit of their theoretical and clinical knowledge. Thanks as well to Barbara Coley, Sheila Felberbaum, Rene Goldman, Jeanine Klein, Laurie Rosen, and Naomi Schlesinger, who reviewed particular chapters and offered me their expertise. I should also like to acknowledge my teachers Gertrude and Rubin Blanck and Jacob Arlow whose contributions to psychoanalysis have informed and inspired my efforts.

This book could not been written without what I have learned from my patients, nor without the help of those many non-patients who shared their own or their patients' sibling experiences with me. To the members of the American Association for Psychoanalysis, the Clinicians Exchange, the New York State Society for Clinical Social Work Clinical Society, and the New York School for Psychoanalytic Psychotherapy and Psychoanalysis, my thanks for the invaluable contributions they made to this effort.

To Julie Kirsch, the editorial director of Jason Aronson, who agreed to publish the book, my warmest thanks for her patience, her understanding, her help, and her support through this long undertaking. I could not have completed the book without the skill, wisdom, kindness, and good humor of Judy Cohen, who edited the book. Thanks also go to Dr. Camille Wortman for her assistance and to my dear granddaughter, Dana Sanders, who helped prepare the book for press.

Finally, I wish to warmly thank my sister, Rosemary Schiff, who has taught me so much about what it is to be a sister and what it is to have a sister, as well as my children and grandchildren, who have afforded me the opportunity to observe siblings in action these many years.

Contents

Acknowledgments

I am deeply indebted to all of those who have encouraged, supported, and facilitated the writing of this book. To Patsy Turrini, Bea Weinstein, Cecily Weintraub, and Diana Siskind, friends and colleagues, my warmest thanks for reviewing each chapter and giving me the benefit of their theoretical and clinical knowledge. Thanks as well to Barbara Coley, Sheila Felberbaum, Rene Goldman, Jeanine Klein, Laurie Rosen, and Naomi Schlesinger, who reviewed particular chapters and offered me their expertise. I should also like to acknowledge my teachers Gertrude and Rubin Blanck and Jacob Arlow whose contributions to psychoanalysis have informed and inspired my efforts.

This book could not been written without what I have learned from my patients, nor without the help of those many non-patients who shared their own or their patients' sibling experiences with me. To the members of the American Association for Psychoanalysis in Clinical Social Work, the Clinicians Exchange, the New York State Society for Clinical Social Work Clinical Society, and the New York School for Psychoanalytic Psychotherapy and Psychoanalysis, my thanks for the invaluable contributions they made to this effort.

To Julie Kirsch, the editorial director of Jason Aronson, who agreed to publish the book, my warmest thanks for her patience, her understanding, her help, and her support through this long undertaking. I could not have completed the book without the skill, wisdom, kindness, and good humor of Judy Cohen, who edited the book. Thanks also go to Dr. Camille Wortman for her assistance and to my dear granddaughter, Dana Sanders, who helped prepare the book for press.

Finally, I wish to warmly thank my sister, Rosemary Schiff, who has taught me so much about what it is to be a sister and what it is to have a sister, as well as my children and grandchildren, who have afforded me the opportunity to observe siblings in action these many years.

Introduction

Ever since Cain killed his brother Abel, the sibling relationship has been associated with envy, jealousy, hatred, and fratricide. So numerous are the accounts of sibling enmity in Genesis that Stephen Mitchell (1996), a modern translator of biblical stories, has suggested that conflict between siblings may be regarded as the theme of that biblical text. Although the Bible also introduces the idea of siblings as one another's keeper, it is the animosity between those ancient brothers that has stood out over time, and with which modern day individuals seem to more strongly identify.

Indeed, Freud (1915–1916) was convinced that the hostility those biblical brothers felt for each other continues to be the earliest and most persistent attitude between siblings in modern times. "A small child," Freud wrote, "does not necessarily love his brothers and sisters: often he obviously does not. There is no doubt that he hates them as his competitors, and it is a familiar fact that this attitude often persists for long years, till maturity is reached or even later, without interruption. Quite oft, it is true, it is succeeded, or let us rather say overlaid, by a more affectionate attitude; but the hostile one seems very generally to be the earliest" (p. 204). Freud tended to regard whatever affectionate feelings siblings develop toward one another, either as a defense against their basic hostility or an expression of aim-inhibited manifestations of early, erotic, incestuous wishes.

In his role as clinician Freud was often confronted with the outcome of troubled sibling relationships, which may have led him to overly focus on the negative aspects of the sibling bond. However, his own experiences with his brothers and sisters are also thought to have influenced his ideas. Freud was the oldest of eight children born to his mother. He had two half brothers that were some twenty years older than he, as well as a nephew, John, the son

of one of his stepbrothers, who was a year older than Freud. In his autobiographical study, Freud (1925) made no mention of his siblings, which has led
to some speculation that he bore them little affection (Coles 2003). However,
he acknowledged elsewhere the impact that his next younger brother, Julius,
had on him as well as the importance to him of his nephew, John, to whom
he related as a brother.

Julius was born when Freud was one and a half. He died at six months of
age, when Freud was just under two. In his self-analysis Freud discovered his
rivalry with Julius and his strong murderous wishes toward him. In a letter he
wrote to Wilhelm Fliess (Freud 1887–1904) Freud acknowledged the guilt he
experienced over his jealousy and ill wishes.

According to Freud (1900b) he and his nephew John had been inseparable
friends as children. They had both loved and hated each other. Freud recognized that their relationship had a significant influence on all of his subsequent relationships with his peers. He wrote,

> All my friends, have in a certain sense been re-incarnations of this first figure.
> . . . My emotional life has always insisted that I should have an intimate friend
> and a hated enemy. I have always been able to provide myself afresh with both,
> and it has not infrequently happened that the ideal situation of childhood has
> been so completely reproduced that friend and enemy have come together in a
> single individual—though not, of course, both at once or with constant oscilla-
> tions, as may have been the case in my early childhood. (p. 483)

Although Freud recognized certain ways in which siblings could contribute
positively to each other's development, as will be seen later in this book, he,
and for many years those psychoanalysts who followed him as well as members of allied professions, remained largely preoccupied with the difficulties
siblings encounter in their relationships with each other (Neubauer 1983).

Some early psychoanalysts conducted extensive research on sibling rivalry
(Levy 1937) and a number recorded their observations of their own offspring,
which showed the intense negative reactions of their older child upon the
birth of a new brother or sister (Neubauer 1982). Through educational means,
several members of the psychoanalytic community tried to lessen the negative impact of the arrival of a new sibling (Buxbaum 1949, Hawkins 1946).

At the same time there was concern about the detrimental impact of mutual
sexual exploration and seduction between siblings (Colonna and Newman
1983). In addition to parents, Freud recognized siblings as the objects of a
child's earliest incestuous sexual strivings and emphasized the necessity for
"the severest prohibitions to deter this persistent infantile tendency from realization" (1917a, p. 335). In part, he attributed the pathology of the Wolfman

(1918) to his sister's sadistic seduction of him when he was a young child, and then, when he was older, to her rejections of his sexual advances.

In those days it was largely left to novelists and biographers to consider the richness and complexity of the sibling relationship. Louisa May Alcott, for example, in Little Women (1868–1869), wrote of intensely gratifying and supportive relationships between sisters. In Jane Austen's writings, the sibling bond often appears to have been more significant in the lives of some of her characters than their marriage bond (Hudson 1999). Hudson introduces her book *Sibling Love and Incest in Jane Austen's Fiction* (p.1) with a quote from *Mansfield Park* (Austen 1814) in which Austen notes that children from the "same family, the same blood, with the same first associations" have a means of enjoyment, which no later relationships can provide. Austen doubted that the impact of that earliest attachment is ever outlived.

The critical role that sisters and brothers can play in each other's lives has been affirmed in the biographies of a number of famous persons. In his book *Blood Brothers: Siblings as Writers,* Norman Kiell (1983) has shown how essential their siblings were to the creativity and success of such writers as James Joyce, Aldous Huxley, and Henry James. It is doubtful that Vincent Van Gogh, despite his remarkable talent, would have achieved his position as an artist without his brother Theo's emotional and financial support (Nagera 1967).

Leonard Shengold (1989), who has written extensively on the impact of abuse on child development, has given a moving account of the way in which the relationship between Rudyard Kipling and his sister, Trix, helped to mitigate the abusive care they received from their foster mother, saving each of them, he thought, from severe pathology. At the age of six Kipling and his three-year-old sister, Trix, were placed in the care of extremely sadistic guardians in England while their parents continued to live in India. Kipling was the primary object of his foster mother's cruelty. Whereas in such situations children often deflect their rage away from their tormenting caretakers and displace it onto a brother or sister, Kipling and Trix treated each other with great care and loyalty. One biographer, Martin Seymour-Smith (1989), wrote of a time when Kipling was forced as a punishment to carry a placard bearing the words "Kipling the Liar." According to her own account, Trix rushed into the street to tear it off.

In general, interest in the sibling relationship on the part of psychoanalysts and members of related professions appears to have remained limited until the 1980s. According to *PsycInfo,* a database used by students and professionals that serves a variety of disciplines, there were less than 150 articles listed on the topic between 1920 and 1980.

One of the first signs among psychoanalysts that the situation was changing was the formation of a study group, associated with the Child Study

Center at Yale University, whose purpose was to conduct a comprehensive study of siblings. Marianne Kris, a leading psychoanalyst, was a key member of that group. The group's findings were presented at the Annual Meeting of the Association for Child Psychoanalysis in Boston, March 28, 1980, and those papers were later published in the *Psychoanalytic Study of the Child* in 1983. By 1988, sufficient interest in siblings had been generated among psychoanalysts that *Psychoanalytic Inquiry*, under the editorship of Elizabeth Agger, devoted an entire volume to articles on siblings.

During those same years Steven Bank and Michael Kahn, both prominent psychologists, and Judy Dunn, a well-known British developmental psychologist, began to study and write extensively about the sibling relationship. The American Anthropological Association held a symposium during that era titled "The Contribution of Siblings to Social, Emotional, and Cognitive Development," and The Society for Research in Child Development agreed to fund a three-day Study Group Conference during May 1985 on the topic of sibling interaction (Zukow 1989).

Interest in siblings has continued to increase during the past ten years. From 2000 to 2010, *PsycInfo* lists more than 5,000 items pertaining to the topic of siblings, contributed by professionals from a variety of disciplines and the PEP Archives of the American Psychoanalytic Association, during that same period, lists more than 800 references from the psychoanalytic literature having to do with brothers and sisters. One of the purposes of this volume is to bring together some of this currently available information.

Although my orientation is psychoanalytic and the treatment model I follow is a psychodynamic one, this book demonstrates how clinicians of other orientations as well as members of other fields such as the social sciences, psychology, social work, psychiatry, ethnology, and history have extended and are continuing to expand our understanding of siblings. The book also draws on memoirs and biographies as well as fiction, which, as Noam Chomsky (1968) has pointed out, often teaches us more about human life and human personality than science itself. Such an interdisciplinary approach is in keeping with a growing interest in unifying knowledge across disciplines, a process known as "consilience" (Valone 2005, Wilson 1998).

The book includes findings from clinical cases studies as well as from interviews conducted with siblings who were not patients. Although systematic, quantitative research is vital to the advancement of the human sciences, case studies are valuable in generating possible explanations for human thought and behavior (Hoffman 2009).They point to certain common demands made upon those who face similar life challenges, and expand our understanding of the multiple determinants that may influence an individual's unique behaviors, attitudes, and ways of relating to others.

Parents remain the critical developmental partners of their children; however, research and clinical experience are showing how siblings may help to foster each other's growth. They can serve as the "object" of each other's wishes, as well as their "model," their "helper," and their "opponent" (Freud 1921, p. 69), roles that Freud regarded as helping to shape an individual's character and personality.

Leaving the consideration of multiple birth siblings to those more experienced with this group of brothers and sisters, chapter 1 explores some of what is being learned today about how single-born siblings in "average expectable" (Hartmann 1939) families perform these developmental roles. Among the issues that are considered in this chapter are the attachments siblings form with one another that help to provide them with a sense of security, the impact that they may have on the formation of each others' personalities, and how their interpersonal exchanges may become internalized and lead to representations in the mind that influence how they relate to others.

In recognition of the diverse population that clinicians and social policy planners are serving today, chapter 2 looks at the influence the larger culture may have on sibling relationships. Chapters 3 and 4 examine the effect that today's non-traditional families may have on determining sibling experiences. The focus in chapter 5 is on those sibling relationships that are marked by excessive envy, rivalry, and hatred that may impede development and in some cases lead to pathology. Chapter 6 concerns sibling sexuality, both the impact of sexual activity between siblings as well as sexual fantasies. Chapter 7 takes up those situations in which a sibling has a developmental disability from birth, a life-threatening illness, or a crippling accident. In chapter 8 consideration is given to the impact that the death of a sibling may have on their surviving brothers or sisters. Chapter 9 offers brief concluding comments.

Throughout, case studies are presented to illustrate the applicability of this increased understanding of the sibling relationship in the clinical situation. This is in keeping with the primary goal of the book which is to show how attention to sibling issues can further the treatment process. This involves gaining a greater appreciation of those transferences and countertransferences (Schechter 1999) that have to do with a patient's brothers and sisters. Too often in the past, when siblings were primarily regarded as displacement figures for their parents, these went unnoticed and unattended to. As a result, patients often left treatment with their relationships with their parents improved, but with little change in their attitudes toward or their interpersonal exchanges with their siblings (Balsam 1988).

I know this from personal experience. Although my interest in this topic was stimulated by an invitation from the New York State Society for Clinical Social Workers to present a paper on siblings at their 1997 conference, it has become clear to me that my continued effort to better understand this relationship has been personally motivated as well. Were it not for certain issues with my own five-year-younger sister, I doubt I would be writing this book. At the time I was analyzed, however, siblings were mainly viewed as stand-ins for their parents. Like many other therapists of the times my analyst tended to interpret my associations to my sister as defensive. "You are more comfortable talking about your sister than your mother or father," he would note. Little attention was paid to the important role my sister played in my development and life as a person in her own right.

That this neglect of siblings in the clinical encounter still occurs in some treatments was brought home to me during the discussion periods that have followed several presentations I have given over the years on the topic. I found many of the participants eager to talk about their own sibling experiences, and at a very personal level. It is likely that most of them had experienced their own treatment, and so I wondered whether as little attention had been paid to their relationships with their brothers and sisters in their therapy as had been the case in mine. I was struck too by the number of participants who noted that they themselves paid little attention to their patients' sibling experiences.

In addition to showing how our current knowledge regarding both the positive and negative sides of the sibling relationship has relevance for our clinical efforts, some consideration is given to its implications for social planning. What has been learned about attachment between siblings, for example, has already proven of importance in the field of child placement. Keeping siblings together has become a goal of many agencies. A broader understanding of the importance of the relationship between brothers and sisters should also be useful to those who make decisions about custody and visitation in divorce situations or to those who are currently involved in creating guidelines for sperm and ova donation as to how many donations a person can make as each donation means the creation of another potential half sibling.

It is important to note that this focus on siblings is not intended to suggest that brothers and sisters are essential for normal development. We know from experience and from studies of only children that this is not so (Arlow 1972, Machman and Thomspon, 1998, Polit and Falbo 1987). However, I will seek to demonstrate that the psychic life of those who do have brothers and sisters is significantly influenced by the experience (Kris and Ritvo 1983), in ways that may be enriching or limiting or in some cases both.

A consideration of sibling relationships is particularly timely today. In this period of high divorce, single-parent families, blended families, and other demographic and social changes in American families (Weisner1982), brothers and sisters are becoming increasingly important to one another, often serving as each other's closest companions and in some families each other's primary caretakers.

At the same time, our current efforts to better understand this critical relationship may shed light on our tragic inability since biblical times to contain our envy, jealousy, and hatred of one another. Although we tend to idealize the concepts of "fraternity" and "sorority" and the idea of brothers and sisters serving as each other's "keepers," exchanges between humans throughout the world today bear a remarkable resemblance to the relationships between those warring siblings in the nursery whose "violent conflicts" Freud wrote about almost a hundred years ago (1915–1916).

Introduction

Ever since Cain killed his brother Abel, the sibling relationship has been associated with envy, jealousy, hatred, and fratricide. So numerous are the accounts of sibling enmity in Genesis that Stephen Mitchell (1996), a modern translator of biblical stories, has suggested that conflict between siblings may be regarded as the theme of that biblical text. Although the Bible also introduces the idea of siblings as one another's keeper, it is the animosity between those ancient brothers that has stood out over time, and with which modern day individuals seem to more strongly identify.

Indeed, Freud (1915–1916) was convinced that the hostility those biblical brothers felt for each other continues to be the earliest and most persistent attitude between siblings in modern times. "A small child," Freud wrote, "does not necessarily love his brothers and sisters: often he obviously does not. There is no doubt that he hates them as his competitors, and it is a familiar fact that this attitude often persists for long years, till maturity is reached or even later, without interruption. Quite oft, it is true, it is succeeded, or let us rather say overlaid, by a more affectionate attitude; but the hostile one seems very generally to be the earliest" (p. 204). Freud tended to regard whatever affectionate feelings siblings develop toward one another, either as a defense against their basic hostility or an expression of aim-inhibited manifestations of early, erotic, incestuous wishes.

In his role as clinician Freud was often confronted with the outcome of troubled sibling relationships, which may have led him to overly focus on the negative aspects of the sibling bond. However, his own experiences with his brothers and sisters are also thought to have influenced his ideas. Freud was the oldest of eight children born to his mother. He had two half brothers that were some twenty years older than he, as well as a nephew, John, the son of one of his stepbrothers, who was a year older than Freud. In his autobiographical study, Freud (1925) made no mention of his siblings, which has led to some speculation that he bore them little affection (Coles 2003). However, he acknowledged elsewhere the impact that his next younger brother, Julius, had on him as well as the importance to him of his nephew, John, to whom he related as a brother.

Julius was born when Freud was one and a half. He died at six months of age, when Freud was just under two. In his self-analysis Freud discovered his rivalry with Julius and his strong murderous wishes toward him. In a letter he wrote to Wilhelm Fliess (Freud 1887–1904) Freud acknowledged the guilt he experienced over his jealousy and ill wishes.

According to Freud (1900b) he and his nephew John had been inseparable friends as children. They had both loved and hated each other. Freud recognized that their relationship had a significant influence on all of his subsequent relationships with his peers. He wrote,

> All my friends, have in a certain sense been re-incarnations of this first figure. . . . My emotional life has always insisted that I should have an intimate friend and a hated enemy. I have always been able to provide myself afresh with both, and it has not infrequently happened that the ideal situation of childhood has been so completely reproduced that friend and enemy have come together in a single individual—though not, of course, both at once or with constant oscillations, as may have been the case in my early childhood. (p. 483)

Although Freud recognized certain ways in which siblings could contribute positively to each other's development, as will be seen later in this book, he, and for many years those psychoanalysts who followed him as well as members of allied professions, remained largely preoccupied with the difficulties siblings encounter in their relationships with each other (Neubauer 1983).

Some early psychoanalysts conducted extensive research on sibling rivalry (Levy 1937) and a number recorded their observations of their own offspring, which showed the intense negative reactions of their older child upon the birth of a new brother or sister (Neubauer 1982). Through educational means, several members of the psychoanalytic community tried to lessen the negative impact of the arrival of a new sibling (Buxbaum 1949).

At the same time there was concern about the detrimental impact of mutual sexual exploration and seduction between siblings (Colonna and Newman 1983). In addition to parents, Freud recognized siblings as the objects of a child's earliest incestuous sexual strivings and emphasized the necessity for "the severest prohibitions to deter this persistent infantile tendency from realization" (1917a, p. 335). In part, he attributed the pathology of the Wolfman

(1918) to his sister's sadistic seduction of him when he was a young child, and then, when he was older, to her rejections of his sexual advances.

In those days it was largely left to novelists and biographers to consider the richness and complexity of the sibling relationship. Louisa May Alcott, for example, in *Little Women* (1868–1869), wrote of intensely gratifying and supportive relationships between sisters. In Jane Austen's writings, the sibling bond often appears to have been more significant in the lives of some of her characters than their marriage bond (Hudson 1999). Hudson introduces her book *Sibling Love and Incest in Jane Austen's Fiction* (p.1) with a quote from *Mansfield Park* (Austen 1814) in which Austen notes that children from the "same family, the same blood, with the same first associations" have a means of enjoyment, which no later relationships can provide. Austen doubted that the impact of that earliest attachment is ever outlived.

The critical role that sisters and brothers can play in each other's lives has been affirmed in the biographies of a number of famous persons. In his book *Blood Brothers: Siblings as Writers*, Norman Kiell (1983) has shown how essential their siblings were to the creativity and success of such writers as James Joyce, Aldous Huxley, and Henry James. It is doubtful that Vincent Van Gogh, despite his remarkable talent, would have achieved his position as an artist without his brother Theo's emotional and financial support (Nagera 1967).

Leonard Shengold (1989), who has written extensively on the impact of abuse on child development, has given a moving account of the way in which the relationship between Rudyard Kipling and his sister, Trix, helped to mitigate the abusive care they received from their foster mother, saving each of them, he thought, from severe pathology. At the age of six Kipling and his three-year-old sister, Trix, were placed in the care of extremely sadistic guardians in England while their parents continued to live in India. Kipling was the primary object of his foster mother's cruelty. Whereas in such situations children often deflect their rage away from their tormenting caretakers and displace it onto a brother or sister, Kipling and Trix treated each other with great care and loyalty. One biographer, Martin Seymour-Smith (1989), wrote of a time when Kipling was forced as a punishment to carry a placard bearing the words "Kipling the Liar." According to her own account, Trix rushed into the street to tear it off.

In general, interest in the sibling relationship on the part of psychoanalysts and members of related professions appears to have remained limited until the 1980s. According to *PsycInfo*, a database used by students and professionals that serves a variety of disciplines, there were less than 150 articles listed on the topic between 1920 and 1980.

One of the first signs among psychoanalysts that the situation was changing was the formation of a study group, associated with the Child Study

Center at Yale University, whose purpose was to conduct a comprehensive study of siblings. Marianne Kris, a leading psychoanalyst, was a key member of that group. The group's findings were presented at the Annual Meeting of the Association for Child Psychoanalysis in Boston, March 28, 1980, and those papers were later published in the *Psychoanalytic Study of the Child* in 1983. By 1988, sufficient interest in siblings had been generated among psychoanalysts that *Psychoanalytic Inquiry*, under the editorship of Elizabeth Agger, devoted an entire volume to articles on siblings.

During those same years Steven Bank and Michael Kahn, both prominent psychologists, and Judy Dunn, a well-known British developmental psychologist, began to study and write extensively about the sibling relationship. The American Anthropological Association held a symposium during that era titled "The Contribution of Siblings to Social, Emotional, and Cognitive Development," and The Society for Research in Child Development agreed to fund a three-day Study Group Conference during May 1985 on the topic of sibling interaction (Zukow 1989).

Interest in siblings has continued to increase during the past ten years. From 2000 to 2010, *PsycInfo* lists more than 5,000 items pertaining to the topic of siblings, contributed by professionals from a variety of disciplines and the PEP Archives of the American Psychoanalytic Association, during that same period, lists more than 800 references from the psychoanalytic literature having to do with brothers and sisters. One of the purposes of this volume is to bring together some of this currently available information.

Although my orientation is psychoanalytic and the treatment model I follow is a psychodynamic one, this book demonstrates how clinicians of other orientations as well as members of other fields such as the social sciences, psychology, social work, psychiatry, ethnology, and history have extended and are continuing to expand our understanding of siblings. The book also draws on memoirs and biographies as well as fiction, which, as Noam Chomsky (1968) has pointed out, often teaches us more about human life and human personality than science itself. Such an interdisciplinary approach is in keeping with a growing interest in unifying knowledge across disciplines, a process known as "consilience" (Valone 2005, Wilson 1998).

The book includes findings from clinical cases studies as well as from interviews conducted with siblings who were not patients. Although systematic, quantitative research is vital to the advancement of the human sciences, case studies are valuable in generating possible explanations for human thought and behavior (Hoffman 2009).They point to certain common demands made upon those who face similar life challenges, and expand our understanding of the multiple determinants that may influence an individual's unique behaviors, attitudes, and ways of relating to others.

Parents remain the critical developmental partners of their children; however, research and clinical experience are showing how siblings may help to foster each other's growth. They can serve as the "object" of each other's wishes, as well as their "model," their "helper," and their "opponent" (Freud 1921, p. 69), roles that Freud regarded as helping to shape an individual's character and personality.

Leaving the consideration of multiple birth siblings to those more experienced with this group of brothers and sisters, chapter 1 explores some of what is being learned today about how single-born siblings in "average expectable" (Hartmann 1939) families perform these developmental roles. Among the issues that are considered in this chapter are the attachments siblings form with one another that help to provide them with a sense of security, the impact that they may have on the formation of each others' personalities, and how their interpersonal exchanges may become internalized and lead to representations in the mind that influence how they relate to others.

In recognition of the diverse population that clinicians and social policy planners are serving today, chapter 2 looks at the influence the larger culture may have on sibling relationships. Chapters 3 and 4 examine the effect that today's non-traditional families may have on determining sibling experiences. The focus in chapter 5 is on those sibling relationships that are marked by excessive envy, rivalry, and hatred that may impede development and in some cases lead to pathology. Chapter 6 concerns sibling sexuality, both the impact of sexual activity between siblings as well as sexual fantasies. Chapter 7 takes up those situations in which a sibling has a developmental disability from birth, a life-threatening illness, or a crippling accident. In chapter 8 consideration is given to the impact that the death of a sibling may have on their surviving brothers or sisters. Chapter 9 offers brief concluding comments.

Throughout, case studies are presented to illustrate the applicability of this increased understanding of the sibling relationship in the clinical situation. This is in keeping with the primary goal of the book which is to show how attention to sibling issues can further the treatment process. This involves gaining a greater appreciation of those transferences and countertransferences (Schechter 1999) that have to do with a patient's brothers and sisters. Too often in the past, when siblings were primarily regarded as displacement figures for their parents, these went unnoticed and unattended to. As a result, patients often left treatment with their relationships with their parents improved, but with little change in their attitudes toward or their interpersonal exchanges with their siblings (Balsam 1988).

I know this from personal experience. Although my interest in this topic was stimulated by an invitation from the New York State Society for Clinical Social Workers to present a paper on siblings at their 1997 conference, it has become clear to me that my continued effort to better understand this relationship has been personally motivated as well. Were it not for certain issues with my own five-year-younger sister, I doubt I would be writing this book. At the time I was analyzed, however, siblings were mainly viewed as stand-ins for their parents. Like many other therapists of the times my analyst tended to interpret my associations to my sister as defensive. "You are more comfortable talking about your sister than your mother or father," he would note. Little attention was paid to the important role my sister played in my development and life as a person in her own right.

That this neglect of siblings in the clinical encounter still occurs in some treatments was brought home to me during the discussion periods that have followed several presentations I have given over the years on the topic. I found many of the participants eager to talk about their own sibling experiences, and at a very personal level. It is likely that most of them had experienced their own treatment, and so I wondered whether as little attention had been paid to their relationships with their brothers and sisters in their therapy as had been the case in mine. I was struck too by the number of participants who noted that they themselves paid little attention to their patients' sibling experiences.

In addition to showing how our current knowledge regarding both the positive and negative sides of the sibling relationship has relevance for our clinical efforts, some consideration is given to its implications for social planning. What has been learned about attachment between siblings, for example, has already proven of importance in the field of child placement. Keeping siblings together has become a goal of many agencies. A broader understanding of the importance of the relationship between brothers and sisters should also be useful to those who make decisions about custody and visitation in divorce situations or to those who are currently involved in creating guidelines for sperm and ova donation as to how many donations a person can make as each donation means the creation of another potential half sibling.

It is important to note that this focus on siblings is not intended to suggest that brothers and sisters are essential for normal development. We know from experience and from studies of only children that this is not so (Arlow 1972, Nachman and Thomspon, 1998, Polit and Falbo 1987). However, I will seek to demonstrate that the psychic life of those who do have brothers and sisters is significantly influenced by the experience (Kris and Ritvo 1983), in ways that may be enriching or limiting or in some cases both.

A consideration of sibling relationships is particularly timely today. In this period of high divorce, single-parent families, blended families, and other demographic and social changes in American families (Weisner1982), brothers and sisters are becoming increasingly important to one another, often serving as each other's closest companions and in some families each other's primary caretakers.

At the same time, our current efforts to better understand this critical relationship may shed light on our tragic inability since biblical times to contain our envy, jealousy, and hatred of one another. Although we tend to idealize the concepts of "fraternity" and "sorority" and the idea of brothers and sisters serving as each other's "keepers," exchanges between humans throughout the world today bear a remarkable resemblance to the relationships between those warring siblings in the nursery whose "violent conflicts" Freud wrote about almost a hundred years ago (1915–1916).

1

Siblings as Developmental Partners

For most of the twentieth century psychoanalysts and members of related disciplines were primarily concerned with the troubling consequences of sibling envy, hatred, and rivalry as well as the harmful effects of sexual activities between brothers and sisters. Yet, Freud recognized certain positive contributions that brothers and sisters might make to each other's development. Viewing curiosity as stemming from a child's desire to find out where babies come from, he saw the birth of a sibling as stimulating an older child's interest in learning. In the case of girls, an infant, he suggested, helps to evoke her "maternal instincts" (1900a). Moreover, a girl's disappointment in not having been the one to have given her mother the baby leads her to relinquish that wish, thereby helping to promote her efforts to separate from her mother and turn to her father (1931). Freud (1921) also traced the development of a social conscience and a sense of social responsibility to the efforts siblings make to deal with their jealousy of one another. Recognizing that their brothers and sisters are loved by their parents as much as they are, children are forced, according to Freud, to control their hostility, which they do by means of reaction formation and identification. These efforts lead to the development of a group feeling and a demand for equal treatment and justice. "If one cannot be the favorite oneself, at all events nobody else shall be" (p. 120).

Despite this recognition on Freud's part that siblings may facilitate each other's growth, it was not until the 1980s, as noted in the introduction, that psychoanalysts and members of related disciplines, for reasons that are not clear, began to explore more fully the roles that siblings may play in each other's development.

THE BIRTH OF A SIBLING

One of the most prolific contributors to the research on siblings is Judy Dunn, a distinguished British developmental psychologist. As an introduction to our topic, I begin with a summary of a study she conducted with Carol Kendrick (Dunn and Kendrick 1982) of children between the ages of one and a half and two years, after the birth of a younger sibling. These were the children of forty working-class, intact English families in which there was a great deal of assistance available to the mothers before, during, and after the birth of their second children. The children were observed in their own homes and their mothers were interviewed at length about them. Each family was seen for four home visits: one during the last month or so of the mother's pregnancy with the second child, one during the first month after the infant's birth, one when the infant was eight months old, and one when the infant was fourteen months old. At least two hour-long visits, often three, were made during these periods.

This study shows how great the changes are in a child's social world when a sibling is born. Not only do the older children face a rival for the love and attention of their parents, but they must now contend with someone who, unlike the adults in their world, is not concerned with their welfare.

Following the birth of their new siblings, all of the older children showed signs of disturbance and unhappiness along with interest in and affection for their new brother or sister. Some became withdrawn, miserable, and clinging. Some were demanding and difficult. In general the children manifested a marked degree of ambivalence. At one time they might serve as comforters and teachers of their younger siblings and at another they might treat them with considerable hostility. There was a strong continuity in these reactions over time. Children who showed friendly reactions during the first three weeks after the birth of their siblings were likely to respond similarly when seen at six years of age.

Almost all of the mothers found the most observable change in their firstborns to be an increase in naughtiness and demanding behavior. Their negative behaviors were primarily directed at their mothers, whereas most of the children were interested in and affectionate toward the baby. Not surprisingly, in those families where there was a close relationship with the father, the escalation of conflict with their mothers was less marked. Almost all of the children were eager to help with the care of their newborn sibling, joining in with great enthusiasm if their mothers encouraged them, and even if they did not. It was noted, though, that the children who were often warm and affectionate toward the baby were frequently those who in other respects were clearly disturbed by the entrance of a rival. On the positive side, over half of the mothers reported increased independence in their children. They became more grown up. Their interactions with their siblings, who like themselves did not have adult power, seemed to facilitate rapid cognitive advance.

Contrary to what one might expect, Dunn and Kendrick (1982) concluded that the extent of jealousy of the new baby was less likely to be determined by the attitudes and behaviors of the parents than by the child's sex and temperament. On a temperament assessment test carried out prior to the birth of a sibling, children who characteristically tended to manifest negative moods were more likely to respond by increased clinging. Boys were apt to become more withdrawn after the baby's birth than girls.

Regardless of their initial discomfort, by the age of three the elder siblings frequently acted as teachers, comforters, and sensitive companions to their younger siblings. They became highly skillful at reading, anticipating, and responding to them. At the same time they were often angry at their small rival who, unlike their parents, was not responsive to their needs and feelings. Under ordinary circumstances, insofar as it led to efforts to deal with frustrating situations between them and their siblings, this anger seemed to further the children's capacities to experience themselves as separate, active, and effective individuals.

Another finding of this study was the way the younger child tended to attach to the older one. As they advanced in age these younger children reported missing their elder siblings, whom they often used as a source of comfort and security. In contrast to first-born siblings, who showed a wide range of differences, younger siblings were more likely to approach older siblings in a friendly rather than hostile way. It was evident to these researchers that siblings growing up in the context of a favorable relationship with their parents are capable of forming a strong attachment to one another.

THE SIBLING STUDY GROUP

The Sibling Study Group (Provence and Solnit 1983), unlike Dunn and Kendrick, focused on just one sibling pair, Mark and Susan. Mark was two years of age when his little sister, Susan, was born. The closeness in age of the two children was of particular importance to these investigators, who recognized the developmental space between siblings as a major factor in how siblings experience each other. When siblings are close to each other in age their developmental tasks and capacities are more evenly matched. When brothers and sisters are separated by more developmental space they may be closer in interests than they would be with an adult, but their ease in communicating, understanding, and identifying with each other is not as great as when they are developmentally closer in age (Solnit 1983).

Mark and Susan were the children of thirty-year-old, middle-class, well-educated parents, who were described as reasonably well related to one another, free of major psychological problems, and committed to being good parents. They had carefully prepared their son for the birth of his little sister.

Mark was enthusiastic about the new baby's arrival, but it was a different story after her birth. He was clear about his wish that she be sent away, and closed his eyes when he walked by her bed. His competitiveness and rivalry were apparent. Yet he also appeared attracted to her and curious. As he watched his mother care for Susan, he enjoyed hearing her tell him about how she had cared for him when he was Susan's age. It seemed as if Mark was re-experiencing his own early exchanges with his mother. He became an expert at knowing what Susan wanted or needed and insisted that his parents attend to her when he felt she required their attention. He seemed to identify with his mother in her caretaking role. Although Mark's behavior may have served to defend against his hostility toward his little sister, it also seemed to these investigators to represent an identification with Susan's helplessness and her need for attention, a kind of empathic response.

Mark's interest in Susan increased when she began to smile, reach out, and move about. His discovery that he could make her smile or become excited became a source of pride to him. He seemed to experience her recognition as a sign of her approval of him. Her pleasure in watching him gave him pleasure and the observers felt that her positive feelings for him helped him develop loving feelings toward her.

By the time Mark was four and a half and Susan two and a half, Susan adored her older brother. She often mirrored his pleasure and pride as he mastered a new challenge. On the other hand she could also be intolerant and envious as well as angry and aggressive toward him.

Mark was often patronizing in his manner toward her, showing off his superior competence and knowledge. He sometimes instructed her and at other times called her dumb. Occasionally he pushed and hit her. Yet by four and a half he seemed to have made some peace with his resentment of her.

At times the children played together. Sometimes they were allies in acts of mischief or anger against their parents. They often appeared to understand each other more quickly than the adults understood either of them, which the group attributed largely to their closeness in age. Despite moments of strife between the children, the study group was impressed by their predominant friendliness and loyalty to each other, by their ability to join together in response to an external threat, and by the way they responded to each other's needs and sought to comfort each other.

The changes in Mark and Susan's attitude as they grew older are a reminder that the relationships between siblings are not fixed, but change over time in accord with each child's changing developmental levels and achievements, alterations in the family context, and changes in the way each sibling relates to other members of the family. For example, two brothers two years apart in age may be close as young children but at adolescence different interests may lead to an increase in the distance between them. A divorce in some families may bring two sisters closer together than they were in the past.

ATTACHMENT

Both of these studies affirm John Bowlby's (1980) finding that brothers and sisters can serve as attachment figures. Under favorable developmental circumstances, they form mental representations of one another as responsive and supportive, enabling them to find comfort and a sense of security when in each other's presence. Bowlby found confirmation of attachment between siblings when he studied a group of children between the ages of thirteen and thirty months who had been temporarily placed in a residential nursery while their mothers were hospitalized. Those children who entered the nursery either accompanied by an older or a younger sibling remained calmer and fared far better than those children who entered alone. They cried less and showed fewer outbursts of hostility. During the early days of the placement, the siblings stayed close to each other and talked and played together. They presented a united front and were quick to remind outsiders that they belonged to each other. Although they did not meet each other's survival needs, the children had clearly developed an emotional relationship with one another that provided them with a sense of safety, leading Bowlby to conclude that attachment behavior can develop and be directed toward a person who has done nothing to meet a child's basic requirements.

Ten years later, Stewart (1983) showed that when children were placed in the Strange Situation with a sibling (when their mother left a room and left both of the children with a stranger) more than half of the older siblings tried to care for their younger brothers or sisters when they showed distress and their younger siblings accepted and were comforted by their efforts.

I am reminded of the experience a friend of mine had when she was taking care of her two grandchildren, four-year-old Jane and her baby sister, Laurel, while their parents went out for an evening. When Laurel began to cry there was nothing this loving grandmother could do to calm her. However, the moment Jane came into the room and called out, "We love you Laurel," she

stopped crying, turned over, and broke out in a smile. As an attachment figure, Jane clearly was not interchangeable with another person (Fonagy 2001).
Only she could help restore her baby sister's feeling of safety (Sandler 1960)
and security in the absence of her parents.

With the achievement of object constancy (Mahler, Pine, and Bergman
1975), a sibling with whom an attachment has been formed becomes a member of a child's inner object world, and may serve as a source of support
whether present or absent. This makes it possible for many siblings who live
at great distances from one another to gain comfort from the knowledge that
they have each other to call upon in times of trouble. V. S. Naipaul, in his
novel *Magic Seeds* (2004), writes of a brother and sister who, although they
had only met once in twenty years, continued to understand each other and
could always count on each other in times of difficulty.

The perception of a sibling as a supportive figure may exist even when a
sibling relationship has been less than harmonious. When a patient's husband
died recently, she advised me that although she and her brother were never
close and at times did not even like each other, he was the first person she
phoned. "I knew he would come immediately, whether he wanted to or not."

EMPATHY

The capacity for empathy, the ability to "feel" into another person, to temporarily identify with the psychological state of another person is primarily
derived from the early mother-child relationship, but siblings may also contribute to its development in each other. Observers have been impressed with
the understanding that develops between young siblings (Dunn and Kendrick
1982, Provence and Solnit 1983, Stewart 1983), the concern they often show
for one another, and the efforts they frequently make to help or comfort each
other. Their close contact, their similarities, and their common experiences
sometimes make it possible for siblings to understand each other better than
their parents do (Stewart 1983). This attunement between siblings does not
necessarily lead to caring and concern. Frequently it enables brothers and
sisters to know precisely what will upset, annoy, or provoke each other.

SIBLINGS AS ALTER EGOS

The understanding that develops between siblings is thought to have an important value in itself. Although Heinz Kohut (1971, 1984) did not, to my
knowledge, write specifically about siblings, he has noted how a person who

is perceived as similar to an individual may be experienced as having a special understanding of them that helps to sustain their self-worth. According to Kohut, the need for such a person can be revived in treatment, leading to what he referred to as an alter ego or twinship transference.

I became aware of this transference in my work with an adult patient, Marjorie, who was an only child. Marjorie was preoccupied with finding or establishing similarities between us. She copied my dress and my hairstyle, and frequently scanned my bookshelves trying to find volumes that she also owned. Initially I thought this behavior might represent wishes for merger or an effort to compete with me. However, we came to understand that her wish for us to be alike, at that time in the treatment, represented a wish for a sibling, who she believed would be like her and therefore better able to understand her. As an only child she had longed for a brother or sister who would share her experiences and as a result would be able to appreciate how difficult her life with her troubled parents was. Were I to be a sister, I would "really" know her, and she would "really" feel understood.

The wish that a therapist be a "good sibling" is not limited to only children. It can sometimes be seen in patients who have had troubled relationships with their siblings or who have had a brother or sister who they could not share their experiences and feelings with. This was true for John, a severely depressed young man who had an older brother who was mentally retarded. Early in the treatment John frequently tried to engage me in highly intellectual discussions, which at first I thought might be a defensive effort to avoid talking about more disturbing matters. However, as we considered this behavior together, we learned that he was trying to engage with me as if I were the strong, healthy brother he had longed for, the brother who would be his equal, with whom he could share ideas, and from whom he might learn.

MENTALIZATION

The capacity to mentalize (Twemlow, Fonagy, and Sacco 2005) refers to the ability to accurately perceive, anticipate, and act on one's own mental states and the mental states of others. When we understand our own actions and those of others as motivated by mental states, behaviors become more comprehensible and predictable. It makes it possible for a child to begin to comprehend the behaviors of others, including their caretakers. If a parent, for example, seems on occasion to be unresponsive, the ability to understand that this may be caused by something within the parent can protect a child from inappropriately assuming that the reaction is in response to his or her behavior and ultimately to the child him- or herself (Fonagy 1998). Mentalization has important implications for affect regulation, self-monitoring, impulse control, and a sense of oneself as agent (Fonagy 2001). Although this capacity develops from a secure early attachment to the primary caregiver, it is thought that the entire family can influence its development (Twemlow et al. 2005).

Siblings play a role in promoting this ability to reflect on the minds of others and to begin to gain an understanding of others' actions and thoughts. Siblings who are fairly close in age have been observed to talk to each other about mental states in both themselves and others at about three years of age. According to one study (Brown, Donelan-McCall, and Dunn 1996) they do so more frequently with each other than with their mothers. This has been attributed to the extensive amount of time they spend in each other's company and the play they engage in together. Moreover, when parents try to mediate arguments between their children, which is perhaps one of the most frequent interventions that parents make, they often tend to talk about feelings and intentions. This helps to introduce the idea that the behavior of others is motivated. The everyday explanations that parents offer in these situations (such as when a mother tells her angry three-year-old daughter that when her younger brother grabbed the first cookie out of the oven, he did not know that mother had promised her she could have it) help a child become aware that there are different reasons people act as they do.

SYMBIOSIS AND SEPARATION

In my use of the concept of symbiosis, I draw on Gergeley's (2000) reconceptualization of Mahler and her colleagues' understanding of the term. Instead of considering symbiosis as a state of perceptual undifferentiation, Gergely has suggested that it be considered in terms of its biological meaning, that is, as a term that refers to a close coexistence between two organisms in which some of the vital life functions of one of the participants are facilitated or fulfilled by the actions of the other. Insofar as the presence of a sibling may at times be psychologically vital to an individual, it seems reasonable to consider that siblings may, as some investigators have proposed (Leichtman 1985; Mahler, Pine, and Bergman 1975), experience a symbiotic-like relationship with each other or as Pine (2004) has proposed "moments" during which one or both siblings may feel as if they are "one" with the other.

Mahler and her colleagues have written about Teddy and his fourteen-and-a-half-year-old older brother Charlie, whose relationship they considered as having a "symbiotic tinge" (p. 171). Around the time of Teddy's birth, his mother lost her father and became less emotionally available. This appears to have led the brothers to turn to each other. Their mother further encouraged their strong tie and treated them as if they were twins. When Teddy was about twenty-two months old, Charlie moved to a different nursery program and Teddy seemed lost. He became more alert, however, when Charlie visited the center where they had once been together.

There was a time when Teddy was asked his name and he replied, "Charlie," and a period when he wanted to wear Charlie's clothes and refused to wear his own. Observers felt that this was not merely a wishful fantasy but suggested some actual confusion in identity. They concluded that at least in Teddy's fantasy life, he and Charlie were interchangeable.

The identity confusion that Teddy experienced has been noted among twins. This "twinning reaction," as Joseph and Tabor (1961) have called it, consists of a mutual inter-identification between twins and a partial fusion of the self and object representations that can lead to a diffuseness of ego boundaries (Ainslie 1999). The twinning reaction, however, is not exclusively a feature of twin relationships. It can occur in other relationships in which there is an unusual closeness between two persons. With Teddy and Charlie, their closeness in age, their continuous contact, and the fact that their mother tended to treat them as if they were a pair, seem to have favored such a response.

Vincent and Theo van Gogh

Vincent and Theo van Gogh appear to have had a symbiotic-like relationship with each other that continued over the years. According to his sister-in-law, the brothers were inseparable as children (van Gogh-Bonger 1913). As in the case of young Teddy, whose mother had lost her father before his birth, van Gogh's mother had experienced a significant loss before Vincent was born. She had given birth to a stillborn infant the previous year. Whether in her grief she had withdrawn from her sons, leaving them to look to each other, we can only conjecture. We do know that the brothers remained extremely close as adults. They lived together for two years and wrote to each other almost daily for many years. Shortly after Theo became engaged to be married, Vincent experienced his first breakdown, and it was following the birth of Theo's first child that Vincent committed suicide. Theo's marriage and his becoming a father may be looked upon as having created greater separateness between the two brothers. After Vincent died, Theo became mentally ill and six months later was buried at Vincent's side, suggesting again how closely intertwined these brothers were.

Marie and Eileen

Eileen Simpson, a psychotherapist (1987), has written about her intensely close relationship with her ten-months-older sister, Marie. The sisters lost their mother when Eileen was eleven months old and Marie was twenty-one months old. Six years later their father died and the girls were orphans. In considering what might make an orphan "reasonably lucky," Eileen put having a brother or sister at the top of her list.

During their early years the girls had been raised as if they were twins. Their hair had been cut in the same way, they were dressed alike, were given the same gifts, were often punished as if they were one person, and when one was sick, both were frequently put to bed.

Eileen could not tolerate being separated from Marie. When she was hospitalized for a mastoidectomy, she only began to improve when her father convinced the hospital personnel to allow Marie to visit her. When Marie eloped at the age of eighteen, Eileen was devastated. She became listless, lost weight, and had other health problems. The loss of her sister, Eileen noted, had been like a death to her.

In her novel *The Member of the Wedding* (1946), Carson McCullers has captured what it may be like when a child forms a symbiotic-like relationship with a sibling. She writes about twelve-year-old Frankie, whose mother died when Frankie was born. When Frankie learns that her brother is to be married, she is inconsolable. She feels alone and abandoned. She seeks comfort in the lap of Bernice, the family's housekeeper, slowing her breath in order to breathe in time with Bernice in order that they may be close as "one body" (p. 97). Frankie develops a fantasy intended to deny her loss. Having declared that her brother and his bride-to-be are the "we of me" (p. 35), she proclaims that she will be a "member of the wedding" (p. 38). According to Katherine Dalsimer (1979), who has studied the play from a psychoanalytic perspective, Frankie seeks to re-create an infantile state of fusion with her older brother and his bride-to-be through this fantasy. Ultimately the fantasy is relinquished and Frankie finds a resolution in the form of her friendship with another teenager. Friendship, Dalsimer notes, allows Frankie a sense of connection without a regression to an illusion of merger.

Such intense ties between siblings seem more likely to occur when, as in the case of the brothers or sisters noted above, a parent is emotionally unavailable or has died or when parents have treated siblings as if they were twins. Yet Helen Meyers (2008) has observed what she has termed a "symbiotic" relationship between sisters two or three years apart in age who had no other siblings, which is sooner or later followed by intense hostility between them and finally by a return to their original closeness. Meyers regards this sequence between sisters close in age as normal and universal.

SEPARATION

Ordinarily, maturational forces and the inevitable frustrations, demands, and restrictions that siblings impose on one another, as well as their conflicts around envy, rivalry, and jealousy (Jacobson 1964) help to promote differentiation between brothers and sisters. Mahler and her colleagues, for example, reported that when Teddy was about three and a half, and the brothers started to assert themselves and fight with one another, Teddy began to gain a sense of himself as distinguished from his brother.

In a study of letters written by preadolescents, Pauline Kernberg and Arlene Richards (1988) share a letter written by an eleven-year-old girl that suggests the struggle siblings may experience in separating from each other. The writer notes that she is eleven and her sister is nine. She complains about her sister copying everything she does. She realizes, she says, that she should feel flattered but it troubles her to have her original ideas copied. Asking her sister to stop has not been effective. She continues on with a few other complaints about her sister but ends by noting that she is a "good friend considering." After reading the letter one gets a sense of this young girl's efforts to separate and be her own person while her sister appears to be trying to hold on to their connection. At the same time the older sister's affection for her younger sibling is clear and there is a suggestion that she too is finding their separation a bit difficult.

The achievement of separation and individuation gains not only from siblings differentiating and separating from each other, but also from the way brothers and sisters help to promote each other's separation from their parents. The very presence of siblings is likely to interrupt or lessen to some extent each individual child's tie with their parents. Older siblings also often support, stimulate, and encourage their younger sibling's efforts to move into the world beyond the family, while the admiration and sometimes envy that younger children accord their older siblings for their independent activities can serve as a developmental stimulus.

INDIVIDUATION

Individuation is the process that leads to the development of one's own personal and unique characteristics and helps to form the core of a sense of identity. Identifications with parents contribute significantly to this process. Older siblings also frequently serve as models for their younger siblings, and younger siblings frequently try to develop characteristics or abilities in order to catch up with or impress or achieve the approval of their older brothers or sisters. In turn, older siblings are likely to find encouragement for their efforts to individuate in the admiration given to them for their achievements by their little brothers and sisters.

Edith Jacobson (1964) has pointed out that individuation also gains from a child's hatred and envy and wishes to surpass that same sibling. In fact, she concluded that individuation actually gains greater momentum from children's more ambivalent relations with their rivals than from their closeness with their mothers.

I am reminded of a young woman, Julie, who loved, envied, and hated her brother. He was an excellent athlete and an outstanding student whom she felt her parents favored over her. Although her love and admiration for him contributed to her desire to be like him, it was my impression that her envy, her wishes to surpass him, and the aggression these feelings mobilized were what fueled her intense efforts to be the athlete he was and that she one day became.

The inability to achieve a brother's or sister's desired characteristics or accomplishments also helps children learn the difference between wishful and more or less realistic self and object images, between what they want to be and what they are capable of being (Jacobson 1964). The sister of an accomplished musician may lack her sibling's talents so that regardless of how persevering she is, she cannot perform as well. Confrontation with one's limitations and the more or less successful acceptance of them are among the developmental struggles that help transform a child's early feelings of omnipotence into a more reality-based view of the self.

Disidentification with a sibling can also affect identify formation. Mary had grown up determined to be as unlike her ill-tempered, aggressive, emotionally disturbed older sister as possible. This led her to inhibit any show of anger and aggression. She became the "good" child in the family, in school, and elsewhere. Although this proved adaptive to the extent that she won the approval and admiration of others, it ultimately limited her capacity for assertiveness and effectance. Moreover, in seeking to fashion a self different from her sister she had developed what Winnicott has termed a "false self" (1960), which sometimes made her feel as if she were an actress rather than a real person.

SIBLINGS AND SEXUALITY

Sexual attraction between siblings, like sibling rivalry, is perhaps the most studied aspect of the sibling experience and I have included a separate chapter on the topic. However, let me say a few words about it here. Despite the fact that Freud concluded that siblings are among a child's first love objects, along with parents, and that incestuous wishes among siblings are universal (Freud 1916–1917), the tendency among psychoanalysts in the past was to view sexual strivings between siblings as representing a defense against the greater threat of incestuous wishes toward their parents. Today we recognize that brothers and sisters can also constitute primary loved and hated figures in and of themselves, not just substitutes for their mothers and fathers (Parens 1999).

Erotic fantasies and sexual play between siblings are common and in the context of a positive relationship they may be developmentally useful. They can pave the way for adult sexuality and help to transform sexual wishes for the parents into age-appropriate wishes directed toward peers (Parens 1988). On the other hand they may seriously interfere with development and lead to pathology.

An Oedipal-like Sibling Relationship

According to Sharpe and Rosenblatt (1994), relationships develop between siblings and between siblings and parents that involve desire and bear the characteristics of the oedipal parental triangle. Oedipal-like relationships may exist parallel to and relatively independent of the parental oedipal constellation. Romantic feelings and fantasies for a brother or sister may exert a strong influence on an individual's later identifications, patterns of object relating, and choice of adult love objects.

Recognition that siblings may be attracted romantically and sexually to each other as people in their own right and not just as displacement figures for parents is important to bear in mind. I am reminded of a young man, Norman, whom I analyzed many years ago. The depression that brought Norman into treatment began following his wife's announcement that she was planning to divorce him. He felt abandoned and humiliated.

Norman had one sister, seven years his senior, with whom he had been close as a child. As adults, however, they each had made very separate lives and saw each other infrequently. This changed after his wife left. Knowing that he was depressed, she and her husband reached out to him and he found them both very supportive.

In speaking of his sister in one of his sessions, Norman told of a game she had played with him when she put him to bed as a little boy. She would bounce him up and down, then kiss him and say goodnight. They referred to the game as "Bedtime Bounces." Norman recalled being very excited during the game and feeling great affection for his sister. She was very attentive to him until she married during his adolescence. He recalled feeling hurt and disappointed at the wedding, as if he had somehow been betrayed.

After Norman's depression lessened and his divorce became final, he began to date one woman after another. He never invited a woman out more than two or three times, and he seemed to experience some satisfaction in the hurt he imagined they felt when he "dumped" them. He took particular delight in telling his sister about each new woman, praising their physical attributes and boasting how quickly he got them into bed. His sister became concerned about his promiscuity, reminding him of the possible danger to his health. Norman was convinced she said this because she was jealous of these women. He came to recognize that he wanted her to be jealous and by flaunting these women in front of her, he was doing what he felt she had done to him when she married.

During those years, I was paying too little attention to siblings. I interpreted these associations to his sister as a displacement of feelings about his mother and his wish for revenge against her. I failed to explore his love for his sister as a person in her own right. As a result, I missed the opportunity to help Norman see that he had had two disappointing loves, one for his sister and one for his mother.

ENVY, JEALOUSY, RIVALRY, AND
HATRED AS FORCES FOR GROWTH

Whereas envy, jealousy, and rivalry are interrelated experiences, they are not the same (Neubauer 1982). Envy is a wish to possess the admired or idealized attributes of a sibling. It involves two persons. Jealousy involves three persons. It has to do with the resentment a child experiences over the love a sibling gains from a parent. Rivalry among siblings involves a struggle between them for exclusive access to the caregiver.

When envy, jealousy, and rivalry are extreme, they may seriously interfere with development and lead to pathology. However, under ordinary circumstances they can, according to Edith Jacobson (1964), help to promote separation and the establishment of a sense of self. Wanting what another sibling has, for example, and making efforts to secure it helps in differentiating self from other. The aggression that is aroused by envy and jealousy also aids the process (Blanck and Blanck 1994) in so far as aggression is understood as a force that "serves to undo connections" (Freud 1940, p. 148).

Competition between siblings, when not excessive, can also further development. Not only does it strengthen demarcation of self from other, but in helping to stimulate the fullest use of an individual's abilities and talents it contributes to the individuation process. A healthy competitive spirit is an advantage in many fields. Science, for example, is an intensely competitive enterprise (Jamison 2004). Harvard geneticist Richard Lewontin (1980, pp. 1–2) has noted, "What every scientist knows, but few will admit is that the requirement for great success is great ambition. Moreover, the ambition is for personal triumph over other men, not merely over nature." He goes on to claim that science is a competitive and aggressive enterprise, "a contest of man against man that provides knowledge as a side product."

Learning to cope with sibling rivalry during the preoedipal period may be helpful when children meet the challenges of the oedipal period. Recognition that one's siblings also cannot win the oedipal struggle may reduce some of the feelings of disappointment and failure attendant on not winning the loved parent. That siblings may play some role in a child's negotiation of the Oedipus complex was suggested by Freud (1916–1917) when he pointed out that in the case of girls the love of an older brother may help her deal with her disappointment in not winning the oedipal love of her father. On the other hand an inability to deal with their sibling envy and jealousy may lead some children to experience more intense conflicts over these same feelings during the oedipal phase (Kris and Ritvo 1983).

AMBIVALENCE

It is ordinarily neither all envy or all admiration, nor all hate or all love that siblings feel for each other. The sibling relationship is perhaps the most ambivalent of all relationships. From early on, affectionate, sexual, and hateful destructive feelings exist side by side. Initially, young children are likely to more or less freely express their hatred of each other verbally and sometimes physically. As they realize that their parents love their siblings and are distressed by any hostility they show toward them, fear of losing their parents or of losing their love generally compels brothers and sisters to try to curb their hostile impulses toward one another. Such defenses as reaction formation and repression help children to manage their ambivalence by intensifying their positive feelings. Later, the development of capacities for tolerating frustration, for understanding what may be going on in the minds of others, for distinguishing thought from deed, for forgiveness, as well as acceptance of the normality of contradictory feelings, makes it easier to hold opposing feelings.

An example of the difficulties siblings can face in contending with their ambivalent feelings toward each other has been beautifully described by Terri Apter in her book *The Sister Knot* (2007). Apter writes of the discomfort of twenty-five-year-old Donna, who describes how painful it was for her to have both loving and hateful feelings for her four-year-younger sister. However much she hated her sister and wanted everyone to see how terrible her sister was, when she discovered some individuals shouting at her sister, she found herself running to comfort her. At the same time she wanted to punch her. In her confusion she started to cry and her sister then tried to comfort her, which annoyed her. Who was she to comfort her? Yet she found her efforts cute and funny and realized how much she loved her, which in turn she says made her feel defeated.

Learning to be able to love and hate the same person is essential if one is to maintain relationships with others. Those individuals who cannot deal with ambivalent feelings are likely to resort to splitting, by which good and bad perceptions and feelings about a person are kept separate. This seems to have been the case with Freud (1900b). As noted in the introduction to this volume, Freud had an extremely close sibling-like relationship with his nephew, John, who was only a year his senior. Inseparable friends, according to Freud's account, they both loved and hated each other. Freud said of John that he had "many reincarnations which revived now one side and now another of his personality" (p. 424). Freud went on to trace his strong need for an intimate friend and a hated enemy back to this relationship. One is reminded of the close relationships that Freud enjoyed with such favored colleagues as Adler and Jung whom he came to view as enemies when they disagreed with certain of his ideas.

DIFFERENCES AMONG SIBLINGS

Many investigators have tried to account for the differences between biologically related siblings despite their genetic similarities. For some, the determining factor has been the order of birth. One of Freud's early followers, Alfred Adler (1928), considered this to be a major determinant in shaping each child's personality. He saw the birth of a new baby as "dethroning" the oldest child, who, if he or she manages to overcome this trauma, does so by serving as a surrogate parent to younger siblings. In this position the eldest child is apt to overemphasize the importance of law and order and become a conservative who is focused on gaining power. The youngest child, Adler suggested, who does not experience this fall from on high, often becomes lazy and spoiled and has problems becoming independent. Overshadowed by older siblings, the youngest child is likely to experience a sense of inferiority. However, if the youngest child does decide to compete, Adler noted, he or she is frequently successful.

A contemporary proponent of the importance of birth order in shaping each sibling's personality is Frank Sulloway (1996), an evolutionary psychologist. According to Sulloway, siblings are impelled by the law of natural selection to develop adaptations that shape their personalities in ways designed to prepare them for the competitive struggle for family resources and approval. In an effort to succeed, they each find a different niche in the family, adopting various strategies that are dependent upon their ordinal positions, and these strategies become embedded in their characters. First-born children, he claims, tend to identify with the parents and to use power and authority to maintain their position and status. Youngest children are left to oppose the status quo and frequently develop into rebels. Among them are the explorers, iconoclasts, and heretics of the world. Middle children, he suggests, tend toward creative mediation and compromise.

Dalton Conley (2004), a sociologist, has concluded that the major differences among children in a family have to do with the particular familial and societal context into which each child is born. What is critical are the social and economic circumstances that confront a family at the time of each child's birth and during the children's early years. One child may arrive in a family when financial circumstances are favorable, another when a father has lost his job. One may be born when a marriage is going well, another when parents are thinking of divorcing. Certain children are thus likely to receive more or less of the emotional and financial resources of a family, and it is what they receive, Conley proposes, that helps to determine who they become.

In their investigations, Dunn and Plomin (1990) did not find a clear link between individual differences in personality or psychopathology and birth order among the siblings they studied. In their opinion, it is only one of many factors that are likely to account for the differences between children in the same family. Among those factors I would include the innate capacities of each sibling, the unique responses of parents to each of their offspring, the impact siblings have on one another, and the cultural, social, psychological, and as Conley (2004) has noted, the economic circumstances into which each child is born in a family. No child is born into exactly the same environment; children are born with different temperaments and innate capacities and are likely to experience and respond to their environments differently, despite having had similar experiences.

Parents also respond differently to each of their offspring. Among the factors influencing their reactions are their children's physical and temperamental endowment. Years ago, as a child welfare worker, I was helping a young, troubled mother prepare her eight-month-old baby, John, for a medical visit. An active little boy, he was squirming as she tried to dress him. She became very angry, calling him a "bad boy" and accusing him of being just like "wild Tom," whom I later learned was her older, hated brother. She admonished her baby for not being like his four-year-old brother, who was a "good" child, as I later learned she had been. At the time of this encounter, I tried to point out that John was actually doing just what he was supposed to be doing at his age. He was using and exercising his muscles and it was clear that he was developing well physically. I went on to suggest that the fact that he could do so was a testimony to the good care she was giving him. I am afraid my words made little difference, and I have occasionally wondered over the years what happened to these brothers. I imagine them as becoming very different, in part, as a result of their different innate dispositions, and in part as a result of their mother's different perceptions and reactions to them.

Siblings may also different develop traits and personalities in order to distinguish themselves from each other and to achieve a sense of uniqueness or to surpass each other or to win more approval from their parents. To this end they may adopt different roles in the family (the good one, the helpful one, the funny one; Apter 2007).

One patient, Roseann, noted that while growing up she was aware that her older brother Felix's much sought-after approval of her depended upon her letting him shine in the family. Felix was a talented, bright, exceptionally accomplished boy. Roseann felt that she could best gain his favor by serving as his admiring audience, and she made little effort to excel in anything herself. As an adult, Felix became an outstanding leader in his field. Roseann became a competent teacher, but did not achieve the success her brother did. However, after her brother died, Roseann, now in her early seventies, began to explore a variety of creative pursuits and discovered an exceptional talent for writing. When her first short story was accepted by a prestigious magazine, she began to wonder if she had not inhibited her own talents for much of her life in order to preserve her connection with her brother. With his death, she had been released from the role of constant admirer and was free to realize her own potentialities.

WHEN SIBLINGS GROW UP

As brothers and sisters grow up, their relationships may change as they themselves change. Two brothers, two years apart, may be very close as little boys but over time they may move further apart as their interests diverge. I can still remember my own five-year-younger sister's unhappiness when I began junior high and she was still in elementary school. Despite our age difference, we had spent a great deal of time together during the years we were in the same school. However, when I moved to a new school, I joined a club of girls and spent most of my after-school hours with them. My sister was distressed and angry. She got her revenge by doing something to embarrass me whenever the club met at our house. Yet when we became adults and wives and mothers we once again had much in common.

Studies suggest that even brothers and sisters whose relationships have been less than harmonious in the past frequently begin to develop more positive exchanges as they mature. Steven Bank (1995), in his review of the literature about siblings as adults, found that almost every study of adult siblings since the 1960s has shown an increase in contacts and closeness between siblings, even as early as college (Cicerelli 1995).

A number of factors may account for this. When development has proceeded favorably siblings are likely to approach their differences with greater maturity. As they make their own lives apart from their families they are less likely to experience the friction or conflict they felt while growing up. Relationships with mates, friends, colleagues, and their own children tend to diminish the role siblings play in each other's lives and help dilute the intensity of past conflicts. Marian's relationship with her sisters suggests how the pattern of sibling exchanges may alter over the years as circumstances change.

Marian

Marian, a wife and mother of a young baby, spoke of how her resentment and anger toward her sisters, Roberta, who was eight years her senior and Rose, who was six years older, had dissipated over time. She envied them for receiving more of their mother's attention than she did. Her mother was forced to give more to Rose, who suffered from epilepsy and mental retardation, and whatever energy she had left, Marian felt she gave to Roberta, who was the smart one in the family. Marian had always felt left out.

When they were children, Marian claimed that Roberta largely ignored her, except to criticize her. She was convinced that Roberta hated her. Her relationship with Rose was that of caretaker. Her mother worked and it was Marian's responsibility to watch Rose when Rose returned from a special program until their mother came home in the early evening. Caring for Rose was difficult. Marian had been warned that Rose might die at any minute if not adequately protected. Keeping Rose safe became a daunting challenge, and fear that she might die on Marian's watch was a constant concern. Rose did not take well to her sister's being in charge of her, insisting that as the older sister, she did not need to mind Marian. Overburdened, anxious, and very angry, Marian tried to encourage her mother to institutionalize Rose, to no avail.

Marian attributed the positive changes in her current relationships with her sisters to the fact that she now had a loving husband and a responsive baby who provided her with the attention she felt she had missed as a child. Her parents had also become more attentive to her since she had provided them with their first grandchild. She no longer had reason to envy her sisters.

Moreover, she and Roberta have arrived at a "truce." Much to her surprise, Roberta offered to help her when she brought the baby home from the hospital. In that week they spent together, they had begun to form a bond.

Marian also found her relationship with Rose much easier since she has been relieved of the responsibilities and frustrations she experienced as Rose's caretaker. The fact that Rose seems happy in the group home where she was placed a number of years ago has also been important. It has freed Marian from the guilt she experienced as a result of her strong wish to have Rose placed in an institution when they were growing up.

Ann

Adult siblings who may not have enjoyed a good relationship as children may be brought closer by life circumstances. This was the case with Ann, a sixty-five-year-old woman and her five-year-older brother, Leonard. Ann sought treatment for her depression after the death of her ninety-five-year-old mother. She had lost her husband the previous year. With the death of her mother, Ann found herself the co-executor with her brother of her mother's estate, which necessitated considerably more contact than they ordinarily had.

Leonard had treated her badly as a child, sometimes attacking her physically, to the point that her parents had to intervene to keep him from hurting her. He was also her father's favorite and an object of considerable envy. She had been particularly angry that he was allowed to attend college away from home while she had to attend a local university and live with her parents.

As adults, brother and sister were cordial but distant. The families got together for holidays but otherwise they saw little of each other. Forced to spend more time with him, she was surprised to find how fair and considerate he was of her.

At one point during her treatment Ann required surgery, and Leonard was extremely attentive to her. Although she was moved by his efforts on her behalf, she was surprised to find that she was also uncomfortable. He seemed so different than in the past. She had always taken pride in the fact that she was the kinder of the two. She had gained a certain sense of self-value from the belief that she was a better person than he was. Now she had to revise her picture of him. This meant modifying her view of herself.

In one session, she remarked that perhaps it was time for her to begin to see her brother as the aging man he now was, a man who had experienced some painful tragedies in the years since they were children. As she began to view the brother of today more closely, she began to reflect on what it might have been like for him to have had her come on the scene after having been the only child for five years. Perhaps his childhood had not been as idyllic as she had thought.

Ann's experience is a reminder that representations of significant others and of our relationships with them that were registered in our minds as we were growing up may exert a continuing influence on how we perceive and relate to them in the present. This occurs despite the fact that who others are in the here and now may be different from how they were once experienced. It is one of the tasks of therapy to help individuals understand how past perceptions of significant persons and their relationships with them may still be influencing—in some instances distorting—their present perceptions and reactions to them.

Fortunately, Ann was open to looking at her brother anew, was able to revise her image of him as well as of herself, and as a result was free to establish a more amicable relationship with him. With her husband deceased, her children living at a great distance, and the loss of close friends either through death or relocation, her brother's friendship made a significant difference in her life.

Of course, things do not always improve. For some siblings, the stresses and challenges of their adult lives expose the fault lines in their relationship. The struggles they face may overly tax their emotional resources and revive childhood rivalries and conflicts. Dealing with the infirmities of aging parents and their deaths may create discord. Resentments on the part of those children who serve as caretakers of their parents against those who do not assist, conflicts over decisions about their care, or difficulties around inheritances are often divisive.

Mitchell

Mitchell, a man in his late sixties, had two brothers, two and four years younger than him. He did not recall them being rivalrous as they were growing up and was surprised to find that when he and his wife offered to share their home with their ninety-year-old mother who could no longer live alone, both brothers became upset. It meant that she would be living at a greater distance from them. Mitchell found that there was more envy and jealousy in the family than he had been aware of. His brothers insisted that their mother be placed in a facility that was equally close to each of them. The only place they could locate that was equidistant turned out to be at a considerable distance from each brother's home. As a result, visits to their mother were infrequent.

In the case of Jeanette and Ruby, their jealousy of each other followed their father to the grave. While he was dying, the two sisters began to argue over where he was to be buried when he passed away. Each insisted that he be buried near them. The argument only ended when they realized that their father had expressed a wish to be cremated. This meant that they could each keep some of his ashes close to them.

SIBLINGS IN OLD AGE

As siblings enter old age their parents have died, they have often lost their spouses, their children have left home, friends may have moved away or passed on, and they are frequently dealing with declining health and facing their own mortality. Under such circumstances the sibling relationship with all its complexity and ambivalence sometimes becomes more meaningful. Some studies (Bank and Kahn 1997, Gold 1987) suggest that although siblings may continue to experience rivalry in their later years, shared memories of family experiences frequently cushion its impact. Some of those interviewed by Gold (1987) who felt they had been hurt by siblings earlier in life indicated that they thought old age was a time for mellowing and forgetting previous conflicts.

The demands and challenges of old age sometimes lead to significant changes in the relationship between siblings. I think here of Maureen, an eighty-year-old woman, who throughout her life had been very close to her three-year-older sister, Emily.

Maureen's mother died when she was five, leaving the sisters with a father who was unable to care for them. Maureen was sent to an aunt and Emily was placed in an orphanage. When the girls were in their teens their father took them to live with him. Unfortunately, what the sisters had so longed for turned out to be a disaster. Their father's household was chaotic. He was inattentive and provided only the bare essentials that the girls required.

As soon as she was able, Emily took a job and tried to provide what she could for herself and for Maureen. It was Emily who purchased a winter coat for her when their father refused to give her the money. Maureen felt very grateful to her. Their roles changed, however, when the man Emily planned to marry, a man she had grown up with in the orphanage, was killed in World War II. Emily was distraught with grief and Maureen recalls thinking, "Now I must take care of her."

As it turned out Emily had much need for Maureen's care over the years. She had several unhappy marriages and at one point was left with a young child and no resources. Maureen provided financial assistance and emotional support through the many crises that her sister faced. She gave, she said, out of love, loyalty, and gratitude, as well as out of respect for her sister's courage and her prodigious efforts to be as independent as she could be under the adverse circumstances of her life. At the same time, Maureen was often angry and resentful, feeling that too much was being asked of her. When she felt this way she saw herself as a "bad" person. She also felt guilty about having more money and material comforts than her sister. She frequently deprived herself of advantages she might have as a way of expiating her guilt.

Nonetheless, the sisters were compatible all through the years. They enjoyed each other's company and shared many interests. However, by the time she was eighty, Emily had lost most of her friends and had become increasingly isolated, withdrawn, and anxious. Her need for Maureen's support and advice increased. At the same time, Maureen began to feel the weight of her years and found it increasingly difficult to listen to Emily's concerns and to deal with her increasing dysphoria. She realized that if they were to continue to have a good relationship, she would have to acknowledge the limitations of what she could do for her sister, and she began to encourage Emily to seek professional help. At first Emily was reluctant, but when Maureen became insistent, she acquiesced. Maureen's role as "good sister" then became that of finding a good therapist for Emily, which she did. In the end, Maureen felt that her ability to relinquish the caretaker role that she had become accustomed to play and Emily's work in her therapy saved their valued relationship.

Fortunately Maureen and Emily were able to change the way they related to each other without serious conflict. One can imagine situations when this might not be the case. Over time, the roles we play tend to become an aspect of our identity, and relinquishing them can be experienced as a disturbing loss.

Old age can also be a time when the disappointment of not having had a "good enough" brother or sister becomes keener. For example, Carlotta, an eighty-year-old woman who had been an important source of support for her chronically depressed seventy-five-year-old brother all through the years, spoke of how troubling it was that she could not speak of her cancer with her brother, much less look to him for support. It would only make him more depressed. He could offer her nothing. One of the reasons she so valued her treatment was because it provided her with an opportunity to speak of her concerns without fear that she would overburden her therapist. Yet, how good it would have been to have had a stronger brother with whom she could share both the pleasures and the difficulties of their old age.

According to Stephen Bank (1995), the development of closeness between siblings during old age can stimulate further development. Working out and accepting one's relationship with a brother or sister is an important achievement.

Unfortunately many relationships between siblings remain frozen in the past. One sees an example of this in the two brothers in Arthur Miller's drama *The Price* (1968) who have had little to do with each other over the years. The brothers are finally brought together by their father's death in order to dispose of his estate. The men are very different from one another. The elder, Walter, has been educated and is rich and famous; the younger, Victor, is a poor, self-sacrificing policeman, who gave up college and his ambition to be a scientist in order to support their father. His hurt and resentment of his brother's failure to assist with his father are always with him. When the brothers meet in the play, Walter has had a breakdown and has been hospitalized. He is trying to rebuild his life and wants to form a closer relationship with his brother. He expresses his regret over what has transpired in the past, revealing that he had in fact attempted to assist their father financially. Their father, however, refused his assistance and never disclosed his offer to Victor. Victor remains unmoved by this information, as far as one can tell, and the play ends without a rapprochement between the brothers.

The audience is given the impression that Walter received psychotherapy when he was recently hospitalized that left him open to and desirous of a new relationship with his brother. However, Victor could not alter his perceptions of his brother and his reactions to him, so strong was the power of his earlier experiences.

Miller has shown us how early unmodified representations of siblings can retain their influence throughout life (Volkan and Ast 1997). Perhaps if Victor had had the opportunity for treatment, as his brother did, a new relationship between these aging brothers might have become possible, one that would allow them to find companionship and support in each other in the years to come.

REMARKS

These and other research findings as well as clinical experience attest to the importance of the attachment siblings form with one another and the role they may play in fostering each other's development. Although obviously not as critical to an individual's development as their parents, brothers and sisters can, as seen in this chapter, help to promote separation and individuation, facilitate the development of such capacities as empathy, mentalization, and promote socialization, as well as influence other developmental achievements. On the other hand, as we shall see in later chapters, the relationship between siblings may impede development, create troubling conflicts, and sometimes play a pathogenic role.

We have seen too how, as with parents, object representations of siblings and representations of the interactions with them are registered in the mind and serve as templates that guide relationships with others (Schore 2003). These inner representations influence the way they relate to mates, children, friends, and helping professionals. Recognition of the important role that siblings play in the development and lives of individuals has implications for both clinicians and social policy planners, as will be demonstrated in subsequent chapters.

2

The Impact of Culture on Sibling Relationships

In the previous chapter on development, the findings presented were largely derived from studies conducted in two Western, industrialized countries, England and the United States, and pertain, as far as one can tell, to brothers and sisters who belong to the dominant culture in these countries, who have grown up in at least average socioeconomic circumstances, and who have been reared in traditional nuclear families.

Whereas children from all cultures face many of the same developmental challenges, there are differing societal and parental expectations, family patterns, and child rearing practices throughout the world. Different cultures favor dissimilar traits and behaviors in their children and often have different expectations of sibling roles and relationships. The customs, laws, and attitudes of a particular society may also exert an influence on the relationships between brothers and sisters. For example, in societies in which the eldest son inherits all of the parents' properties or those in which younger sisters have to wait to marry until the eldest sister is wed, siblings are likely to relate to each other somewhat differently than in societies that do not observe such practices.

Today, mental health professionals in America are increasingly serving clients of diverse backgrounds, whose family structures, customs, values, and expectations vary considerably. In recognition of the multicultural nature of our society, "cultural competence" has been added to the general requirements for helping professionals. This is in recognition of the fact that unfamiliarity with the normal variations in behavior, belief, or experience particular to an individual's cultural background may lead to inaccurate diagnoses of pathology. This appreciation of the importance of culture is reflected in the decision of the Accreditation Council for Psychoanalytic Education, developed by a consortium of psychoanalytic organizations (American Academy of Psychoanalysis; American Psychoanalytic Association; American Psychological Association, Division 39; American Association for Psychoanalysis in Clinical Social Work) to make the understanding of the role of culture in development and pathology a curriculum requirement for psychoanalytic training institutes.

Sensitive attention to cultural factors is requisite to avoid pathologizing attitudes and behaviors that are normative in a person's culture of origin and to understand and form a working alliance with individuals who are different from ourselves (Akhtar 1995, Mishne 2002). Although some individuals might prefer to be treated by clinicians of similar backgrounds, the reality is that there are not enough health care practitioners for this to be practical. Fortunately, there have been countless successful treatments in which the backgrounds of patient and therapist were different. What is needed is recognition of the importance of cultural influences and a willingness to learn from those we work with how they understand the role that their particular background has played in their development and lives. Each individual's experience is unique. Nonetheless, some familiarity with the patterns of sibling relationships in different cultures and the roles that siblings are expected to play in each other's lives can help clinicians avoid making erroneous assumptions.

It is of course impossible to acquire more than a limited understanding of the many different cultures in which our clients have grown up and the role that cultural factors may have played in determining their relationships with their brothers and sisters. Moreover, there are significant differences between people of the same culture, and generalizations are likely to be misleading at least and stereotyping at worst. However, there is a growing body of literature that focuses on the influence of race, ethnicity, nationality, gender, and socioeconomic factors on the bond between siblings. Although writings cannot inform us about any one patient's experiences, they can increase our knowledge of this area of our patients' lives and encourage us to pay greater attention to it.

AUTONOMY

One of the most significant differences between industrialized and non-industrialized nations is the way in which they regard autonomy. Salvador Minuchin (1974), a family therapist, has proposed that healthy families are connected but have a good sense of individual separateness whereas unhealthy families lack a well-defined sense of separateness or are disengaged, lacking a sense of connection. Although we in the United States value the capacity for relatedness to others, we accord a high priority to the ability to tolerate separateness and the achievement of independence in our extremely mobile, competitive society. We expect our children to grow up and make their separate lives. We tend to evaluate the mental health of individuals on the basis of their capacity to live and succeed on their own. Although American parents would like their children to remain close as adults, it is not imperative that they do so.

In many areas such as Southeast Asia, the Middle East, Africa, and Latin America, individuation from the family is likely to be seen as an aberration. It is the "familial self" (Akhtar 1995) that is valued. It is expected that siblings will play a significant role in each other's lives throughout their lifetimes. In certain Asian societies, for example (Nuckolls 1993), adult brothers are often expected to live with each other and with their parents in multigenerational households and to share work and resources. They remain closely involved in each other's affairs and frequently share strong economic ties in adulthood. Even when they do not, they are likely to feel entitled to call upon each other for support and assistance at any time. They continue to share social obligations. These obligations are not optional or temporary, as they frequently are in the United States, but expected role attributes.

Rita Ledesma (2003) has written of the close ties between members of Latino and Native American families. She identifies herself as Chicana and Oglala Lakota and works with both groups of families. Ledesma notes how family is the central reference point for Native American and Latina women. This focus on family necessitates a reconceptualization of such psychological concepts as separation, individuation, autonomy, and boundaries, lest we pathologize attitudes and behaviors that are highly valued in these groups.

In her own life Ledesma notes how family takes priority. She describes an occasion when a colleague at the university where she taught overheard a phone call she made to her home during which she asked whether her husband or sons had eaten breakfast. If they had not she offered to return home and prepare the meal for them. After the call, her colleague suggested that her dissertation would be completed sooner if she devoted herself to working on it more and let her family prepare their own meals. Ledesma goes on to say that her colleague did not understand that her academic activities were not the driving force in her life and that the ability to return home to her family and engage in traditional caregiving was an important source of affirmation, validation, intimacy, and mutuality.

An example of the importance of sensitivity to cultural differences has been offered by Marsha H. Levy-Warren (2001) in her description of work she did with a young Southeast Asian Indian couple. Dr. Levy-Warren's intent in offering this case illustration was not to demonstrate the value of cultural sensitivity, but it has stood out for me as a fine example of such.

Pilar and Musaf (the fictious names Dr. Levy-Warren gave to her young patients) sought help after the birth of their infant daughter, Leila. Leila's birth was one of today's medical feats. Conceived through a donor egg and a mix of Musaf's sperm and a donor's, Leila was carried by Pilar. Unfortunately the sperm bank had not matched them properly, and Leila was born with fair skin, light hair, and blue eyes. Among the young couple's concerns was the fear that their parents and their siblings would not accept Leila because she was clearly not of their background.

Dr. Levy-Warren understood Pilar and Musaf's concerns about their family's possible rejection of Leila. However, she reminded them that in some ways their parents had actually shown greater flexibility over time than they seemed to appreciate. They had, after all, permitted their children to be educated in America. Although Musaf's parents found his move to this country particularly difficult, she reminded them that his mother and father were planning a visit the following year, which suggested some change in their attitudes. Perhaps news of Leila would be met in the same way.

Dr. Levy-Warren was well aware that these young parents' concerns were multidetermined. However, she began where they were, and her understanding of the importance to both of them of their family's attitudes played an important role in fostering the excellent working relationship that developed between Dr. Levy-Warren and Pilar and Musaf.

COMPETITION

In addition to cultural variations in the value placed on autonomy, significant differences in attitudes are likely to exist among industrialized and non-industrialized nations with respect to competition. Although sibling rivalry, competition, jealousy, and conflict can arise in all countries, the feelings among different cultures about these attitudes vary. In Western nations sibling rivalry is more or less accepted when not excessive. Its contribution to the development of a competitive attitude is even viewed to some extent as a preparation for success in our capitalistic society. In other parts of the world, however, particularly in Asian societies (Nuckolls 1993), rivalry and competition are not valued. Instead cooperation, interdependence, and working for the good of the family are of primary importance.

SIBLING RESPONSIBILITIES

In many societies siblings participate jointly with their parents in activities that are essential for survival, reproduction, and the passing on of cultural and social values (Weisner 1982). They perform important, responsible domestic chores. They are involved in child rearing, in protecting the family and the community, in arranging marriages, and in providing marriage payments (Cicerelli 1995, Weisner 1982). Considerable emphasis is placed on sibling cooperation, family solidarity, and the authority of older over younger children (Weisner 1982). In the traditional cultures of India (Nuckolls 1993, Weisner 1982) brothers are likely to feel obligated to check on the welfare of their married sisters and their children throughout their lifetimes.

Older children in these societies are frequently expected to serve as the major caretakers of their younger siblings (Weisner 1982). They learn to take care of their brothers and sisters and to respond favorably to their siblings taking care of them. In Thailand (Nye 2005), the eldest sister assumes special responsibilities for her younger siblings and is highly protective of them. She deserves and demands respect. She is expected to be tolerant, understanding, benevolent, and caretaking. Indeed, social workers in that country are said to model their relationship with their clients on the relationship between older sisters and their younger siblings.

A pattern of sibling caretaking has been found to lead to a different affective style and pattern of attachment from that which occurs in those countries in which parents are major caretakers. Children cared for by siblings tend to develop a more diffuse affective style and pattern of attachment to both adults and other children (Weisner 1982). They are less involved with adults and more oriented toward multi-age groups of peers of either sex. On the whole there also appears to be less fighting, less quarreling, less competition, increased social responsibility, and an increased capacity to nurture, as well as earlier and stronger sex-role identification among those children who have grown up caring for or in the care of their siblings. Yet, according to Weisner, sibling exchanges are not always congenial and fights, rivalries, and conflicts do occur.

To the extent that these caretaking arrangements decrease involvement with adults, children in such societies have been found to have less chance to acquire skills that are dependent upon adult models (Weisner 1982). Whereas children cared for by adults tend to learn through highly verbal modes, children cared for by other children appear to learn by imitation and mimicry and through sharing and cooperation. This can place such children at a disadvantage when they immigrate to Western countries where verbal skills are essential.

In the United States, caretaking of younger siblings has tended in the past to be an optional practice in middle-class families. A study of 168 families more than fifteen years ago (Bryant 1992) showed that among middle-class families, sibling caretaking in America tended to be episodic rather than continuous. Older siblings were largely called upon to entertain their younger brothers and sisters for short periods of time or to watch them when parents were busy, but their responsibilities for them were usually limited.

When adult caretakers have relegated greater responsibility for child care to their older children, it has ordinarily been because the family is contending with economic, psychological, or health problems. In the case of the working poor, for example, the lack of affordable day care often forces parents to assign child care responsibilities to older siblings. There are also certain troubled or seriously ill parents who are unable to assume the care of their young children and it is left to siblings to take on parental responsibilities. However, today, with the increase in the number of families in which all of the adults are employed and away from home during the day, older children are more likely to be responsible for their younger siblings than in the past.

When the caretaking activities are limited they can contribute positively to the development of both younger and older children. Younger children learn from their older siblings, who may serve as models for them. The older ones learn from their roles as teachers and often develop a sense of self-worth from contributing to their younger siblings' achievements.

In immigrant families, older siblings frequently play an important role in helping their younger brothers and sisters with academic encouragement and assistance, and often help to convince their parents of the importance of allowing them to have educational opportunities However, there is some research that shows that when these older siblings reach junior high school (Cooper, Denner, and Lopez 1999) their own academic performance declines, possibly as a result of the time they expend on helping their younger brothers and sisters. In some instances they leave school or do not do as well as their younger siblings whom they had assisted.

Patti

This was true for Patti, a twenty-four-year-old Chinese college student, who was given almost full responsibility for the care of her three younger siblings when she was not at school. This included tending to her four-year-old sister, Sue, who suffered from autism.

Patti served as a translator for her parents in their contacts with the school for emotionally disturbed children that Sue attended. Most family sessions were held with her alone, as her parents found it difficult to leave the small grocery they operated. It was during those sessions that Patti's depression became evident. She shared how hard she was finding life. Her father became enraged, sometimes beating her if she came home from college with less than an A average. She found it impossible to achieve the grades he wanted her to, given the extra demands that were made upon her at home. Not only did she care for her siblings, but she was expected to help out in the store and as the only one with a driver's license, she did the shopping and chauffeuring for the family.

Patti was overwhelmed, but she did not think her situation was anything out of the ordinary. She had been taking care of her younger siblings for as long as she could recall. In China, she recalled looking out for them while her parents worked nearby in the rice fields.

Although her social worker understood that this had been the family pattern ever since Patti was little and one that was common in Patti's homeland, she tried to help Patti understand that her father's wish for her to do well at college suggested that he also had other goals for her. What he and she did not understand yet was that she could not achieve his aspirations for her as well as her own wishes for herself and at the same time assume all the other responsibilities she was expected to meet. No one could do all that she was trying to do.

The goal of this short-term work was to try to modify Patti's expectations of herself and, if possible, those of her father. In an interview with Patti and her parents, the worker tried to convey her appreciation of all they were trying to do for their family and her recognition of how hard it must be moving to a new country with new ways. She understood how important it was to have Patti's help at home and in the store. Encouraging her to go to college suggested, though, that they also wished her to achieve outside of the home. An effort was made to help them see how Patti could not effectively do both at the same time and to help the parents consider some practical ways of relieving Patti of some of her responsibilities.

Whether this and similar efforts helped these parents understand Patti's situation better and alter some of their expectations was never clear. However, the sessions did enable Patti to modify some of her own expectations of herself. She was not a "bad" daughter or a "bad" person if she could not fulfill the roles her family expected her to assume in China and those she was being called upon to fulfill in America. As a result she became better able to assert her needs and to say "no" occasionally when she could not meet all of her parents' demands.

Patti's experience reminds us of the role that cultural factors play in helping to shape a child's ego goals and aspirations (Jacobson 1964). We can see how different societal expectations in a new country can tax the ego's adaptive capacities and lead to conflict within the superego and the ego ideal (Akhtar 1995). According to the customs of her native land, Patti's self-esteem depended, at least in part, on her fulfilling her role as a caretaking sibling. Although education is highly valued in China, as it is in the United States, as a farm worker during the Cultural Revolution, it is unlikely that Patti's father or those around him would have expected their children to attend college. After the family moved to this country a college education became a possibility for Patti and she and her father increasingly appear to have identified with American expectations and goals. As a consequence, Patti's father's valuation of her and her own self regard became increasingly dependent upon Patti's ability to meet American goals for success. It was not possible to fulfill both these expectations. Patti's sense of shame and failure for not living up to her ideals contributed to her depression. For Patti, like many other immigrants, the therapeutic challenge is to help them integrate those self-representations that are being shaped by experiences in America with those developed in their native country, that is to develop what Berzoff, Flanagan, and Hertz (1996) have referred to as a "bicultural identity." This identity state needs to encompass the positive aspects of both the old and the new identities (Chung 1999).

PARENTAL PREFERENCES

Gender

Different cultures value different features in their children. In many countries boys are valued more highly than girls. Martin, a nurse, shared what it was like for him to be the preferred male in an Italian-American family with a little sister nine years younger than he.

Martin regarded his position in an Italian family as typical. Whereas his parents insisted that they treated him and his sister, Gale, equally as they were growing up, both he and Gale agreed that he was the "prince." Gale was cared for and loved, but there was no question who held the place of honor in the family. From Martin's perspective his parents' preference for a male child proved in some ways to be disadvantageous insofar as it led his parents to be overprotective and overinvolved with him. His sister's birth helped to diminish some of his parents' intense preoccupation with him and left him freer. He could not recall whether he had been envious or jealous of Gale or not, but imagined he might have been at first. Yet it was always clear that he was the more important child in the family. However, had she not been born, he believes he would have had a much harder time gaining his independence and achieving a more realistic view of himself.

Martin could not, of course, speak for Gale. He supposed she envied him as the valued male in the family and as the much older sibling who was accorded many more privileges than she during her growing up years. She was a difficult child, stubborn and demanding, and perhaps he was part of her problem. However, he also thought that as she grew older she used him as a model in some ways, and he hoped that that had proven an advantage for her. As an adult she had successfully pursued a career similar to his. They are close as adults, enjoy each other's company, and have a number of common interests.

He especially values Gale now that their elderly mother is ill. He hates to think about what it would be like if he had been an only child and did not have his sister to share the responsibility and the pain that they both experience watching their mother decline.

Li

A young college girl, Li, tells what it was like for her growing up in a Chinese family in which male children were highly favored. She had a brother two years her senior. Li says of herself, "I was not the favored child in my family." As in other traditional Chinese families, boys are preferred over girls. Boys grow up, get married, and bring their wives into the family, whereas girls are a lost investment.

> I hated my older brother because he always received preferential treatment. I hated being a girl and wanted to be a boy. I did the traditional female chores in the house. I hated domesticity and all that it entails. I was jealous of my older brother and wanted to be like him. I didn't have my own sense of identity because I had rejected it. I ran errands for my mom and acted as a liaison for her to the outside world. Nothing I did was good enough. My mom had high expectations. It was a no-win setup for me.
>
> I excelled at school, not because of my love for education but because it brought me momentary praise and attention. Once that wore off, the motivation to excel did not last.
>
> My older brother was pampered and spoiled. He got whatever he wanted and his sense of entitlement was cultivated very early on. As he grew up he became lost too. He was angry at the world when he didn't get what he wanted.

Appearance

Skin color and hair texture may determine which children are favored in some African American families (C. L. Thompson 1996, Watson 2003). There are parents who prefer a lighter-skinned child, whereas in other families it can be the darker-skinned youngster who is more valued. Cheryl L. Thompson has noted how her own struggle with skin color has helped her appreciate the complexity of this issue in her work with her African American patients. Because lighter-skinned African Americans are often more likely to achieve greater success regardless of education, family background, or occupation, this is a desired attribute in many families. "Skin color," she writes, "becomes the variable around which hope or despair for the next generation is aroused" (1996, p.127). However, as can be seen in a case reported by Martha Watson, an African American psychotherapist (2003), in some families the preferred siblings are those who most closely resemble a parent in appearance regardless of whether their characteristics are regarded as desirable or not in the wider culture.

Martha Watson (2003) writes of a thirty-five-year-old woman, Mary, who had four siblings, two older brothers, one older, and one younger sister. Both parents were professionals. Her father was light brown and her mother was a darker shade. Mary herself was medium brown. Mary felt her mother favored her sisters, who were darker complexioned, like their mother herself.

Though her mother and her sisters envied her straight hair, in fights with her sisters they would deride her for having "white" hair. Her difference from them made her the least favored child in the family.

Intellect

In some families in which intellectual prowess and academic achievement are highly valued, the most accomplished child often becomes the more valued one. Morna, a forty-year-old Jewish woman, who was accomplished in her field, nonetheless felt that all of her life she had suffered in comparison to her four-year-older sister, Joan. Joan was an outstanding student who won many prizes during her school years and as an adult is a leader in her field. Morna's parents doted on her sister, boasting of her exceptional abilities and accomplishments to anyone who would pause long enough to listen. When they had to decide how to spend their limited resources, they chose to send Joan to a private college, believing it would mean more to her than to her sister. Morna was obliged to enroll at a city college, which she thought was inferior to her sister's school. Morna has continued to envy and resent Joan and her parents, blaming them because she finds herself today in a less prestigious field than her sister. Even more troubling is the fact that she has identified with her parents and measures her achievements against those of her sister's. She always comes up short.

Despite the fact that our society favors the achieving child, in some cultural groups scholarly, academically successful children may actually enjoy less favor (C. L. Thompson 1996). They are sometimes viewed as rejecting their group and family, and their accomplishments are depreciated rather than praised. In some African American families, for example, doing well in school, speaking standard English, and pursuing intellectual activities may elicit scorn and rejection, rather than encouragement, pride, and acceptance. This occurs in other groups as well.

Rose

Such was the case in Rose's family. Rose, a twenty-four-year-old Latina, masters degree student, sought treatment at the counseling department of the large university to which she had won a full scholarship. She had been referred by one of her professors, who was concerned about the changes he saw in her following her mother's death several months previously. Rose had uncharacteristically begun to miss classes, and when she did attend, frequently fell asleep.

Rose came from an impoverished, multi-problem family. Her father was an alcoholic and had been incarcerated for much of her young life. An older brother, who had dropped out of school, was involved with drugs and was a member of a gang. As far back as she could recall he and her father had teased her for what they referred to as her "high and mighty ways." Her mother, on the other hand, had encouraged her to do well in school and was proud of Rose's accomplishments. She was careful, though, not to let her son and husband see how much Rose's academic success meant to her. It would have made the other family members even more critical of Rose. With her mother's death Rose lost the only person who cared that she make something of herself. Attending school seemed less important to her once her mother was gone.

In Rose's sessions it became apparent how high a price she had paid for her accomplishments. She was ridiculed and rejected by her father and brother, as well as other family members. She was the "odd-ball." In one session, when she was trying to decide whether she would visit her father and her brother over the school holiday, Rose spoke of the dilemma she faced.

Rose: I'm going to go home for a month. It'll be really strange. I'm afraid of losing my freedom. I feel free here, lately, anyway. It's just so backward back home. There's an education barrier with the people I'd be around. I've been in school for so long that going back there, I'd be around family members who can't talk on my level and don't know the things I know. I would feel isolated there. I don't feel isolated here at school.

Therapist: I'm reminded of your cousin whom you've mentioned here. Might you visit her?

Rose: Yes. She's not afraid to live her life, to move forward. That's why she's an outcast too. A lot of people in my family, especially my brother, don't like that. They want you to stay where they are. Or they say, "Are you trying to be better than us? Are you trying to show us up?"

Therapist: It seems as if you and your cousin, by being different from the rest of your family, are threatening to them.

Rose: Yes, and they try to make us afraid a lot of the time.

Therapist: What do you find frightening?

Rose: Well, my biggest thing was that these were the only people I had, that they were given to me. So if I wanted to be with people, I had to monitor my behavior so that I could stay with them. But now that I'm getting older, I realize I don't even want to be with these people. Why should I stunt my growth? I have to get my own family and build my own friends and I'm doing that. I don't want to be a part of their group anymore. I was raised to believe that your family is all you have. That's not true. There are people out there that you can connect with that will care about you the same or even more than your blood relatives! There are kind and loving people who show concern for you. My father and brother have not phoned me once since my mother died. I call them, and ask about them, but they don't ask about me. I guess after my mom passed away and my family didn't seem to have any interest in me, I finally asked myself, "Do I really need it? Can't I be happy with other people?" It's my friends who seem to understand the pain I'm in and try to comfort me.

Louise

Cheryl Thompson (1996) writes of an African American patient, Louise, who came from a family that enjoyed considerable status in their community as a result of her father's position and biracial heritage. Unlike her siblings, who were light skinned and had wavy hair as well as European features, the model for attractiveness in her family, Louise had thick lips, a wide nose, and kinky hair, which she felt created distance between her and the other members of the family. Though they were pleased that she had graduated from college (the first one to do so in the family), Louise found that her accomplishments further increased the distance between her and the rest of her family. She was deeply conflicted about succeeding, for success only meant further separation from them.

Whereas Thompson regarded these familial attitudes as contributors to Louise's conflicts about success, it is important to note that she emphasized that Louise's resistance to defining herself as an educated, independent, and socially mobile black woman was determined by a number of other factors, such as her unconscious concern that self-sufficiency would somehow compromise her femininity. We are reminded that although culture is important, it may be only one of the determinants of a person's personality and behavior.

IMMIGRATION AND SIBLING RELATIONSHIPS

Immigration is a challenging experience for all concerned, involving painful losses of family, friends, and professional affiliations, as well as familiar places, customs, and activities (Hoffman 1989). Ties with the past are interrupted. In many instances siblings are parted, never to see each other again. Immigrants who have prospered here often feel guilty over leaving other brothers and sisters living in dire circumstances in their home countries (Mehta 1997).

Eva Hoffman (1989), an immigrant herself, has pointed out how immigration frequently upsets the patterns of family life and the transactions and balances among family members. Immigrant children usually assimilate into their new cultures faster and more easily than their mothers and fathers. They tend to learn English and assume American ways more quickly than their parents. As the English-speaking members of the family, they may assume a premature sense of authority, and brothers and sisters may share together in ways that exclude their parents. While strengthening the bond between siblings, this arrangement may lessen respect for parents and weaken the ties between parents and children.

Sonia Nazario (2006) studied a group of young people from Latin American countries who came to the United States unaccompanied in search of their mothers, who had left them at home in order to earn money. She detailed the dangerous and seemingly impossible journeys many of these children take, some as young as seven, though the average age is about fifteen. In many cases those children who finally locate their mothers discover that their mothers have formed new families and that they now have half siblings. Anger at their mothers for abandoning them and resentment of their new siblings, who have had their mother's attention since birth, frequently follow these young people's initial joy at reunion. Their American brothers and sisters are in turn often threatened by their newly discovered siblings, who ordinarily receive considerable attention when they first reunite with their mothers. Some of these American children refer to their immigrant siblings disparagingly as *mojados,* or wetbacks. There have been instances in which the hostility on the part of these American-born siblings has been so intense that they have threatened to summon immigration authorities to return these brothers or sisters to their homeland.

REMARKS

It is clear that different cultures view sibling relationships differently and have different expectations of the roles siblings play in each other's lives. It is therefore essential that psychoanalysts and other helping professionals explore with those they serve the influence their particular backgrounds have had on their relationships with their brothers and sisters.

Yet, even as we seek greater knowledge about cultural influences we need to remain mindful that the peoples of the world have much in common. Whereas different cultures offer unique possibilities and challenges for resolving conflicts, children from a variety of cultural backgrounds face many similar developmental tasks, and many of our concerns and conflicts are universal (Erikson 1963). Whatever one's nationality, economic background, race, class, and gender, we are all familiar with feelings of love and hate, of envy and jealousy, and of guilt and humiliation, though what evokes these feelings may differ. Mothers and fathers may prefer one child over another for a variety of reasons other than cultural values, and resentment and hatred of a preferred child occurs all over the world. What we hope to achieve is a balance, to appreciate its importance while at the same time remaining aware of the myriad factors that bear on who our patients are, the struggles that they have faced in the past, and the challenges they are presently encountering.

3

Siblings in the Families of Today

The American family has changed dramatically in the last fifty years or so. The nuclear family, which forty years ago was described as a "family composed of adults of both sexes, at least two of whom maintain a socially approved sexual relationship, and one or more children, own or adopted" (Murdock 1960, p. 37) was considered to be universal. This is no longer so. In 2003 it was estimated that 68.7 percent of American youth were living in non-traditional families, that is seven out of ten children (Rainbows, www.rainbows.org/statistics.html). These include divorced families, step or blended families, families in which both parents are of the same gender, families in which children are of different ethnic groups than their parents and/or each other, and one-parent families created either by choice, divorce, abandonment, the death of a partner, or by unplanned pregnancies.

The ways in which families are formed, which will be considered in the next chapter, has undergone significant changes over time. Foster care and adoption, which have long been ways of building a family, serve different children and parents and involve different procedures than years ago. Through the development of new reproductive technologies, medical science has provided options for building a family that were never imagined in the past.

Although there have been studies of children growing up in these non-traditional families, little attention, as far as I can ascertain, has been paid to the relationships among siblings in them. This chapter considers issues that may arise for siblings who grow up in divorced families, in single-parent households, in gay and lesbian families, and in step families. The next chapter discusses sibling issues in families formed by foster care, adoption, and the new reproductive technologies.

SIBLINGS OF DIVORCE

One of the most significant changes in the family over time has been the increase in the number of divorces. It is generally estimated that around 40 to 50 percent of marriages in the United States today end in divorce. Separation and divorce rates are at least as high in second marriages, so that many children face family disruptions more than once.

Divorce means loss for all members of the family. Even when both parents continue their involvement, children are likely to see the non-custodial parent less frequently than they once did and whatever the circumstances, children lose the family that they have known in the past, as well as their parents as they once were. Both parents are likely to be in a different place emotionally, socially, and economically after a divorce and the pattern of family life including such everyday routines as who puts the children to bed, who drives them to school, or who sets the limits are more often than not altered.

Many children in divorced families provide each other with support and continuity that help to ease the transition. Mara, who was seven, and Jennifer, who was four when their adoptive parents divorced, recalled in an interview with me how important it was for them to have each other when everything in their lives seemed to change. Jennifer spoke of how Mara's presence made her feel safer when she visited her father in his new apartment. She could count on Jennifer to braid her hair and to encourage her father to buy the foods she liked. Things did not seem so different with Mara there to help her.

When their parents eventually remarried, Mara and Jennifer found it easier to deal with their stepparents because they had each other. If they thought they were not being treated fairly they had each other to complain to. The support these sisters offered each other during their parents' divorce and re-marriage led to an extremely close bond between them that continued through their adulthood.

Wallerstein and Kelly (1980) found in their study of children of divorce that, as in the case of Mara and Jennifer, many siblings turned to each other for comfort and support and developed a strong relationship. However, this was not always the case. In some families siblings became more envious and hostile toward one another as they competed for scarce resources of parental love and attention. Some brothers and sisters formed a small group and helped each other to deal with the adults in the family, whereas in other families the children sided with different parents, which led to conflict between the siblings. Older children were frequently given more responsibility for their younger siblings. Some younger children valued this care as Jennifer did, but some felt deprived of parental care.

The latter was the case with Felicia Reiss, whose mother consulted me about therapy for Felicia. Following her divorce the preceding year, Mrs. Reiss had taken a full-time job, and had relegated the after-school care of her ten-year-old daughter, Felicia, to her twelve-year-old daughter, Martha. When she was married Mrs. Reiss had only worked part time and had a housekeeper to help her with the home and the girls. The family was affluent and she could have afforded household assistance, but Mrs. Reiss believed that it was time her daughters learned responsibility. However, the arrangement was not working out. The girls were constantly fighting and calling her at work to settle their arguments. She was at her "wit's end." She felt that the problem really was with Felicia and had decided that perhaps she needed therapy.

I tried to get a picture of how Mrs. Reiss and the girls had experienced the divorce, and whether she thought that the difficulties the sisters were having might have something to do with their feelings about the changes in the family. She adamantly denied that the divorce had any negative impact on any of them, insisting they were all better off since the divorce. She saw the problems they were facing as a family as due to the fact that she had "spoiled" the girls earlier, particularly Felicia, as the younger.

A session with Felicia about a week later revealed a somewhat depressed young girl who found her older sister "very bossy" and who wished her mother was at home. She thought her sister was too young to be a "mother." She definitely did not want to see a therapist. She did not think she was "crazy." She thought that since the divorce things were just "crazy" at home.

Although I believed Felicia would have benefited from an opportunity to share her feelings in treatment, there seemed to be no point to making such a recommendation at this time. Not only was Felicia opposed to the idea, but it seemed unwise to designate her as the one in need of assistance when each member of the family appeared to be contributing to the difficulties among them. A suggestion that perhaps Mrs. Reiss herself might find counseling helpful in dealing with her daughters was immediately rebuffed and the idea of their meeting with a family therapist was also rejected. I finally decided to suggest a change in the situation and proposed that before we considered treatment for Felicia, which she did not seem ready for, Mrs. Reiss might want to consider a homemaker, as she once had had, during the hours when the children were alone.

Mrs. Reiss was resistant to this idea as well, insisting that the girls needed to learn to work together and assume greater responsibility for themselves and the house. I agreed that this certainly was a worthwhile goal, but they just did not seem ready yet. When they became more accustomed to their new arrangements—their separation from their father and the fact that she herself was now less available—they might more easily assume the responsibilities she wished of them. Perhaps it was something she could try for awhile. I noted that we could reevaluate what was needed if the arrangement did not prove helpful. Mrs. Reiss reluctantly said she would think about this. It was clear, however, that this idea did not sit well with her, and when she left I thought I was unlikely to hear from her again.

Much to my surprise, about a month later Mrs. Reiss phoned to say that her mother had spent a week with her in the interval and she had not received one call from the girls. She could see where it made a difference to have someone there in the home when they returned from school and until she returned from work. She was currently looking for a homemaker.

For most divorced, single parents such an arrangement is not an option. Few have the financial resources that this family had and there are very few after-school programs to provide the care that many children need today. Moreover, this intervention did not address Mrs. Reiss's difficulties in considering the impact that the divorce had had on her daughters, on their relationship with one another, and on herself.

Changes in Parental Preferences Following Divorce

There is some evidence to suggest that following divorce, some parents begin to develop a stronger preference for one child over another that had not been evident during the marriage. A study by Wallenstein and Lewis (2007) found that many of the noncustodial fathers narrowed their interest and attention to one child in their first family. Sometimes it was the youngest child. Sometimes it was the child who shared the father's interests or the child whose talents made him or her more attractive. The preferred youngster was often rewarded with more expensive gifts and with funds for higher education. The less favored children received little emotional or educational support. This differential led to those children feeling neglected and rejected and proved detrimental to their development and well-being.

According to this study, mothers, too, often shifted their attention to one child in the family after the divorce. Some focused on the child who needed the most care, often the youngest. In some families a mother gave her fullest attention to the child who made his or her needs known and who demanded her attention. There were also mothers who became closer and more responsive to the child who helped them the most, often the oldest girl.

Wallerstein and Lewis cited the case of a young mother whose husband left her with three young children. She had to work full time and relied on her oldest child, age nine, for help in supervising the younger children and running the household. She rewarded her with warm praise and privileges. At the same time she was unable to attend to her other two children as she did in the past, leaving them feeling abandoned. When these investigators followed up this family after ten years, they found the oldest child doing well, whereas the development of the other two children had been seriously compromised.

SINGLE-PARENT FAMILIES

In 2002, 9 percent of America's children were growing up in single parent households (U.S. Census Bureau 2007). In addition to those parents made single by divorce, there are those who are widowed, those who are separated from their mates, those who have had unplanned pregnancies, and those who have chosen to be single parents.

Whatever the reason, single parents generally face certain practical challenges, which are likely to have a bearing on the emotional state of the family. They more often than not must balance child care with work, run a household alone, arrange for substitute child care, and carry all the responsibilities that two parents ordinarily share. As a result, they are likely to be less available to their children and to need their children to assume increased responsibility for their own care. As in the case of the Reiss family, siblings frequently become responsible for each other's care. It is not unusual for younger siblings to come into the care of children not much older than themselves.

The Death of a Parent

Although there is considerable variability in responses to loss, the process of mourning is slow, agonizing, and emotionally and physically demanding. When one parent dies, the remaining parent often must bear all the everyday responsibilities alone at a time when the family is struggling to deal with the traumatic impact of the loss they have sustained. The way the surviving parent and each of the children deal with their grief can have a significant impact on the relationship between siblings in the family. In some families, the support that family members provide each other with, including those that the siblings offer one another, is of enormous value, and helps to foster closer relationships between them. In others, the death of a parent, may severely strain family relationships, adversely affecting the development of one or more of the members.

Loretta

In this connection I think of Loretta, whose father committed suicide when she was two and her older brother, Russell, was nine. After her husband's death, their depressed mother left the children in the care of relatives for long periods of time while she traveled around the country visiting friends. Sometimes she took Russell with her, leaving Loretta at home, generally in the care of her seriously depressed grandmother.

When she was home, Loretta's mother had little interest in Loretta, and gave most of her attention to Russell. She appears to have tried to put him in the place of the husband she lost and looked to him for help in raising Loretta. He determined what clothes Loretta wore, what friends she was permitted to make, what privileges she enjoyed, and other matters.

With the loss of her father and the lack of attention from her mother, Loretta turned to her brother from an early age for attention and affection. He rebuffed her best efforts to engage him, was intensely critical and disdainful of her, and generally treated her as if she was in the way. As a child, Loretta interpreted his responses as a sign that there was something wrong with her. She also internalized his harsh, critical view of her, and came to see herself as she thought he saw her. While this was a source of considerable discomfort, viewing herself through her brother's eyes unfortunately became a way of feeling close to him, and helping her relinquish that image of herself proved to be a difficult therapeutic challenge.

As an adult Loretta continued to seek her brother's notice and approval and was hurt, disappointed, and enraged by his indifference and rejection of her. She dealt with her rage by turning it back on herself. It became clearer in her treatment that whereas her efforts were motivated in part by the hope that eventually he would change and respond positively to her, the pain associated with these efforts itself became a vehicle for feeling connected with him. Like those patients Arthur Valenstein (1973) has written about, Loretta became attached to pain.

An effort was made in her treatment to help Loretta begin to appreciate how her brother's responses to her were likely to have had little to do with her. As a much older brother, he must have appeared to her to be an adult. It was understandable that under the circumstances she had turned to him for attention and affection. However, only a child himself, traumatized by the death of their father, and burdened by the demands their mother made upon him to take his father's place, he was ill equipped to provide her with care and love. She had mistaken his inability to give her what she longed for as indicating that something was wrong with her.

Single Parents by Choice

Single parents by choice contend with the same demands as all single parents, as well as with whatever challenges may be associated with the ways in which they have formed their families, whether through adoption or through one of the new reproductive technologies. Determining whether to provide their only child with a brother or sister is often a difficult decision for these parents to make. Worry about what it will mean for their youngster to be an only child is common among this group of parents. Many are concerned about what it will be like for their single child to grow up alone. They also worry about how it will be for their child to deal with an aging parent by themselves and, be left alone when their one parent dies. Such concerns lead many single parents to feel a pressing need to enlarge their family, even when adding another child may be more than their emotional or financial resources can bear.

In the newsletters of the organization Single Mothers by Choice (www .singlemothersbychoice.com), I came across writings by single mothers noting some of the difficulties this decision posed for them. One woman wrote about how essential she thought it was for a single mother who has chosen to have a child alone to provide a sibling for that child, someone who can also write "not applicable" when asked for the father's name on a school form, someone with whom to share complaints about her as a parent, and someone to be close to when she dies. Another mother pointed to the difficulties of adding another child to the family when resources and parental time are limited. She found herself besieged with the additional burdens of a second child and felt guilty over her inability to give both children the energy and time she felt that they needed. Yet she appeared to feel she had made the right choice in adopting another child.

Victoria

I am familiar with some of the difficulties that one single mother, Victoria, a forty-eight-year old woman, faced in determining whether she should adopt a second child. Victoria had adopted her three-year-old son, Roger, from overseas when he was nine months old. Despite the fact that she was struggling with health problems and financial difficulties, she was determined to adopt another youngster.

Even before she adopted Roger, it had been Victoria's intention to adopt two children. As an only child herself, who after her father's death had cared for her ailing, elderly mother before she passed away, she did not want Roger to have to care for her in her old age by himself or be the only survivor in the family when she dies.

Despite the rigors of tending a baby who was somewhat developmentally delayed, as well as working full time and trying to arrange competent child care, Victoria had thoroughly enjoyed her first year as a mother. However, Roger proved to be a difficult toddler, and increasingly, despite the pleasure she gained from him, she found his care physically and emotionally draining, especially in the light of the health problems she was facing. Rather than considering that a second child might place a strain on her resources, she nonetheless concluded that having a sibling would prove helpful to Roger and therefore ease her situation.

Victoria was convinced that some of Roger's difficulties were due to his being the only child. If he had a brother or sister, she reasoned, he would be forced to share and adjust to not being the center of the world. A brother or sister would be company for him and he would require less time and attention from her. Although Victoria recognized that she was having considerable difficulty managing one child, she could see nothing but positives in adding to the family. She dismissed the therapist's efforts to point to some of the hurdles that she might face with a second child and denied the possibility that instead of providing companionship a sibling might prove to be an unwelcome rival to Roger.

It soon became apparent in the therapy that behind Victoria's conscious reasons for seeking a second child, there were unconscious factors that impeded any realistic consideration of the potential difficulties she and Roger might face if she enlarged her family. As an only child of a depressed, extremely critical mother with whom she was always in conflict, Victoria was convinced as a child that her life would be easier if she had brothers and sisters. They would be companions and would understand what she was going through with her mother. Moreover her mother would have someone else to attack.

In the absence of a brother or sister Victoria provided herself with imaginary siblings. She pretended she had numerous brothers and sisters with whom she engaged in imaginary play during the many hours that her mother and father left her alone to work in their store.

As she learned more about Victoria's own wish for siblings, her therapist sought to convey her appreciation of Victoria's longing for brothers and sisters when she was a child and how, given her needs, she had come to idealize the role that siblings could play in each other's lives. At the same time Victoria's experiences seemed to be making it difficult for her to assess what Roger's needs might be and to consider how she might deal with more than one child under the challenging circumstances of her life.

Efforts to help Victoria assess her capacity to add to her family appeared to be in vain. She seemed unable to relinquish the fantasy that she would have been "saved" by a sibling and that Roger, too, would be helped by a brother or sister. Yet while she continued to speak about starting the adoption process, she took no action. In time she became too old to meet the agency's eligibility requirements. Talk of adopting a second child seemed to abate, particularly during the termination period of her treatment, when ending brought up new issues. Only in one of her very last sessions did she express her regret that she had not been able to have more than one child.

Since her treatment ended six years ago, Victoria has continued to keep in touch with her therapist through holiday cards. In a recent card she wrote of how well Roger was doing and how much she was enjoying him. He is very talented musically. Victoria has encouraged him and given him opportunities for training that she would have been unlikely to have afforded had she had an additional child, though she has never expressed this thought. However, the wish for another child appears to have persisted. In her last holiday card, Victoria noted she still wished she had been able to adopt another child, and she believes that Roger would have liked that as well.

STEP AND HALF SIBLINGS

Many single parents are only single for brief periods of time. Divorced, widowed, and single parents by choice may marry and establish new families. In 2004, 17 percent of all children under age eighteen lived in stepfamilies or what sometimes are referred to as blended families. Forty-six percent of the children in these families lived with at least one stepparent (Krieder 2008).

Traditionally, the word "stepchild" meant a child who came to be related to a person through marriage to one of a child's parents, but today the words "stepchild" and "stepfamily" may include some families that are formed by cohabitation. A stepfamily may include full siblings, stepsiblings from the stepparents' earlier marriages, and half siblings produced by the marriage between a child's biological parent and their stepparent. Stepchildren have generally experienced significant losses and changes in their lives. They are often members of two households, and need to adapt to both families.

Who can forget Cinderella's wicked stepsisters? Martin Daly and Margo Wilson (1998) in their book *The Truth about Cinderella* have pointed out that all over the world in such countries as Russia, Japan, and India, stories similar to that of Cinderella exist about mistreated stepchildren and stepsiblings.

Anna Burt, editor of *My Father Married Your Mother,* (2006) recalls an occasion after her divorce when she was caring for her own little daughter and the daughter of her fiancé. After reading the story of Cinderella to them, and concluding with the words "and Cinderella lived happily ever after," one of the children added, "With no sisters!"

Stepfamilies ordinarily face a set of complex challenges and adaptive tasks which are likely to place a strain on the relationships among family members (Hetherington, Henderson, and Reiss 1999). Parents must develop a bond with their new partners. They must maintain their relationships with their own biological children, and if there are stepchildren they must develop positive relationships with them. The children in turn must deal with the loss of the family they once had and the many changes they face, contend with the alterations in their relationship with their own biological parent, and to the development of a new relationship with a stepparent. They may also be faced with developing or maintaining relationships with their biological siblings, half siblings, and stepsiblings, those living within the same household and those who are living separately.

There is some evidence to suggest that step- and half siblings may be less likely to develop lifelong ties than full brothers and sisters. In one study (White and Riedman 1992), the contact between them was only several times a year compared to one to three times a month for full siblings. Contact was more frequent when the stepchildren had no full siblings, when they spent more of their childhood years in a stepfamily, and when they lived with a stepfather rather than a stepmother.

Nonetheless other studies suggest that many stepparents and stepchildren form warm, reciprocal relationships (Hetherington and Clingenpeel 1992). Jane Addams, for example (Gottesfeld and Pharis 1977) lost her mother when she was two and a half and her father remarried when she was eight. She and her stepbrother, George, who was six months younger than she, were said to be devoted to each other and inseparable. Addams believed that George had helped her grow up, claiming that having him as a brother had made it possible for her to separate from her father, to whom she felt she had been overly attached.

Rebecca

Less fortunate was Rebecca. Her half sister, Phyllis, was seven years her senior. Phyllis's mother had divorced Phyllis's father and remarried. Rebecca was born four years later. Phyllis was never able to accept her new stepfather and she resented Rebecca from the start. Rebecca longed to be close to her older sister but Phyllis avoided her as much as possible, leaving Rebecca feeling as if there was something unworthy about her. As adults the stepsisters had little contact, much to Rebecca's regret.

Rebecca was in her thirties when she entered treatment. At that point she started to rethink her relationship with Phyllis. She began to consider how difficult it must have been for Phyllis to cope with her parents' divorce, relate to a stepfather, and contend with a new baby in the family. Might Phyllis's anger at her been caused not only by her jealousy of a stepsister, but might she, Rebecca, have been the recipient of Phyllis's angry feeling toward her mother, for leaving her biological father, and toward her new father who had taken Phyllis's biological father's place? This consideration of possible motives for her sister's hostility toward her led to Rebecca's feeling better about herself. It helped to alter her belief that there was something wrong with her that made Phyllis hate her. She decided that one day when she felt strong enough to face Phyllis's possible rejection, if that were to be the outcome, she could share with her stepsister some of what she had been thinking. Perhaps by her opening up to Phyllis they might eventually develop a more positive relationship.

GAY AND LESBIAN FAMILIES

Perhaps the newest of the non-traditional families are those headed by gays and lesbians. Among them are both single- and two-parent households. Although researchers have begun to study the development of children in these families, as far as I have been able to ascertain there has been little attention paid to the sibling relationships in them. Most of the research has focused on identifying possible differences between children growing up with gay and lesbian parents and children growing up with heterosexual parents. So far the findings suggest that there is little difference and that the family environments provided by gay and lesbian parents are as likely as those provided by heterosexual parents to support and facilitate their children's healthy growth (Golombok, Spencer, and Rutter 1983; Patterson 1992).

There is no reason to believe that those developmental circumstances that favor or impede positive relationships between brothers and sisters in traditional families are any different in gay and lesbian families. Those children who were either conceived or adopted in the context of a heterosexual marriage that ended in divorce or in a gay or lesbian union that terminated, face the pain of loss as do their counterparts in a heterosexual family. Those who have been adopted or conceived through one of the assisted reproductive technologies, face the same challenges as those who have been similarly conceived in heterosexual families. Siblings in gay and lesbian families may also carry the weight of discrimination as siblings often do in interracial and transcultural heterosexual families. According to the National Lesbian Family Study (Gartrell, Banks, and Reed 2000), all of the eighty-four lesbian mothers interviewed were concerned about the impact of discrimination on their children.

At this writing a few states have decided to legalize gay and lesbian marriages, attesting to some change in attitudes, but gay and lesbian families continue to struggle with discrimination. How, if at all, this intolerance may affect sibling relationships has not been studied, as far as I know. Like children who face discrimination growing up in transcultural families (a matter that will be addressed in the next chapter), siblings in some families may be brought closer as they seek to protect each other from the outside world. In other families experiences of discrimination may strain the sibling relationship.

An additional factor among gay and lesbian families is the fact that in those families formed through the assisted reproductive technologies, the biological relationships between siblings are likely to vary more than in heterosexual families similarly formed. In some lesbian families, for example, one woman may bear all of the children whereas in others each woman may bear one or more of the children. Each child may be conceived through the assistance of the same donor or they may be fathered by different donors. In gay families a father may be biologically related to all of his children or each partner may father a different child. Given the variety of techniques employed, the children in these families may be full siblings, half siblings, or biologically unrelated.

It is also important to note that both partners do not necessarily have legal rights to a child born to one of them. There are states in which co-parents in gay and lesbian families have no legal status. Unless a co-parent lives in one of the few states where the couple may be married or in which he or she is legally able to adopt the non-biological child, there is the danger that a co-parent may lose the non-biological child if the parents decide to separate. This may mean that siblings may lose each other, as well as a parent.

What, if any, effect such circumstances may have on the relationships between parents and children or on the relationships between siblings in these families remains largely unexplored as far as I can tell. Certain questions come to mind, however, which invite study. Might some parents develop a stronger bond with or a preference for the child they gave birth to or fathered? In families where one mother does more of the caretaking might there be greater envy of the sibling who was born to that mother on the part of the child who is not biologically related to her?

This last question came to mind as I thought about a young lesbian couple with whom I am familiar. Each of the women bore a child and adopted the other's biological child. The donor was the same for each conception. One mother, Sylvia, who gave birth to their first child, Sam, worked and supported the family. Mathilda, who gave birth four years later to Wayne, was the primary caretaker of both children.

Sam was intensely jealous of Wayne and the parents had to watch him carefully lest he harm his little brother. The mothers attributed the intensity of Sam's resentment of Wayne to his having become accustomed to being the center of their lives until his little brother was born. Yet, Sylvia wondered whether the fact that she had given birth to Wayne had somehow affected her treatment of the two children. Might she have unknowingly and subtly favored her biological child over her adopted son? Might the fact that she was the biological mother of one son and not the other have made any difference to either boy? Such questions may bear some consideration on the part of those who seek a fuller understanding of sibling relationships in these families.

REMARKS

How siblings get along together in some of today's non-traditional families and the role they play in each other's development and lives are determined largely by the same factors as those in traditional families. However, brothers and sisters in these families are likely to face certain challenges that may influence the relationships between them. Until we pay more attention to sibling relationships in these families, we have little reliable information to draw on as to what that impact might be. This chapter has been an effort to consider some of the limited knowledge that I have been able to access on the topic in the hope that it may encourage further study of sibling relationships in these families.

It is essential that we learn more about these families in general. This is especially so for clinicians whose understanding of psychological development has long been drawn from findings having to do with children in traditional families. Since an increasing number of individuals seeking treatment are likely to have grown up in the families considered here, we clearly need to know more about them. It is they who are becoming some of today's traditional families.

4

Foster Care, Adoption, and the New Reproductive Technologies

Foster care has changed considerably since I was a child welfare worker, more than forty years ago. Unlike in the past when it was not unusual for siblings to be separated, efforts are now being made to place brothers and sisters together whenever possible. This is more important than ever, for the children requiring foster care today have frequently grown up in troubled families and many have suffered from neglect and/or abuse. Having the support of brothers and sisters, when they are placed, can be very helpful, though, as will be noted later, that is not always the case.

The needs of children being placed for adoption, the families who are eligible to adopt them, and current adoption practices have also changed over time. Older children and children who suffer from emotional, physical, or cognitive problems, once considered "unadoptable," are now beginning to find permanent homes. Many older parents, single parents, and gay and lesbian parents have opportunities to adopt that were denied them in the past. There are now international and transracial adoptions, which bring parents and children of different cultural backgrounds together. Adoptions may be "open," with children remaining in contact with their birth families from the beginning. Those children, in what once were termed "closed adoptions," in which the identity of parents and siblings were kept confidential, can more easily locate the members of their biological family, or be located by them. Today it is not unusual for an adopted child to either know and sometimes form a relationship with their biological siblings from early on or later in life.

In addition to adoption and foster care, many individuals are forming their families through one or another of the new reproductive technologies (ART). The children in these families may have half or full siblings they are unaware of who are growing up in other families, as well as siblings in their immediate family. These brothers and sisters may have been conceived naturally or through ART or they may have been adopted. A child conceived through ART may also be one of a set of twins, triplets, or quintuplets. One of the consequences of these reproductive technologies is an increase in the number of multiple births. It has been reported that 45 percent of the pregnancies among those treated for infertility in 2003 resulted in twins while 7 percent resulted in triplets (Wright, Schieve, Reynolds, Jeng, and Kissen 2004).

SIBLINGS IN FOSTER FAMILIES

In 2008, it was estimated that there were 463,000 children in foster care in the United States (U.S. Department of Health and Human Services, Administration for Children and Families October 2009). According to a study conducted in 2005 (Shlonsky et al.), 70 percent of the children in foster care had at least one sibling in care. Many of them were separated. A study of children in foster care in California indicated that 55.6 percent of the children in placement in that state were separated from at least one sibling; 32.8 percent were separated from all of their brothers and sisters. This, despite the fact that California, along with Illinois and New York, is considered a leader in legislation and policymaking on the issue of siblings in out-of-home care (Shlonsky et al. 2005). Many of these siblings are separated for the remainder of their childhoods. More adults are thought to search for their siblings than for their biological parents. Children are suing child placement agencies to release information that will aid their search for their brothers and sisters and are winning (Barbell 1995).

Separation occurs for a variety of reasons. It is often very difficult to find families that will accept a sibling group. Brothers and sisters frequently enter the foster care system at different times. Sometimes the children's problems may seem too severe for one set of parents to deal with, and the family of the first child placed is unable to provide for an additional child. In some instances separation seems indicated for the welfare of the children, as in families in which there has been sibling abuse or to give an older child who had parented his younger siblings a chance to be a child. This rationale for separation has been questioned, for practice has shown that frequently the younger children have a more difficult time with placement when separated from a familiar figure to which they have been attached. At the same time, many of the older siblings who have felt responsible for the care of their younger brothers and sisters suffer severe anxiety about what is happening to them when separated from them. It has proven more advantageous to place these families together and help them begin to develop a relationship in which they can all be "children" (Casey Family Programs, www.casey.org).

Studies have shown that in general separating siblings heightens the trauma of foster care placement and increases the loss of identity, self-esteem, and security that children are already feeling from being separated from their family. This contributes to these troubled children cycling through one foster home after another (Jane Addams Hull House Association, Executive Summary 2001).

Recognizing how important it is, a growing number of agencies are making every effort to place siblings together, and, as previously noted, some states are mandating such efforts. One of the leading agencies in this effort is the Jane Addams Hull House (www.hullhouse.org/programsandcenters/program/neighbortoneighbor.html) In 1994, this Chicago agency established a program called Neighbor to Neighbor, which has been replicated in several other states. This agency makes special efforts to recruit foster families that will accommodate sibling groups and offers considerable support to those families that do. In the overwhelming majority of cases Hull House has found that siblings placed together experience more stable placements and healthier development than those who are separated. They tend to have fewer emotional and behavioral problems, are more likely to remain in their first placements, and are less likely to experience placement disruptions (Newberger 2001).

Lynn Price, once a foster child herself who had been separated from her older sister and only learned of her sister's existence when she was eight, has attempted to bring separated siblings together through the establishment of a national nonprofit organization Camp To Belong (www.camptobelong.org). This program affords separated siblings in foster care, many of whom live in different foster homes in the same community, a chance to reconnect for a one-week camping experience. It has also become something of a sibling advocacy organization.

WHEN FOSTER CARE CHILDREN ARE ADOPTED

Agencies like the Northeast Ohio Adoption Services (www.noas.com) are receiving special funding from the federal government to support their efforts to aid families that will adopt family groups. One of the mothers, who adopted three siblings from that agency, wrote on the agency's website of the importance she saw in keeping her children together. She noted that they had formed a strong bond before she adopted them. They had no one but each other when living with their biological family and needed each other to survive. She felt

that to separate them from the only people they trusted, would have been dev-
astating and would increase their mistrust of other people (Riggs 1999).

Many foster children, however, are still placed in separate adoptive homes,
for some of the same reasons that children are placed in different foster
homes. When the children are separated, adoptive parents are then faced with
the question of whether they should promote contact between the siblings.
Some parents seek to end contact (Schooler 2002), fearful that it will make
their child's life more difficult, open up old wounds, and in some cases make
it more difficult for the children to bond with their new adoptive families.
Other parents see their children's contact with their biological siblings as
helping them realize that they were not alone in losing their parents but
that they have siblings who experienced the same problems. They may also
believe that the siblings can serve as a support to them when they grow up.

ADOPTION

Adoption is a complex and challenging experience. It involves loss, grief,
and mourning on the part of all involved. For the biological parent or parents it means relinquishing their child. For the children, it means contending
with loss and rejection as well as feelings of not belonging and difference
(Siskind 2006). For the adoptive parents it means dealing with their inability
to conceive a child. Considerable attention has been paid to these and other
psychological stresses related to adoption (Brinich 1990; Brodzinsky and
Schechter 1990; Hushion, Sherman, and Siskind 2006; Shapiro, Shapiro, and
Parent 2001) and I will not address these here.

To date, little information is available about sibling relationships in these
families. One study that included siblings in forty-one adoptive families
(Stocker, Dunn, and Plomin 1989), does suggest that brothers and sisters in
these families are no less close than siblings in non-adoptive families. However, there is some indication that families composed of adopted and non-
adopted children and families formed by transracial and international adoption may face challenges that impact on the relationship between siblings.

WHEN BIOLOGICAL AND ADOPTED
CHILDREN GROW UP TOGETHER

Several adoption experts have suggested that the presence of adopted and
biological children in a family may lead to increased difficulties for various family members (Hoopes 1982, Kraus 1978). Yet a study conducted by

Brodzinsky and Brodzinsky (1992) failed to support that finding. Nonetheless these families are likely to face certain challenges. Differences in appearance between the biological and adopted children in a family, for example, frequently draw stares and questions from strangers. Biological children sometimes experience concern about the permanency of the family knowing that their adopted brother or sister has been "given up"? There is also the possibility that parental preferences may be influenced by the adopted or biological status of their children.

When Strangers Question

Years ago adoption agencies often went to great lengths to match children in appearance to members of their adopted family. Today this is seldom the case. Siblings in a family, whether they are the biological children of the parents or adopted brothers and sisters, may be strikingly different in appearance. This often means that families find themselves troubled by stares, questions, and comments by complete strangers when they are out in public. Young Beverly, an adopted ten-year-old with a three-year-older non-adopted sister, expressed her discomfort when the family went on outings and people repeatedly inquired as to whether they were "real" sisters. "I have no privacy," she said. "I feel like everyone knows I'm adopted."

Concerns about Loss

An adoptive mother, a friend of mine, shared how taken aback she was when her biological son, who was born when his adopted sister was five, began to repeatedly seek assurance that he would always be "her boy." She realized that he had only recently begun to understand what it meant that his sister was adopted.

Jeanette and Liza

There may also be a fear on the part of some biological children that their adopted siblings will look for and return to their birth family, leaving them behind. This was true in the case of Jeanette, whose three-year-younger adopted sister, Liza, had expressed her wish to find her parents, since she was a little girl. When Liza actually began a search in her late twenties, Jeanette sought constant reassurance that Liza would still consider her, her "real" sister when she found her family. Liza did locate her biological mother and father and her two half brothers, and much to Jeanette's surprise, Liza remained as close to her as ever.

In some cases, the adopted child's possession of another family may, as Theodore Jacobs (1988) has pointed out, be regarded as an advantage. Jacobs has written about a biological child, Henry, whom I will discuss shortly. Henry was born after his parents had adopted two children. Henry envied them and longed to have been adopted himself. Having another set of parents to go to when life in the family proved difficult seemed to him to be highly desirable.

The reality of an adopted sibling's situation can give a sense of possibility to what Freud discovered to be a common childhood fantasy, in which children imagine being adopted and replacing their parents with better ones. This "family romance fantasy" (Freud 1909c), helps children deal with normal frustrations and disappointments as well as oedipal issues.

Preferred Siblings

Henry

Henry, as the biological child in the family, was also preferred over his adopted siblings. When parents have not come to terms with their inability to conceive a child, they may not be fully satisfied with their adopted child. In the case of Henry, whose parents had considered themselves infertile, his birth was experienced as a miracle. Although Henry enjoyed the special treatment he received, he felt guilty about having a better life than his brother and sister. His wish to be adopted stemmed in part from his feeling that then he would be treated as his siblings were. Jacobs compared Henry's plight to that of a child who survives the loss of a sibling and feels undeserving of good treatment.

Marsha

In some instances it may be the grandparents or other significant relatives who favor the biological child over the adopted child. Having a child who continues their blood line and promises them a kind of immortality may prove of great importance to them. Marsha, a dark-skinned, brown-eyed, ten-year-old girl, for example, was keenly aware of her grandmother's preference for her four-year-older non-adopted sister. In speaking with her school counselor, Marsha wistfully noted that her grandmother much preferred her sister, Lucy, who had blonde hair and blue eyes like her grandmother had. She realized she could never really please grandma like Lucy did.

In some families it may be the adopted sibling who is the favored child. Having desired a child so strongly, having gone through a difficult adoption process, whether domestically or overseas, having waited so long for their child, their adopted son or daughter may have seemed like a miracle. At the same time, it is also possible that parents may overvalue one or another child defensively. Realizing that they prefer their biological child, they may focus more of their attention on him or her, or vice versa.

Alison

Sue Sherman (2006) has written about her treatment of a young African woman, Alison, who had two brothers, one three years younger and one five years younger, both the biological children of her parents. Alison saw herself as the favorite child in the family and as being very special to her mother who referred to Alison as her "soulmate." It did indeed seem as if the mother preferred Alison, her adopted child, over her sons which might simply have been related to the fact that she preferred girls. Yet, it was not clear how real this feeling of mother-daughter closeness was. Dr. Sherman questioned whether Alison's feeling that she was special to her mother might have been a wish or perhaps a reaction formation on the part of both daughter and mother, defending against less positive feelings. She also considered the possibility that this mother's seeming preference for her adopted daughter might have been a defense against favoring her biological children, and Alison's feeling that she was special to her mother might have served as a way of protecting herself from feeling different and rejected.

Samantha

Disappointment in either a biological or an adopted child who fails to meet the expectations of a parent may lead a parent to prefer the child who they feel is more likely to do so. At the 2009 Conference of the American Association of Psychoanalysis in Clinical Social Work, Kathi Hushion presented a case of a family who, after their efforts to conceive were unsuccessful, adopted an eleven-month-old baby. Their biological daughter, Elizabeth, who had a learning disability, was six at the time.

Mrs. X's decision to adopt a child from China had been influenced by seeing an adopted Chinese girl in her community who she thought was adorable, and who seemed to show a good deal more promise than Elizabeth. So influenced was this mother by the image of that child that she was shocked when Samantha arrived and she found her to be a malnourished, developmentally delayed little girl with rashes and scabies instead of the cute little child with pigtails she had expected.

Mrs. X had grown up with two older sisters and a younger brother and sister. Her younger sister had learning disabilities and asthma and required much of her parents' attention. Her two older siblings were highly competitive and talented and though Mrs. X was successful in her own field, she never felt equal to her more accomplished older sisters.

Mrs. X developed an idealized image of Samantha, and seeing her as exceptionally able, devoted herself to encouraging her talents. She was unable to see her as she was. When Samantha was in second grade the school began to express concern about her inability to accept limits and her aggressive behavior with other children. Mrs. X could not accept their picture of her daughter and their recommendation that she seek treatment for her. Mrs. X was convinced that the teacher was young and rigid and did not understand Samantha. When, for example, the teacher complained about Samantha throwing tissues into the fishbowl, Mrs. X insisted that she had not understood that Samantha was conducting an experiment and meant no harm to the fish. Instead of appreciating that Samantha had the mind of a scientist the teacher was trying to squelch her. The difference between how Mrs. X viewed Samantha and the way others, including her therapist, did was dramatic. Unfortunately her idealized view of Samantha made it impossible for her to understand the child and interfered with her ability to respond to her needs appropriately.

Ms. Hushion did not directly address the question of how Samantha's being adopted might have contributed to her mother's idealization of her. Perhaps, in the face of her sister's and her biological daughter's difficulties, Mrs. X found it easier to idealize a child who did not carry the family genes.

Interestingly, Elizabeth seemed to benefit from her mother's preoccupation with Samantha. She grew up to be a confident, sociable preadolescent. Ms. Hushion speculated that the idealized fantasies Mrs. X had about Samantha took some of the pressure off her older sister.

Regardless of whatever preferences their parents have, we are reminded that children are likely to have their own ideas and fantasies about who is the favored child in a family. For some adopted children the baby who grew in "mommy's tummy" may seem to be the preferred one, while the "chosen baby" may seem to be the special child in the eyes of some biological children.

Special Needs Adoptees and Their Healthy Biological Siblings

As noted earlier, one of the changes in adoption procedures has been the increase in the adoption of children with special needs. According to one study, the large majority of these adoptions have proven successful (Brodzinsky, Lang, and Smith 1995). However the addition of an adopted child with a disability may pose challenges for their healthier biological siblings. This is true, of course, in families in which children have biologically related siblings with special needs. However, in the case of adoptive families, children are or become aware that their parents have chosen this situation, which may make some difference in their attitudes toward their adopted special needs sibling.

The James Family

The James family is a case in point. When their older child, George, was four and their younger son, Daniel, almost two, they adopted Peter who was just a few months older than Daniel. Peter first came into the James family as a foster child and was adopted several years later.

Howard James was a pediatrician on the attending staff of a small group home for HIV-infected infants and his wife, Ellen, was a nurse in that facility. They both developed a strong attachment to Peter, who had been cared for in the program since he was seven months old. At the age of eighteen months, when Peter no longer tested HIV positive, he became ineligible for the facility, and Ellen and Howard arranged for his placement in their family. Both parents were aware of the challenges they were likely to face, but their deep feelings for Peter, along with their professional training and experience, led them to believe they were well prepared for the tasks ahead.

Initially Peter tested at a retarded level, had a chronic physical condition, and was extremely hyperactive and demanding. Peter's positive emotional and intellectual development in the care of these two devoted, capable parents is an inspiring story.

Although Daniel and Peter got along fairly well, George found the adjustment to another sibling very difficult. At one point, George declared that his parents' adopting Peter had been the worst thing that had happened to him in his life.

Throughout their childhood George remained angry with Peter. Daniel was more accepting of him. Peter developed some of the same interests as Daniel, which brought them closer when they were young.

However as the children grew older, the distance between Peter and his siblings increased. George and Daniel were very successful academically, and though Peter's I.Q. increased over the years, he had serious academic difficulties. Both George and Daniel went away to college, whereas after high school Peter went on to a community college and continued to live at home. Over time Peter and his siblings had less and less to do with each other, although Daniel continued to be more accepting of Peter than did George.

George's animosity toward Peter may partly be understood as the consequence of having so little time to deal with the birth of one new sibling before he had to contend with another brother who required an inordinate amount of attention from both parents. Had George been older and more advanced developmentally with less need for parental attention, perhaps it would have been easier for him to accept Peter and even to empathize with his difficulties.

Yet here was a child who clearly needed a home and parents who were uniquely fitted to care for a special needs child, who had formed an attachment to him, and had a deep desire to care for him. One could imagine how difficult it would have been to deny a child such benefits.

Transracial and International Adoptions

In 2004, it was reported that 4,200 children were placed transracially, an increase of 14 percent over 1998 (Clemetson and Nixon 2006). According to the Office of Children's Issues of the U. S. Department of State (http://www .adoption.state.gov.news/notices.html) there were 12,753 children adopted from other countries in 2009.

Many of these adoptive parents feel it important to provide their children with siblings, particularly siblings of their own ethnic group. An Irish mother married to a German husband noted how meaningful it was that her three Korean children had each other. Not only did this lessen any discomfort they might feel about their difference from the other children in their neighborhood, but she believed their common background drew them closer to each other.

One young black girl (Simon and Roorda 2000), whose adoptive parents were white, pointed to the advantage of having black siblings. She noted that they made her feel less different than a black friend who was the only black child in her family. She felt good when her whole family was together and she knew she was not the one who stood out in the crowd.

Children adopted internationally and transracially can expect to "stand out" and be noticed by others in the community, often in ways that are discomforting to them. One mother (Register 1991) who adopted two Korean girls found numerous people coming up and asking her if the children were really sisters. She sometimes responded that they were now, but found that adding the qualifier was troubling. After much experience, she offered an answer that she felt clearly confirmed siblinghood: "Well, they fight in the backseat of the car."

Not only are strangers apt to question the relationship between children in these families, but they are known to ask what happened to the children's "real parents," even to ask how much they paid for their children (Raible 2006), and to give their opinions on the way these parents have developed their families, sometimes praising them, sometimes sympathizing with them, and sometimes criticizing them.

Most troubling is the prejudice that these families are all too often confronted with. Paula, who had adopted a son, Craig, domestically, adopted a little daughter, Muriel, from South America some three years later. Paula feared what would happen when Muriel entered school the following year. Just recently an adopted Latina daughter of a friend found a sign on her back, "Go Back to Mexico." Paula was worried about the hostility that Muriel was likely to face and that Craig might experience being her brother. She was also troubled by the fact that the school appeared to have low academic expectations of children from Spanish-speaking countries and she was concerned that the teachers would not offer Muriel the same attention that they had offered Craig. Most of the Latinos in her town were employed in low-level jobs, and other families who had adopted from Spanish-speaking countries were finding that the school expected too little from their children.

In his study of Caucasian people between the ages of twenty-one and forty-nine, who had grown up with adopted African American or Korean siblings, John Raible (2006) found that many were deeply troubled by the prejudice their African American brothers or sisters were subjected to. They were extremely discomforted by the racist comments and jokes and the difficulties their siblings encountered. They were often unclear as to how to respond. Some spoke up and acknowledged how offended they were by the remarks. Others let the comments slide. Sometimes they tried to educate the offending person, and there were times when they found themselves in fights defending their brother or sister.

Joel and Sally

On the other hand, one young mother, Fran, noted how she realized her little son Joel derived some satisfaction when people outside the family teased his adopted sister, Sally, about her Korean appearance. At the same time she knew he felt conflicted for he also had positive feelings for his sister and he knew he should not feel pleased and should stand up for her.

Fran and her husband, Jim, had adopted Joel, who was born in the United States, when he was three months old. Four years later they adopted Sally from Korea. Joel was extremely resentful of his little sister during her first years, which Fran attributed to the fact that Sally required a tremendous amount of care. She had arrived in the family with serious physical and developmental problems. It was clear that Joel resented the time and attention his parents had to give to his little sister, though they tried their best to attend to both children equally. Although the relationship between the children improved with time, Joel remained highly ambivalent toward Sally.

Societal intolerance can also find its way into the family itself. Parents as well as extended family members may discover prejudices in themselves they had never suspected themselves of having. These can influence parental preferences and lead to sibling rivalry being played out around ethnic lines.

Where they reside can be of great importance to these families. William Feigelman (2000) concluded that African American and Asian transracial adoptees who lived in racially mixed areas experienced less discomfort than those living in predominantly white areas. The presence of other families of mixed ethnic backgrounds in a community can make a significant difference in the comfort of these families. So important is this factor that many parents, if they have not already located in such neighborhoods, are advised to consider relocation to more culturally heterogeneous areas if they wish to provide their children with a more congenial environment.

Rosalie and Charlotte

The importance of place was brought home to me when I recently attended the funeral of a member of my small community. Her two grown daughters, Rosalie, her adopted black child, now a mother of several children, and her non-adopted Caucasian sister, Charlotte, sat at opposite ends of the church. I knew from more intimate friends of the family that the sisters had little or no contact with each other once they left home. They had each visited separately to tend their ill mother before she died.

Their parents were motivated to adopt an African American child by their deep commitment to the development of an integrated society. They were active participants in the Civil Rights Movement. Unfortunately there was considerable racial strife in their community at the time they were establishing their family. When the sisters attended high school, Charlotte was accused of being a "nigger lover" by her white classmates, and Rosalie was derided by her black classmates for trying to pass as white. Neither was accepted and their school days were a torment for both girls. They directed their anger at what was happening toward each other. Although other factors are likely to have contributed to the troubled relationship between these sisters, the societal prejudice they faced took its toll on their relationship.

In the light of these and other possible challenges, parents and children involved in transracial and international adoptions need to be prepared for a sometimes difficult road ahead, especially in view of the racism they are likely to encounter. It is not possible to protect children from racism, but families can talk about race and racism openly and honestly. They can establish contact with other families who are facing similar challenges. Children can be helped to find ways of responding to insensitive comments about themselves or their siblings from others (Vonk 2001). Some of these parents may need help and support for some time after the initial adoptive placement to deal with some of these issues (Raible 2005). It is important to bear in mind, though, that many of the roadblocks these children and their families encounter are normal under the circumstances (Pavoa 2005) and should not be pathologized.

Despite such hurdles (Simon and Alsten, 2000), studies point to warm, rich relationships between siblings of different nationalities and races. Joyce Ladner (1977) conducted in-depth interviews with 136 white parents who had adopted black children. In many cases the families already had biological children. She found that in most instances the relationships between the siblings, as described by their parents, seemed typical. They were envious of each other and there were the expectable arguments and fights between them. At the same time they played and shared like other children.

In Dr. Raible's study (2006) the young white siblings he met with expressed deep affection and love for their adopted black brothers and sisters. Some noted how much they had gained from their identifications with their sibling and the black culture he or she had introduced them to. One young person remarked that although he knew he was white, he felt he was something more. He was able to forge personal connections with African Americans outside of the family, and achieve a greater understand of the dynamics of race in our society, as well as a deeper appreciation of the struggles against racism. Dr. Raible has given the term "transracialization" to the development that can occur when individuals participate in long-term caring relationships with people of another race or nationality, and can use them as a springboard to form friendships with others beyond the family. For Dr. Raible, transracial adoptions may be one way to promote the transracialization, he deems necessary if we are to ever fully integrate our still segregated society.

THE NEW ASSISTED REPRODUCTIVE TECHNOLOGIES (ART)

The advances in the field of reproductive technology continue and are dramatic and rapid. Stephen, E. Levick, a psychiatrist (2004), proposes that whether it is desirable or not, the likelihood is that reproductive scientists and physicians will one day make cloning humans possible. In a volume considering the possible psychological and social consequences of cloning, Levick has noted some of the ways this will affect siblings. He points out, for example, that when a clone's sibling is also cloned from the same rearing parent the children will be twins but of different ages. He also notes that a non-cloned child who dies may serve as a progenitor of a sibling, leaving that brother or sister as a replacement child, a role that will be considered later in the book.

The degree of biological relatedness in children formed by the new reproductive technologies varies. Depending on the techniques employed, children conceived through ART may be full biological siblings, half siblings, or unrelated biologically. When all of the children have been conceived through in vitro fertilization, they are full brothers and sisters. Those children conceived through gamete donation are likely to have half siblings growing up in other families. The chances are high that children who have been conceived through donor insemination may have a number of half siblings, as men who donate sperm are likely to father more than one child, sometimes many more. Children who have been conceived through embryo donation may have full siblings growing up in other families.

There is research (Golombok et al. 1996, 2008; Murray 2003) that suggests that parents who have conceived through in vitro fertilization and donor insemination enjoy good relationships with them, and that their preschool and school-age children manifest the same degree of emotional health as children who have been naturally conceived or adopted. A study of early adolescents bore out these findings (Golombok et al. 2002). However, a study by the Institute for American Values (Marquardt, Glenn, and Clark), which was released June 3, 2010, found that among 485 adults between the ages of eighteen and forty-five conceived through sperm donation, a significant number reported concerns about their origins and their identity, and experienced feelings of confusion, loss, and tension.

One concern that seems to weigh heavily on a number of families who have used donor gametes is whether to tell the children about how they were conceived. In the 2002 study referred to above, only 10 percent of the parents of children conceived through donor insemination had told their children. Currently, most of the children resulting from gamete donation grow up without knowing that their father or mother is not their genetic parent (Murray 2003). Among the reasons advanced for secrecy are concerns about the effects on children of discovering that their parents are not their biological parents and a fear that the children or others will reject the parents when they discover their infertility.

Those who favor information sharing (Cooper and Glazer 1998) do so for some of the same reasons that have been advanced for telling children they are adopted, such as the danger that children will learn of their origins from persons other than their parents and the importance to the children of knowing their genetic history. There is also some concern, that given the large number of children fathered by some sperm donors, some half siblings may be in danger of mating when they are unaware of their common biological parent.

When children conceived through ART have been advised of the circumstances of their birth, many of them, like adoptees, have shown great interest in locating their biological half siblings. There is a Donor Sibling Registry (www.donorsiblingregistry.com) that helps individuals conceived as a result of sperm, egg, or embryo donation to make contact with their siblings. The World Wide Web also lists at least two other such registries, one maintained by the California Cryobank (www. sibling-registry.com/why.cfm) and one offered by Single Mothers by Choice (www.singlemothersbychoice.com/sibling.html).

Siblings as Gamete Donors or Surrogate Mothers

Many donors are anonymous; however, it is not unusual for a brother or sister to donate gametes to help a sibling form a family or for a sister to serve as surrogate mother to her sibling's child. Many couples prefer this arrangement insofar as it offers them an opportunity to assure the continuation of their blood lines. Cost may be a factor in the selection of a sibling as a donor or surrogate. Reproductive technologies are expensive and frequently not covered by insurance plans

The American Society for Assisted Reproductive Technology (2003) has raised concerns about such intrafamilial reproduction. They note, for example, that if a brother donates sperm to help a sister conceive or a sister donates eggs to help a brother form a family, the child would have the same genetic relationship to the participants as children of consanguineous and incestuous unions between first-degree relatives. This places such children at risk for birth defects and genetic diseases. Such arrangements may also prove disruptive to the emotional well being of those involved. The society strongly recommends against such donations.

The society can make recommendations, *but* they are only recommendations. Assisted reproductive technologies are almost completely unregulated in the United States (Meyer www.rockinst.org/pdf/healthcare/2009 -07-StatesRegulation_ART07.pdf, Rosato, 2009). The extent to which fertility clinics follow the society's recommendations is unknown. Moreover, it is not unusual for families to make informal arrangements that leave them free to secure donations from whomever they choose.

What prompts a sibling to assist a brother or sister in having a child? Sperm donation is a relatively easy procedure; however, ova donation and carrying a sibling's baby are emotionally demanding, time consuming, often physically uncomfortable, and sometimes dangerous. It is unlikely that any sibling whether consciously or unconsciously, undertakes such a procedure without some concerns. However, it appears that, at least consciously, siblings seem to be largely motivated by their love and empathy for their brother or sister. They are aware of the deep anguish their siblings are experiencing, and they want to help make parenthood possible for them. On the website of the Organization of Parents Through Surrogacy (OPTS), Joan Merchlinsky (2007) explained her reasons for enabling her sister to have a child. She wrote that she and her sister had always been the best of friends. She could not recall anything they hadn't shared over the years, except for the joys of parenthood. She found the decision to contribute her eggs and become a surrogate for her sister's baby easy. It was her sister, she claimed, who needed convincing.

After the birth of a baby boy Ms. Merchlinsky said that she felt she had the best of a surrogacy situation. Her sister's family lives out of state and she thought the distance helped her deal with any difficulties she faced by the separation, while at the same time she had photos and visits and the assurance that she would always be a part of her sister's child's life. Most important, she noted, was the satisfaction she gained from sharing the pleasures and tribulations of parenthood.

The family plans to tell the child the circumstances of his conception and birth, but at the time of writing Ms. Merchlinsky noted she enjoyed being called "Auntie" and hearing the happiness in her sister's voice when she speaks about her little son.

We do not know what other conscious or unconscious factors might have prompted Ms. Merchlinsky's decision to help her sister. We are aware that in some families there is often strong pressure on would-be donors from family members, particularly parents who want to see their children form a family. Some siblings may be moved to help their brothers or sisters largely to please their parents and to win their favor, even though they may have reservations. Some may find it difficult to say no out of love for their sibling, whereas others may assent in order to defend against less positive feelings. Given what we know about how common sexual feelings are between siblings (a subject to be considered in a later chapter), we can conjecture that for some siblings helping their brother or sister have a child may involve unconscious incestuous wishes on the part of either or both siblings.

Those who screen and counsel donors recognize the importance of helping siblings understand their motivations, concerns, and conflicts about the process, as well as enabling them to consider some of the challenges they are likely to face in the future. Not only must donors and surrogate mothers anticipate how they are going to handle the relationship with the child, but there are other exigencies that may arise. For example, if a sister has not yet had a child herself, what will her feelings be about the sister to whom she "gave" her child, if she finds herself unable to have a child later? What if the child turns out to have a handicap? What if she does not approve of the way her sibling is raising "their" child? What if the child seeks more of a relationship with the donor or surrogate mother than was planned or if the child is angry and questions what has been done? (Cooper and Glazer 1998).

Allie and Beth

Judith Kottick (2005), a consultant on these issues, has written about two sisters she worked with who sought infertility treatment together with their husbands. She shows some of the complexities that may be involved when siblings seek to help each other achieve parenthood. Allie and Clark, her husband, had had a previous course of infertility treatment and Allie had become pregnant on their fourth in vitro fertilization. Unfortunately, in her eighth month she delivered a stillborn. Several months later they returned to the clinic to utilize cryopreserved embryos, but Allie did not become pregnant.

Meanwhile, Beth and her husband, Dave, were also experiencing infertility. Beth was referred for ovum donation. At this point, the two sisters realized they could both benefit from Allie's ability to produce viable eggs and they wanted to share them. From a medical standpoint there were no issues, as donation between sisters has been standard practice and is one of the arrangements that the American Society for Reproductive Medicine (2003) approves of.

However the psychological implications of this plan troubled Kottick. What if Beth became pregnant with the help of her sister's eggs and Allie did not? Allie and her husband were still mourning the loss of their baby less than a year earlier. How would they cope with the possibility of being responsible for the birth of a niece or nephew while childless themselves? What if they never conceived? Among the other concerns Kottick had was the effect this might have on the relationship between the two sisters.

Kottick was apparently the only member of the clinic staff who felt deeply concerned about this arrangement. She suggested an alternative plan of giving Allie and Clark the chance to have a baby first before helping Beth. The couples, however, were unwilling to wait what might be years to become parents. Moreover, the physicians were not willing to deny the couples' requests to proceed on the chance that psychological problems might develop.

REMARKS

Child welfare experts have already given considerable thought to the importance of sibling relationships and, as noted, are making great efforts to place siblings together. Attention is also beginning to be paid to sibling issues in international and transracial adoptions. Our understanding, however, of the sibling related issues among children conceived through the assisted reproductive technologies and their parents is limited. We do know that many of these children are interested in locating their half or full siblings. The Institute for American Values study (Marquardt, Glenn, and Clark 2010) found significant concern on the part of their respondents that without knowing who their siblings were they might unknowingly become romantically attached to someone biologically related to them. Two-thirds of the respondents supported their right to know about the existence and number of their half or full siblings, to know their identity, and to have the chance to form some kind of relationship with them.

As the technology of reproduction continues to progress, we hope to see advances in our understanding of its ethical, social, and psychological implications for the children, the parents, and those siblings who helped their brothers or sisters form their families. There are many questions to explore. In what ways, for example, might being conceived through ART affect the relationships between siblings in these families? What effect might it have on the relationship between brothers and sisters who share the same rearing parents to have been parented by different biological parents? What might it mean to a child to have an aunt who is his biological mother or an uncle who is her biological father and cousins who are half siblings? What might be some of the issues that arise when siblings reared in different families find each other? Might concerns about incest arise among some of these donors or recipients or, for that matter, their children?

Each child's and parent's experiences are unique, but knowing more about how some individuals are experiencing and reacting to these new methods of conception should prove valuable to those who screen and counsel donors and recipients, to those clinicians who treat members of these families, and to those who seek to regulate these medical interventions for the protection of all participants.

5

Sibling Discord

I stood over my mother, guarding her body like a soldier. All the while my father was hounding me to go home. He could never understand why I would want to stay with her through this, how much it meant for me to have her for myself, just this once, not with my older and younger brothers and sisters all fighting for a piece of her.

Thus spoke one of Sheila Felberbaum's patients after having stood vigil over her dying mother (2007).

One cannot consider sibling discord without acknowledging the deep yearning to have one's parents all to oneself, to be the "only" one and to be free of those who stand in the way. Whether a person has had to relinquish his or her place as an only child to a new sibling or has never had the opportunity to be the "only" one, those of us who have had brothers or sisters can empathize with that young woman's longings, even as we may consider her fortunate to have siblings to share her grief in the days of mourning ahead.

Envy, jealousy, and rivalry among siblings are ubiquitous. They are the price humans pay for their attachment to their caregivers. In the absence of attachment, wishes for exclusive possession of the other are unlikely to develop, as Anna Freud and Sophie Dann (1951) found in their study of six children, ages three to four, who lost their parents during the Holocaust shortly after they were born. Moved from one facility to another, including Terezin, a concentration camp, they were finally sent to England and placed in a nursery, Bulldog Banks, where Dann and Freud observed them.

At the start the children were either indifferent or openly hostile to the adults who cared for them. However, they were strongly attached to each other and were deeply troubled when separated. More than eager to share whatever they had with each other, they made no efforts to compete. When they did begin to relate to staff members more positively, they showed none of the demanding, possessive behaviors that young children ordinarily show toward their parents or parent substitutes. Even when they sought a more exclusive relationship with a caretaker, their attachments were weak. Only one child developed a close relationship with a member of the staff and sought her exclusive attention. Freud and Dann attributed this little girl's tie to her caretaker to the fact that she had experienced an earlier close relationship with a staff person at Terezin.

A NEW BABY ARRIVES

The birth of a new baby in a family is well recognized as a major event in the life of an older brother or sister. Feelings of envy, jealousy, and hostility to the new baby are expectable. Yet, Juliet Mitchell (2003), a British psychoanalyst, suggests that we have minimized or overlooked the serious threat that the arrival of a new sibling poses for the older child. According to Mitchell, older brothers or sisters not only feel displaced by a new baby but feel *replaced*. Someone else now occupies the position they have had, leaving them feeling in a state of nothingness, of non-being. The experience is felt, Mitchell avers, as a "death" of the sibling's self. The child has lost not only his previous self but the mother as the person she was before the new baby was born. So traumatic is this threat of annihilation that it leads older siblings to wish to obliterate their replacement. Because this murderousness is forbidden, it normally becomes transmuted over time into aggressive play and healthy rivalry.

The new baby, Mitchell claims, registers this threat to its existence from an older sibling and develops a fear of being killed. Normally, this response also becomes transformed into hate and love as well as friendship and rivalry.

The presence of siblings also confronts children with the realization that they are not unique or even irreplaceable, but ordinary. This loss of uniqueness is part of what leads the child to feel annihilated. The development of healthy self-regard depends upon a child's ability to more or less successfully mourn this loss and accept his ordinariness. Accepting that one is ordinary does not, Mitchell adds, mean that one is not unique. It simply means that one's brothers and sisters are also ordinary and not unique.

Jeanine M. Vivona (2008) has referred to this loss of uniqueness as a "universal crisis of non-uniqueness." This crisis may be precipitated by the actual birth of a sibling, as it does in the case of an older child, or it may occur when a younger sibling becomes aware that she is not the only child in the family. Sibling rivalry, Vivona proposes is not simply a contest for the love of the parents but for recognition of the child's value and specialness. Vivona (2007, 2010) regards the efforts children make to regain their feeling of being special with respect to their siblings as an important component in identity formation. She points to the efforts children make to be different from their rivals as a means to establish their own unique self.

To return to Mitchell (2003), it is important to note that she appreciates that there is a positive, loving side to the sibling relationship and writes of the lateral bonding between brothers and sisters that she observed in a kibbutz nursery where she once worked. However, she emphasizes the traumatic and hostile aspects of the relationship out of her belief that they contribute to the prevalence of violence in our society, both individual and collective.

Given the violence and wars that continue to plague humankind, some of which are between peoples who are culturally and ethnically related, the idea that we might look to sibling relationships to help us understand the plight our world is in is intriguing. Clinically, the recognition that a child may feel replaced as well as displaced by a new sibling provides another vantage point from which to view some children's reactions to their new brother or sister. However, clinicians like me, who regard development as dependent upon a unique interaction between the innate endowment of a child, maturational forces, and the conscious and unconscious attitudes and ministrations of their caretakers, may question the inevitability and universality of the specific responses Mitchell delineates.

Instead, I would suggest that the response of older children to the arrival of a new baby is likely to be determined by a variety of factors such as the age and developmental level of the older child, the nature of the relationship with their parents before and after the arrival of a sibling, the difference in ages between them and the new baby, the degree to which ego functions such as frustration tolerance and the ability to wait have developed, the adequacy of the older child's narcissistic resources, and the child's fantasies about the new baby. A young child, for example, may be more sensitive to the loss of parental attention with the arrival of a new sibling whereas an oedipal child may be concerned at not having played a part in creating the baby. A child who has been overvalued by his parents and extended family, such as one conceived when parents thought themselves infertile, may suffer a greater narcissistic loss at the advent of a new brother or sister than a child who has not been regarded as a "miracle."

New infants also play a role in their older sister or brother's responses to them. A healthy infant who meets a family's hopes and expectations, who responds positively to older siblings and whose needs for parental attention leave room for the parents to continue to focus on their older brothers and sisters is likely to be responded to differently than a sickly infant or one with developmental disabilities, who requires a great deal of time and attention and causes great stress and worry to the parents.

PARENTAL RESPONSES

One of the most critical factors in determining siblings' reactions to each other, not only at the time of a new baby's birth but throughout life, are the parents' responses to each of their offspring. Parental favoritism plays a major role in creating strife between siblings. It was the Lord's preference for Cain's gift that moved his brother Abel to kill him. Throughout Genesis sibling conflict is generated by the preference of a parent for one child over another.

Children are extremely sensitive to the differences in attention paid to them and their brothers and sisters and to any perceived injustices in the treatment accorded them. Dunn and McGuire (1994) found that even when older children have experienced the same affection or attention when they were at the same stage of development that their younger sibling is currently at, witnessing their parents' differential behavior toward them may have an important impact. Children vary both in the degree of their sensitivity to perceived differential treatment and the strength of their responses to it. Siblings may also misperceive parental preferences. A younger child may experience the activities and privileges of older siblings as evidence of parental favoritism without understanding that the prerogatives they enjoy have to do with their age and more mature capacities. Temperament, cognitive capacities, and the ability to utilize defenses are among the factors that help to determine how a child experiences and deals with differential treatment (Dunn and Kendrick 1982).

Parents who have more than one child are challenged to find a way to love each of their children as the unique individuals they are (Kris and Ritvo 1983) and to respond to the many differences between them without seeming to favor one over the other. It is neither possible nor desirable for a parent to treat each child exactly the same way. A new baby, for example, must be protected and attended to in ways that older children do not require. With advances in their little brother's or sister's development, older children need their parents to assure them their place in the family and to see that their possessions are safe from intrusion. Although "good enough parents" (Winnicott 1953) try to be loving, appropriately responsive, and fair to each of their offspring, it is inevitable that at times one child or another will receive more of a parent's attention than another. Ordinarily this is balanced out in the long run. It is impressive how for the most part parents do succeed in valuing each of their children equally, although their children are often unconvinced of this. The wish to be the only one loved or the most loved exists no matter how equally loved each child is.

For some parents, however, loving all of their children is not possible. Parental preferences are dictated by factors within the parents and in some instances are shaped by cultural values, as was noted in an earlier chapter. Different children elicit different responses in their parents. Some parents find a baby they can hold close most rewarding. Others may value an independent child who has less need of them. Some parents prefer a boy and others a girl. Some parents may find in one child features that remind them of an important loved or hated figure from their past, or may see in them a "good" or "bad" aspect of themselves, leading them to favor or reject that child. There are families in which a child does not "fit together" (Hartmann 1939) well with a parent, because of marked differences in temperament, abilities, or appearance. An outgoing, active son, for example, may be valued by one mother for being "all boy," whereas another mother may find such a child wearing and annoying.

Little Hans and His Sister Hanna

As important as it is, parental preference is not the only factor that may negatively influence an older child's response to a new brother or sister. A review of the case of five-year-old Hans (Freud 1909b), whose treatment by his father Freud supervised, suggests how the interplay between parental behaviors and attitudes (both conscious and unconscious) and the innate capacities and personalities of a child may influence a youngster's response to his new sister or brother.

Freud recognized the important impact of a new baby on an older sibling when he averred that the birth of Hans's sister Hanna, when Hans was three-and-a-half, was the most influential factor in his development. Although he considered oedipal issues to be foremost in the etiology of Hans's neurosis, Freud also regarded Hans's jealousy, rivalry, and death wishes toward Hanna as playing a significant role in the development of his phobia of horses when he was four and a half.

The recent release by the Sigmund Freud Archives of previously restricted interviews with Hans himself and with his father suggests how certain developmental circumstances may intensify the traumatic effect of the arrival of a new sibling. We now know that Hans's family was deeply troubled. The parents had a difficult marital relationship, and after the children grew up, they were divorced. Hans's mother, Olga Graf, had had a traumatic childhood (Chused 2007). According to Harold Blum (2007), Olga had many of the features we associate today with a borderline personality. Blum also thought that Olga might have suffered from postpartum depression following the birth of her little daughter. As a mother, Olga was inconsistent in her treatment of her young son. At times she overstimulated him, and at other times she was unavailable and hurtful, threatening to abandon him or send him away if he displeased her. She also seriously neglected and abused little Hanna. Hans was aware of the unhappy relationship between his mother and his sister. In his treatment he made repeated references to his mother's beating Hanna when she must have been less than eighteen months old. Fortunately Hans's father, Max, was very attentive to his son and assumed a good deal of responsibility for his care. Their relationship appears to have compensated to some degree for the difficulties Hans encountered with his mother (Chused 2007). Yet, according to Blum (2007), Hans's poor relationship with his mother and the family circumstances in general interfered with his achievement of separation-individuation and autonomy, leaving him prone to the separation anxiety that contributed to the development of his phobia. Jerome Wakefield (2007) has concluded that Hans's fears of abandonment and separation, brought about by the disruption of his attachment to his mother with the arrival of Hanna, were, in fact, more significant in the etiology of his neurosis than his oedipal rivalry.

This new information about Hans's early experiences sheds some light on why the birth of his little sister might have contributed to his neurosis. In the face of the difficulties in his relationship with his mother, it would have been hard for him to develop those inner resources that ordinarily help to cushion, to some extent, the disruption caused by a new baby in the family. An inconsistent, frequently unavailable mother who threatens abandonment makes it difficult for a child to develop that degree of "confident expectation" (Benedek 1973) that is necessary to assure him that he, too, will be cared for when his mother becomes preoccupied with a little brother or sister. In such a context, it is impossible to develop and maintain an inner representation of a reliable caretaker. In the absence of this representation that Daniel Siegel (1999) refers as the "virtual mother" and that Mahler and her colleagues (1975) long ago recognized as the indicator of object constancy, a mother's focus on a new baby may be experienced by an older sibling as a loss of mother and of self.

Hans's mother's mistreatment of his little sister also bears consideration. Although it may be satisfying to see a rival beaten, for a child to find his own destructive wishes acted upon by another person can lead to anxiety and guilt: anxiety that the same fate may befall one as retribution for one's wishes and guilt over the pleasure that one has escaped the hurt or that one has not protected the unfortunate sibling.

Such was the case with Theresa, an adult patient who when she was a child witnessed her two-year-younger brother, Brian, being beaten regularly with a belt by their parents until he was about thirteen years old. At times Theresa was aware of feeling pleased to see her brother hurt. At other times she felt ashamed that she did not stand up for him. Her guilt over her own destructive wishes toward her brother. which she witnessed her father acting out, and her satisfaction in seeing him beaten, as well as her remorse for not having stood up for her brother, contributed to the development of her masochistic personality.

ABANDONMENT AND LOSS

There are families in which a mother seems to abruptly withdraw from her older child when she gives birth to her next child and may even do so during her pregnancy, leaving her eldest child feeling abandoned. This appears to have been the case with Rita, who experienced her sister as if she had actually replaced her (Mitchell 2003).

Rita sought psychotherapy at a time when her daughter, Alice, was about to be married. She attributed her dysphoria to the fact that she was losing Alice. Her sister, Nancy, was involving herself in the wedding plans and she saw her as taking over her role as mother of the bride. She felt she was losing her place as mother to her daughter. Who, she wondered, was she if she was not her daughter's mother? She acted as if her very existence was threatened.

Rita, I learned, was two years old when Nancy was born, and according to her, her mother turned away from her and focused all of her attention on her sister. Although her mother continued to take care of her physical needs, Rita experienced their connection as having been "severed." She has been told that she withheld her feces for some time after Nancy was born, and a previous therapist had interpreted this behavior as a way of expressing her rage at her mother and her baby sister.

Her sister and her mother continued to be extremely close as adults. They lived within blocks of each other and were in touch daily either by phone or visit. Rita felt she had no place in that twosome. Even when her mother was old and ill, her efforts to help out were rejected.

At the beginning of her treatment, Rita was so convinced that she was losing her daughter that she failed to register any evidence to the contrary. Even as she reported events that showed that Alice was seeking and valuing her advice about the wedding plans, Rita did not feel as if she was being involved. She was confusing past and present, feeling as if her daughter would be the mother who had abandoned her in the past and her sister, the new baby who

she believed stole her mother away from her. Gradually she began to understand her confusion with the past and to appreciate that Alice would always
remain her daughter and she would always retain her place as her mother.

Two years after Rita concluded her treatment, she phoned to say that Alice
was pregnant. Rita spoke of her delight and excitement and the layette she
was assembling for the baby. Then, with a laugh, she noted that Nancy had
also prepared a layette. Her humorous response suggested that what once
would have been a calamity had become an anticipated annoyance, but one
that she could deal with.

Harriet

Harriet, too, experienced her mother as withdrawing from her after the birth
of her sister, Maeve. Harriet was three at the time. Once her sister arrived, the
closeness she once had had with her mother was lost and everything changed.

At the time she began treatment Harriet was anxious, depressed, and overwhelmed by difficulties in her marriage and in her parenting. She thought
that some of her problems had to do with her discomfort about her daughter's
increasing independence. She hated to see her grow up.

For the first year or so the treatment appeared to be progressing well. Then
her sister Maeve, who had made several suicidal attempts over the years, tried
once again to kill herself, and Harriet became very upset. She spoke of her
having been responsible for Maeve's difficulties. She had treated her sister
badly when they were children. She used to tell her that she smelled bad and
was ugly and that she hated her. From the day Maeve was born, Maeve had
taken her mother away from her and she continued to be her mother's favorite
throughout their lives. To this day her mother has eyes only for her sister.
Although Harriet felt her father loved her, he was uninvolved with the family
for the most part, something that Harriet felt had not bothered her much. It
was her mother's attention and love that mattered.

Harriet's depression increased after she spoke of her resentment of her
sister and she began to insist that she, too, needed to be hospitalized. Her
therapist drew Harriet's attention to what she had been saying in her recent
sessions about her guilt over her envy, jealousy, and hurtful behavior toward her sister. Therapist and patient then began to consider that the recur-
rence of Harriet's painful symptoms so similar to Maeve's represented a
way of punishing herself for her guilt over having made her sister suffer.
This understanding proved helpful, although it was not the whole story. A
few sessions later, Harriet added what she thought was probably another
reason for her increased discomfort. She had always entertained a fantasy
that if she were to be as troubled as her sister, her mother might begin to

be more attentive to her and they would regain the closeness they had once had before Maeve was born.

WHEN PARENTS DON'T UNDERSTAND
THEIR CHILDREN'S RESPONSES

For some older children their parents' failure to understand the difficulties they face in adjusting to a new baby and their intolerance of their older child's increased neediness intensifies their child's adverse reactions. This seemed to be true in Sheila's case.

Sheila, a twenty-six-year-old depressed young woman, sought treatment eight months after being hospitalized briefly for a transient psychotic-like episode. At the time she was working at a menial, poorly paid job. She was convinced that she was stupid and was hopeless about her future. When seen in consultation, she was dressed in a childlike fashion, in overall shorts and a shirt, and behaved as if she was much younger than her years.

Sheila was the oldest of three girls born three years apart. In the first consultation session, she noted that following the birth of her first sister, Lottie, she was so upset that she did not speak to her mother for a week.

Sheila appears to have responded to the birth of this rival by trying to become a baby herself. Her mother was unable to tolerate Sheila's infantile behavior and reprimanded and made fun of her. She was particularly harsh in her efforts to make Sheila stop sucking her thumb, grabbing her thumb out of her mouth, and spanking her. Her mother also became enraged when she discovered Sheila stroking a soft, cuddly doll that her grandfather had given her after Lottie's birth. Frightened that her mother would take the doll away from her, Sheila hid it during the day, bringing it out after her mother left the room at night and putting it away before her mother came in the morning.

The doll was a source of comfort and served as a transitional object (Winnicott 1953). Although, we think of the transitional object as acquiring its ability to help a child self-soothe because of its connection with the primary caretaker, in Sheila's case it seems to have connected her with a caring, understanding grandfather.

After several months of treatment, Sheila's therapist took a week's vacation. When sessions resumed, Sheila stopped talking and continued to remain silent for the next seven months except for terse responses to questions, such as "I have no ideas to talk about," "I'm stupid," and "The treatment is stupid."

Her therapist recalled Sheila's silence after the birth of her first sister and suggested that Sheila seemed to have experienced the therapist's leaving her and going off on vacation as she had her mother's leaving her to go to the hospital when her sister was born. Her not talking now to her therapist seemed similar to the way she had expressed her hurt and anger when her mother had left her.

Through this intervention and a variety of other efforts to bring Sheila out of her silence, Sheila gradually began to be more responsive and engaged in the sessions. At first her involvement was limited to expressing her contempt for the therapist and the treatment. Whereas, as she later reflected, not speaking made her feel powerful and as if she were destroying the therapist's ability to be effective, now she could verbally express her contempt for the therapist's lack of skill and the uselessness of her efforts. As she did so she imagined the therapist as feeling humiliated and helpless. The therapist interpreted this behavior as an effort on Sheila's part to do to her therapist what she felt had been done to her by her mother. Through this identification with the aggressor, Sheila was not only expressing her rage, but the therapist felt that Sheila was helping her understand what it had been like for Sheila when she was left, by inducing in her feelings similar to those Sheila had experienced.

A FALL FROM ON HIGH

Many years ago Alfred Adler (1928) who, as noted earlier, was convinced that birth order was an important factor in shaping a child's personality, saw the birth of a sibling as "dethroning" the older child. This seems to have been an important factor in the case of Tracy, who lost her sense of uniqueness when her younger brother was born (Mitchell 2003, Vivona 2008).

When Tracy sought treatment for her chronic depression she and her husband had one adopted daughter, Sara, age five. Tracy had never tried to conceive a child, fearing she would die in childbirth. Four months after her first consultation an opportunity to adopt a newborn baby girl arose. Tracy was ambivalent. Although she had always wanted more than one child, she now feared that Sara would feel, as she expressed it, "betrayed" by their adding another child to the family. Yet her husband and Sara, who knew about the baby, were eager for the infant. Tracy felt she, too, would probably regret not accepting the child and so the couple decided to proceed with the adoption of Katie.

Tracy herself had been born after a long period in which her parents believed themselves unable to conceive a child. Her birth was regarded as a "miracle" and she became the "queen bee" of the entire family. Aunts, uncles, cousins, and grandparents doted on her. To her parents' great surprise and to

Tracy's consternation, four years after her birth her mother conceived again. The delivery was very difficult and it was thought her mother might die. Fortunately she lived, but she was left with a serious, chronic health condition.

Tracy's brother, Rudy, then became another "miracle" child in the family, having survived a difficult birth and being a boy in a family in which males were highly valued. Tracy recalled how unhappy she had been when he was brought home. She had been sent to nursery school shortly after he arrived and became so upset that her parents had to withdraw her from the program.

Due to her mother's poor health the household was chaotic. She began to depend increasingly upon Tracy for help with her brother's care. On one hand Tracy resented her caretaking tasks. On the other hand she enjoyed the praise she received from her parents and relatives for her efforts, as well as the admiration she received from her brother, who to this day admires and looks up to her. I believe these factors, as well as Tracy's wish to be the one to have the children in the family, helped to account for Tracy wanting to have children despite her fear of giving birth to a child.

It became clear to Tracy early in the treatment that her fears about Sara's response to a new baby derived from her own feelings of betrayal at the birth of her brother. Her parents, she said, led her to feel she was the most important figure in their lives and then they showed her she was not. Not only did she fear that Sara would hate her new sister, but she also was concerned that Sara would hate Tracy for bringing Katie into the family as she herself had hated her mother for having her brother.

When Katie joined the family, Sara appeared to take her in stride and for the most part seemed to derive pleasure from her new little sibling, who from early on seemed delighted by her "big sister." Tracy's anxiety about Sara's reactions dissipated as she came to understand how she had projected her own feelings on to her older daughter.

However, Tracy found herself increasingly uncomfortable mothering Katie. She was having difficulty getting close to her. When the baby sitter was feeding Katie, Tracy became hungry. She realized she wanted to be the one to be taken care of, not the caretaker.

One day, Tracy arrived at her session extremely upset. That morning she had found herself wanting to throw Katie off the changing table. Consideration of this led to an understanding of how she had wanted to kill her little brother, so hurt and angry had she been at his part in toppling her from her role as "princess."

Through a consideration of the transference, and countertransference, and Tracy's associations, the impact on her of the birth of her brother became clearer. We came to recognize that her routine arrival ten to fifteen minutes late, sometimes more, for both of her twice-a-week sessions were a way of acting out a number of unconscious intentions. On one hand her tardiness served to help her avoid meeting any other patient leaving the office, enabling her to maintain the fantasy that she was my only patient, as she had wished to be the only child of her parents. On the other hand it showed how little I mattered to her. She would make me feel as unimportant as she had felt once her brother was born. By limiting our time, Tracy also fantasized she was destroying the therapy, which to her meant destroying me. As she once wanted to destroy her mother for having another child, she wanted to kill me for having other patients.

I was aware of my frustration and anger as I waited for Tracy to arrive for her hours and troubled that I could not find a way to effectively deal with her lateness. I reasoned that my response was due to the limitations Tracy was imposing on our work. However, it did not take long before I realized that my anger was also rooted in my own past.

At the time I was seeing Tracy my first grandchild was born. One day while I was visiting, my daughter suggested I might take the baby for a walk if I wished. I was delighted and started to look for the carriage to place him in. No carriage was needed for that younger generation of mothers! I could just carry him. I suddenly felt slightly anxious as I left the house with him in my arms. Why, I wondered? Was I afraid I would drop him? I did not recall being fearful of dropping my own children. As I was pondering this, I suddenly had a recollection of my five-year-younger baby sister asleep in my parents' room. She was born at home and slept in a beautifully decorated bassinet. Had I wanted to toss her out of it? I rather think so. Tracy and I were both repeating our pasts. We were engaged in an enactment, with Tracy the parent who was preoccupied with other children and I the frustrated, angry little girl that Tracy had been.

Joseph Sandler (1976) has proposed that such a response on the part of the therapist, which he termed "role-responsiveness," is an important aspect of the therapist's countertransference. He has called attention to how much can be learned from such enactments that occur under the pressure of the therapist's unconscious compliance with the role that a patient unconsciously assigns him or her.

In time the opportunity to express her hostility toward her brother and parents without being judged, to understand some of the reasons she had been so upset by her brother's birth, to see how since childhood she had confused her wishes with deeds, and the chance to learn how she had been experiencing Sara as the child she was and Katie as the brother she had, helped Tracy gain greater comfort as a mother to Katie and to develop a more secure attachment to her.

One matter that was not touched upon in Tracy's treatment was her fear of pregnancy. Although I waited for her to do so, she never raised this as an issue in the treatment. However, I have hypothesized that her wish to kill her brother and destroy her mother for having borne him played a significant role in generating Tracy's concerns about bearing a child. Jacob Arlow (1972) has noted how some children who welcome their only-child status entertain a fantasy that when they were in their mother's womb, they destroyed their potential rivals. The fear that they will be punished and an unconscious fantasy that a sibling in the form of a fetus within their own body will retaliate and destroy them lead to a fear of pregnancy. Although Arlow did not, as far as I know, address this conflict in the case of an older child who wishes to destroy a baby sibling, it seems to me that this may have been the case with Tracy.

The fact that her mother experienced severe health problems following the birth of Tracy's brother may also have contributed to Tracy's fear of pregnancy. Having experienced hostile feelings toward her mother for bearing her brother, she may have entertained an unconscious fantasy that she was responsible for her mother's difficulties and anticipated that she would be destroyed in retaliation if she bore a child.

OEDIPAL OR SIBLING CONFLICT?

It is often difficult to distinguish between oedipal and sibling issues at any given moment in a treatment. Oedipal and sibling rivalry coexist. Conflicts with parents are often displaced onto siblings and vice versa. When one of my patients borrowed her sister's dishes and silverware for a family party and then did not invite her to the gathering, it was difficult to determine whether she was unconsciously getting rid of her sister as a rival, or whether she had displaced on to her sister her wishes get rid of an oedipal rival. In Tracy's case, when she spoke of being betrayed, was she expressing her reactions to having been made to feel so special and then finding that she was not or was she feeling betrayed by her mother and father creating a child together rather than with her? The birth of a baby is evidence of the parents' sexual relationship and their ability to have babies together, experiences the child is excluded from. It disproves the frequently comforting fantasy, often entertained by children, that the only time their parents engaged in sex was the one occasion when they were conceived. In Tracy's case, addressing her oedipal conflicts was an important part of the treatment. However, her identification with her older daughter, her longing to be the baby, her wishes and fears of harming a baby (as evidenced in her associations as well as what we drew from the transference and countertransference) led me to believe that her sibling conflicts were paramount during the period in treatment I have described.

In thinking about whether a conflict may be sibling or oedipally determined, Prophecy Coles (2003), a British analyst, has also noted the difficulty that a therapist may have in making this distinction. She has written about a depressed man who sought treatment in his late forties. The middle child of seven siblings, he had been cared for largely by his two older sisters, who mistreated him. On one occasion when he was a little boy, they were walking him home from school and ran off without him, leaving him feeling abandoned and lost. As an adult, the idea of not being able to find his way filled him with dread.

This man was extremely anxious during his sessions, hyperventilating on occasion. He was unable to lie down on the couch, explaining that if he could not see his analyst's face, he didn't know what she was doing. Based on her patient's extreme anxiety about his sexual fantasies, Coles initially interpreted it as related to oedipal longings for her, his analyst. However, the patient was convinced that his fear had to do with his experiencing her as one or the other of his cruel sisters. For example, he saw her dismissing him at the end of a session as leaving him to wander off alone as his sisters had. After he revealed that one of the "games" his sisters played with him was to suddenly pull down his pants to see if he had an erection and that he never knew when they might do this, Coles recognized that at that point the transference was to her as a sibling. She understood that the sexually arousing fantasies that so frightened him, which she had thought to be oedipal, were related to the cruelties his sisters forced on him.

WHEN PARENTS AND CHILD DO NOT FIT WELL TOGETHER

A poor fit between parent and child is another factor that may lead to an unsatisfying relationship between them. I understood this to be the case with Melanie and her family. Suffering from feelings of inadequacy and shame, despite her accomplishments as a biologist, Melanie sought treatment for depression. She partly attributed her poor self-esteem to having been the least favored child in her family. Something was never right between her parents and herself. They took good care of her and were never unkind but somehow she just never felt she belonged to them. She could not understand why. Was it her plain appearance or her seriousness? What was there about her that did not suit her parents?

Melanie had grown up with a two-year-older sister and a two-year-younger brother. Neither parent had completed high school. They both worked at low-level jobs. Her brother and sister were both considered "slow learners" at school. Melanie, on the other hand, was extremely bright. She was skipped in school. She won a prestigious high school award and was a recipient of a full scholarship to a university. The contrast between her abilities and those of the rest of the family were dramatic. During the course of the treatment her therapist suggested that the differences between her and the other members of the family might play a role in her feeling that she did not fit in. This led Melanie to think about how difficult it had been for her parents and siblings to understand her great love of books and the considerable amount of time she spent in the local library. Perhaps they were uncomfortable with her because they had no interest in the things that interested her.

In reviewing the past with this understanding in mind, Melanie seemed to gain a better appreciation for the efforts her parents did make to respond to her needs, even though they did not quite understand them. She recalled their sending her to a camp for gifted children that was recommended by one of her teachers. She realized now that they could ill afford such a program. Looking at her family in this way helped Melanie feel better about her family and about herself. Being different was not the same as being bad or ugly or unworthy.

THE FAVORITE CHILD

It is important to note that it is not only the least preferred child in a family who may suffer from parental favoritism. The preferred child may also be negatively affected. Kurt, for example, was valued far more than his younger sister, Serena. He was overly indulged and pampered. As a boy, he was excused from any chores about the house. He chose the outings the family took and dictated much of what went on in the household. Kurt grew up with a sense of entitlement that left him unable to tolerate not getting what he wanted. He was enraged with others who did not recognize him as the superior being he believed he was, and as a result was unable to make friends or hold on to a job for any length of time.

Moreover, not all preferred children enjoy their position. For some it feels unfair. One patient noted how her parents' preference for her cost her brother psychologically. She felt guilty and found it difficult to enjoy her more advantaged life, sometimes compromising her own achievements.

AFTER THE FIRST SIBLING

Envy, jealousy, and rivalry are not limited to a child's first encounter with a sibling, although no matter how many children follow and how old and developed the older brother or sister may be when a new baby is born, each subsequent birth in the family may revive that first experience with a new baby, at least initially.

Disturbances in the sibling relationship may occur or be exacerbated at any point during the life cycle. Children, parents, family circumstances, and sibling relationships change. A child may be more sensitive at one age than at another. Siblings may pose greater problems as they grow older. A once revered older child's increasing privileges and activities may arouse greater envy on the part of a younger brother or sister who cannot or is not permitted to do the same things as he does. Accidental events or crises may shift the balance in a family. A healthy brother or sister may become ill and require far more of the parents' attention than earlier. A parent may die and a child may lose the parent whose favorite he once was. A cute, endearing, devoted little sister may grow up to annoy and provoke her older brother. A father may withdraw his attention from a previously treasured little daughter and become engrossed in his older or younger son's athletic activities. The relationship between adult siblings may also be impaired by parents shifting their attention from one child to another. I think here of a family in which the parents died and left more money to their unmarried daughter than their married daughter, thinking she would need more resources. As it turned out the married daughter and her husband lost their business some years after their parents died. They requested that the sister give part of her inheritance to them to equalize things, which she refused to do. This created years of discord between these siblings.

Diane and June

Diane is a woman whose early positive relationship with her sister, June, became more troubled as she grew older. This seemed to be partly due to the fact that June, who had been their father's favorite, had lost her place of importance with him, while Diane remained her mother's favorite.

The family had emigrated from Europe and for the first years of her life, Diane did not speak English and had little contact with other children. She longed for a sibling to keep her company. When she was nearly six, her sister June was born. Before June's birth, her mother promised Diane that she could be her "little helper" with the baby. When the nursemaid she hired refused to let Diane into the baby's room for fear she would carry germs, her mother fired her and replaced her with a nurse who allowed June to help her.

Diane took great pleasure in teaching and supervising June. She helped with her toilet training, pushed her in her stroller, and eventually taught her to read. The girls remained very close until June was around four and Diane ten. By then Diane spoke English well and had made friends. Now she had little time to attend to June and she resented June's following her around. At the same time, June was beginning to resent and resist her older sister's "bossiness."

Their father, according to Diane, lost interest in June when she was about seven and was no longer the cute, appealing little girl she had once been. Diane had had the same experience with their father, who turned away from her as she grew older. However, Diane always had her mother, whereas June had no one once her father withdrew his favor. As a result of their father's withdrawal, June's jealousy of Diane's relationship with her mother became intense.

The relationship between the sisters became more strained during their teens after their father died. Diane recalled hitting her sister when June insisted that Diane had no right to cry at the funeral because she had not loved their father as June had.

Tension between the sisters increased over the years, but they continued to stay in close contact nonetheless. As adults they traveled together, saw each other frequently, and shared many interests and activities. According to Diane they had an "unbreakable bond." When Diane was in treatment, her therapist had referred to the sisters as "enmeshed" despite the fact that they frequently disagreed and argued.

When the sisters were in their fifties their mother died, and tension increased between them. June became very needy and demanding of Diane and seemed to want her to play the mothering role she had assumed when they were little girls. Diane found this burdensome and resented her sister's demands. Finally, their relationship was so disturbing to Diane that she unsuccessfully tried to persuade June to see a therapist with her. After this the sisters continued to do things together, but the friction between them was a source of ongoing distress for Diane.

When they were in their late sixties, June developed cancer and Diane helped with her care. There were nights when June became frightened and would ask her to come to her. Many a night she slept at her side. Yet, June was frequently irritated with her, and never acknowledged that she felt good about Diane's help. She didn't know whether June realized that, despite all, she loved her. It was a great relief when Diane learned from a mutual friend that before her death, June had noted how important Diane's care had been to her, and how much she loved her. She regretted, however, that June could not express those feelings directly to her.

WHEN FEELINGS FOR A PARENT ARE DISPLACED ONTO A SIBLING

Fearful of losing a parent or a parent's love, fearful of being punished for hostile actions toward the parents, or a need to maintain an image of a parent as "good," children may displace their anger, hate, and murderous wishes toward their parents onto their siblings. Leonard Shengold (1989) writes of such a patient, whose alcoholic parents humiliated, neglected, and mistreated all of their children.

Shengold quotes his patient, "A" (as he referred to him): "My parents despised their children: I despised my brothers and I despised myself" (p. 7). As an example of the mistreatment "A" was subjected to, Shengold describes how each year at Christmas, when he was a young boy, "A" was permitted to play with the expensive toys he was given right after he received them. The next morning, though, he had to help his father pack the toys back into their boxes so that they might be sent to "poor children." "A" came to abhor those poor children and instead of hating his father, according to Shengold, he came to hate his younger brothers. So intense was the hatred that "A" displaced onto his brothers that he usually remembered the past as if he were an only child. Not only did this defensive effort help to protect him from expressing his hostility against his parents and incurring their wrath, but it also enabled him, as a child, to maintain a positive image of his father. His father became a "benevolent" man who did Christ's work by giving to the poor. By means of the defense of splitting, "A" was able to sustain an image of his father as "good" by assigning all the "bad" to his siblings. It should be noted that Shengold does not say whether "A's" brothers were permitted to keep their toys, which if it were the case, might also have contributed to "A's" hatred of them.

TRANSGENERATIONAL SIBLING CONFLICTS

Several psychoanalysts (Abarbanel 1983, Agger 1988, Coles 2007) have noted how a parent may stimulate or encourage certain patterns of relationship between their children that resemble those experienced with their own sibling. As a way of satisfying unconscious needs and fantasies from the past, they may convey their expectations of how their children should relate to each other by directing their behaviors. They may treat their children in ways that lead to or encourage the envy and discord that characterized their own childhood sibling relationships.

Joyce Abarbanel (1983) has written about a mother, Mrs. C., who, when she became pregnant, withdrew from her little daughter, Caren. She continued to avoid her little daughter after her son was born, leaving her largely in the care of a maid.

Caren became increasingly troubled and troubling. She refused go to bed at night, pulled off her diapers, and made it difficult for her parents to care for her. When Abarbanel last interviewed Mrs. C. and Caren six weeks postpartum, both Caren, who was then two years of age, and her mother seemed depressed, and Abarbanel was concerned about the kind of relationship this brother and sister were likely to have as they grew up.

Abarbanel understood Mrs. C.'s treatment of her older child as determined by the relationship that Mrs. C. herself had had with her fourteen-month-older sister. The sisters had been playmates during their childhood, but they had been strong rivals for the limited affection accorded them by their unavailable and distant mother. Mrs. C. felt that she had received even less attention than her sister and that her mother considered her to be her "second best" daughter. As adults, their rivalry was a constant theme in Mrs. C.'s interviews. Abarbanel understood Mrs. C. as unconsciously responding to Caren as if she were her own older sibling, thereby creating conditions that were likely to lead to the rivalry between her children that she and her sister had experienced.

Grace

Grace, a middle-aged mother of two daughters, believed, in retrospect, that her mother had wanted she and her three-year-younger sister Elise to have a poor relationship. At the time I spoke with Grace, Elise had shut her out of her life, much to Grace's distress. In her first consultation she noted that her family had a history of sibling strife. Her grandmother and her grandmother's sisters never got along, and Grace's mother and her sisters were constantly battling. They went months without speaking to each other. Eventually they would make up, only to fight again. According to Grace, her mother was usually the instigator of those fights.

As described by Grace, her mother was a greedy, angry woman who verbally and sometimes physically abused Grace as a child. After hurting her, she would then hug and caress her. As an adult, Grace recognized that her mother had been a seriously disturbed woman, but when she was growing up she simply thought of her as cruel.

As children, she and Elise got along well. Grace recalled with much pleasure some of the games they engaged in together. She also remembered how when her mother made Elise, who was a poor eater, sit at the table until she ate everything, she, Grace, would either eat the food or throw it away. As the girls grew older they developed separate friends and began to distance from each other. Yet, they continued to share a bedroom, even when they had the opportunity to have their own rooms.

As teenagers they both realized that neither of them could shield the other from their mother's wrath. Elise avoided their mother while Grace would fight with her. Although their father was kinder to them, he rarely intervened, and Grace felt he, too, was fearful of invoking their mother's wrath. Both girls left home as soon as they could. Grace married at eighteen, and when Elise went off to college, she never returned to the family.

In their early years, it was clear that Grace was mother's favorite, although that did not spare her from mother's rage. She was valued, she thought, because she was the prettier of the two girls. Her mother could not tolerate the way her sister looked and was constantly criticizing her for her lack of attention to her appearance. When Grace was an adolescent her mother forced Grace to dye her hair another color,

The situation changed when the girls became adults. Their mother became very angry at Grace for divorcing her wealthy husband and in a way that left Grace and her children in poor financial circumstances. She made it clear that she was not there to help support her. She turned away from Grace, and Elise, who by then had become a very successful businesswoman, became the "good," loved daughter.

Eventually the sisters moved to different parts of the country. They saw each other infrequently, although originally there did not appear to be hard feelings between them. As time went on, however, Elise made it increasingly clear that she was not interested in any contact with Grace. She even went so far as to exclude Grace from the traditional family meal after the unveiling of their mother's headstone.

In her talks with me, Grace kept coming back to the history of sibling discord in their family, feeling that there was some connection between her relationship with her sister and her mother's past relationships with her own siblings. In her mother's family there was always one sister who was excluded by the others. She recalled how when they held the unveiling for her mother, they also unveiled her mother's sister's grave. As they stood by the graves, Elise noted how displeased their mother would have been to know that she was sharing the day with her sister.

Grace had the sense that her mother would be satisfied to see that the relationship between her daughters was as troubled as her relationships were with her siblings. In looking back, she felt as if her mother had somehow encouraged discord between them. Grace remembered a birthday party when she was a child. Her mother had told her that she need not invite her sister. They lived in a very small apartment and her sister was forced to remain in the bedroom alone with the door closed while the party went on in the next room. At some point, Elise was allowed to come in and watch the party. To this day Grace can recall her sister sitting on the side, not participating but watching the other children as they enjoyed the games. She was sure Elise must have hated her that day. Perhaps, her sister was shutting her out of her life as she had felt shut out by Grace.

Thinking about the transmission of patterns of sibling relationships from one generation to another raises any number of questions about the dynamics of this process. Was Grace's mother identifying with a sister who had excluded her, thereby turning what she had once passively experienced to something she actively brought about? Was this her way of showing what she had once endured as the rejected sibling in her family, by inducing similar feelings in one or the other of her children?

Todd

Parents who have suffered from sibling conflicts may also foster conflicts among their children in order to satisfy their narcissistic needs and to gratify their aggressive wishes (Agger 1988). This seemed to be so in the case of Todd and his brother, Simon. These brothers were bitter rivals while growing up and fought constantly. Their father appears to have encouraged the competition between his sons. He constantly compared them to each other. Both sons fought to gain their father's favor. Sometimes he showed his preference for one brother, only to turn away from him and focus all of his attention on the other. When Todd looked back, he felt that his father gained considerable pleasure from their rivalry for his favor. Todd was aware that his father was the least preferred child among his own five siblings. It seemed to him that having his sons fight over his attention probably helped his father feel better about himself. He was no longer the least preferred child but instead he was the much sought after father whom each boy wanted to possess.

FATHERS

In some of the families considered above, the fathers appear to have played a negligible role. However, in families when fathers are involved with their children, as in the case of Little Hans, they can often help to compensate for a poor mother-child relationship. This appeared to be the case with Margaret Mahler, an outstanding child psychoanalyst and researcher of child development (Coates 2004, Stepansky 1988). She had been a sickly infant whom her mother seemed unable to relate to. When her little sister, Suzanne, was born four years after her birth, her mother doted on Suzanne, leaving Mahler feeling her mother's rejection even more intensely. Although she was in touch with her hurt and anger, Mahler appears to have adapted to these circumstances in a way that ultimately benefitted her and the field of child psychoanalysis. According to Mahler, her observations of her mother's loving relationship with her sister and the way it contrasted with her own treatment led to her lifelong efforts to understand the mother–infant relationship. That she was able to make such a positive adaptation seems to have partly been made possible by the love and support of her father. He was said to have been very proud of her intellect, and to have gained much pleasure from the fact that even at a young age he could engage her in discussions on such adult topics as politics and mathematics (Stepansky 1988).

Patsy Turrini, a psychoanalyst who founded the Mother's Center movement in the United States, recalls Mahler telling a study group that as a four-year-old watching her mother nurse her baby sister, she had placed her hands on her hips and angrily proclaimed, "I was born from my father." In her memoir, Mahler (1977) does mention her impulsivity, her overly strict conscience, and her propensity for depression, suggesting that being her mother's less favorite child was not without cost.

SIBLING PHYSICAL AND EMOTIONAL ABUSE

In some families, conflict between siblings leads to physical or emotional abuse, as well as sexual abuse, which I will consider in the following chapter. It is difficult to accurately assess the extent of sibling physical and emotional abuse because it is so often dismissed as normal sibling rivalry. Several studies, however, suggest a high degree of physical violence among brothers and sisters. According to Straus, Gelles, and Steinmetz (1980), it has been estimated that one in five American children between the ages of three and seventeen who have a sibling at home commit at least one violent act against a brother or sister during a typical year.

A study ten years later by Straus and Gelles (1990) found that 53 percent of children ages three to seventeen committed acts of severe violence (such as kicking, stabbing, punching, or attacking with objects) against a brother or sister. Vernon R. Wiehe (2000), in his qualitative study of 150 individuals (130 females, average age thirty-seven, 127 Caucasian) also found these to be the most common forms of physical abuse among siblings.

In many instances violence among siblings is viewed as normal and goes unrecognized and unattended to by parents. Frequently parents fail to distinguish it from normal sibling rivalry and leave the children to fight their own battles. All too often parents deny the suffering the abused child experiences, or even blame that child for what has happened.

More prevalent and sometimes more damaging than physical abuse is the emotional abuse sustained by many brothers and sisters (Wiehe 2000). Such abuse includes destruction of a sibling's personal possessions, exacerbating a sibling's fears, ridicule, degradation, and name-calling.

Emotional abuse is difficult to identify. It ordinarily leaves no physical marks so it can go unnoticed by those outside the family. Within the family parents often tend to view teasing, or ridicule, or other forms of emotional abuse as normal expressions of sibling rivalry. Yet the taunts and insults of siblings may have a pervasive impact on the development of a brother or sister. The harsh superegos of some patients may be traced back to the internalized taunts and demeaning insults of a brother or sister.

Children frequently experience all three forms of abuse, emotional, physical, and sexual. Fifty-five of the adults in Wiehe's study (2000) have been abused by their siblings in all of these ways.

Sibling abuse is frequently associated with dysfunctional families, with parents who abuse each other (Hotaling, Straus, and Lincoln 1990), and with families in which one or the other parent or both suffer from mental illness or addiction. There is often little supervision in the families in which abuse occurs. The abusing sibling is often an older child who has been burdened by considerable responsibility for younger brothers and sisters. Parents also frequently play favorites in these families. The abuse of the more preferred child by his less valued sibling may not only express rage at the envied brother or sister but also the anger the child feels toward the parent who has rejected him. We shall see a case of sexual abuse that illustrates this in the next chapter.

In some families the parents feel helpless to control their offspring. In others the abuse serves some unconscious need or wish of the parents themselves. For example, when Roy wondered in his treatment why he had sat by while his younger son, Phillip, viciously kicked his two-year-older brother to the point of injuring him, he realized, to his great discomfort, that he had in some way enjoyed the scene. Having been abused by his own older brother, he realized that he found satisfaction in witnessing his younger son as the victor. Unconsciously, he identified with him and was replaying his past, but now it was he as the younger sibling who was the stronger.

In families in which a parent or parents mistreat one child, the other children may identify with their parent's aggression toward that brother or sister, and they may experience their parent's behavior as giving them implicit permission and encouragement to mistreat that sibling. In some families abusing parents actively demand that their other children join in the abuse of their sibling.

Richard. B. Pelzer (2005) has written about his relationship with his brother, David, who was subjected to unspeakable acts of cruelty by their seriously disturbed, alcoholic mother until he was taken from the family by the court and placed in foster care. Richard writes of his lifelong regret over his own participation in his brother's torture. He and his three other brothers were not only allowed to abuse David but were encouraged and rewarded for doing so. Their mother demanded that they treat David as less than human and she chose Richard to be her informer against him. Living in constant fear that his mother, who to some extent abused all of her children, would treat him the same way she treated David, Richard sought her favor by becoming her ally. Many times Richard falsely accused his brother of some act that he knew his mother would beat David for or even try to kill him. He believed that by keeping her hatred focused on his brother, he could keep it away from himself. Actually he was correct, for once his brother was removed from the home, Richard became the target for her abuse.

On the other hand, there are families in which the other children actively protect their mistreated or abused brother or sister. So it was with JoAnn and her two-year-younger brother, Ron. For some reason that JoAnn was unable to fathom, her father seemed to have always hated her younger brother. He constantly criticized and demeaned him, and often compared him unfavorably to her. When her father was drunk, which was often, he would beat Ron unmercifully for such insignificant things as leaving his toys around or having a dirty face. Their mother was frightened of her husband and did nothing to stop him. As early as when she was five, JoAnn could recall running around to pick up Ron's toys before her father came home from the bar after work. Sometimes when he would begin to yell at her brother, she would rush down into the cellar with him and hide until she thought her father had fallen asleep on the couch. Then they would sneak upstairs and go to bed.

Dominick

Another young man, Dominick, whom I interviewed for this volume and who had been both emotionally and physically abused by his three-and-a-half-year-older brother, was extremely concerned that the relationship between his two sons not become abusive, and made great efforts to try to curb their expressions of hostility toward each other. An account of Dominick's experience suggests some of the dynamics of sibling abuse and its potential for interfering with the establishment of a positive sense of self, the capacity to comfortably relate to others, and, in Dominick's case, to concerns about parenting.

Dominick was forty-five, married for fifteen years, and the father of two sons, ages eleven and seven, when he sought the help of a psychotherapist. He had begun to worry about how best to deal with his boys. He was finding it difficult to distinguish between what might be normal roughhousing and teasing and what went beyond that. As a result of his own experience of being abused by his brother, he became extremely anxious when the boys fought. He was worried that in his efforts to prevent them from hurting each other, he was probably "on them too much" and actually created more discord between them.

Dominick's own older brother, Francis, who was three years his senior, seems to have resented Dominick from early on. Although there were times when Francis was friendly, most of the time he treated Dominick with tremendous disdain, made fun of him, taunted him, and physically attacked him. His occasional friendliness was confusing for Dominick, who would think they were getting along well when suddenly Francis would attack him with ferocity. He never knew what to expect of his brother. This left him with an inability to trust anyone. He was never sure where he stood with someone and worried that as friendly as people seemed, they might be harboring a hatred of him that he needed to be prepared for.

Dominick described his mother as overwhelmed by her responsibilities and ineffectual in dealing with her sons. Although she insisted that they could not hit each other in the back or in the face, she was unable to control Francis. Their father was an alcoholic who played little part in the life of the family.

When their father was drinking he was extremely critical and deprecating of both his sons. However, he was harder on Francis than on Dominick. His parents had always found his brother difficult to deal with. Francis was stubborn and opinionated, which troubled his father greatly. Seeing the strife between his brother and his parents, Dominick had made every effort to be as different from Francis as he could be. He became the "good" son, the diplomatic one, an adaptation he thought served him well in his work and personal life, but which extracted a price from him emotionally

The physical fighting stopped when Francis was sixteen and Dominick, thirteen. After one violent fight Dominick injured Francis severely. Although this ended his brother's attacks on him, the experience left Dominick frightened of his own anger. He feared becoming uncontrollable and inflicting serious harm on another person. This suppression of his anger has proven a handicap; he avoids conflict and has difficulty being appropriately assertive.

In looking back, Dominick attributed his brother's abuse not only to Francis's resentment and hatred of him, but also to the poor image Francis had of himself. Francis was an unattractive boy with very poor eyesight. He wore thick glasses. Despite his ability to hurt Dominick when they were young, Francis was not strong. He was frequently teased by his peers for being weak and was called "four eyes." Dominick thought Francis's power over him when they were small probably made Francis feel stronger and more adequate.

As an adult Francis has never married, lives alone, and is socially isolated. The brothers live at some distance from each other. However, they have developed a better relationship over the years and phone each other regularly. They get together in person once or twice a year. Dominick noted that it seems as if they have changed places in these last years. Francis reaches out to him for advice and it is as if he, Dominick, is now the older brother. However, Dominick believes if he were in need, Francis would try to help him. They are there for each other, he said.

We see in the case of Dominick some of the dynamics that are often present in cases of sibling abuse: an alcoholic father who emotionally abused both sons, although one more than the other; an overwhelmed mother who seems to have given up on controlling her sons; and an abusing sibling who himself had been emotionally abused. As it frequently does, the abuse left Dominick with difficulties in trusting others, with intimacy, with problems in self-assertion, and with a lack of self-confidence, which was partly reflected in his uneasiness about his parenting abilities.

Yet, Dominick felt that certain positives had come from his experience with his brother. He saw his capacity to tune into other people, to read them with accuracy, as related to his need to sense his brother's moods for self-protective reasons. This sensitivity to others has been an advantage in his work and social relationships. He also felt that his difficulties as a child have contributed to his wish to make life better for other people. He does not want others to be mistreated as he was. Dominick added that his past experiences had strengthened his religious faith by giving him hope and a sense of purpose when he was struggling.

Dominick found his psychotherapy of great value in helping him deal with the impact of his relationship with his brother. It enabled him to develop more positive feelings about himself, and to relate more easily to others. He had found it extremely helpful to share his experiences in a safe environment, to be able to talk about his rage and his love of his brother and everything in between. He noted that he had a chance to sort his feelings out, whereas "initially it was like one big stew." In finding that he could trust his therapist after testing him in every way, he gradually gained more trust in others and began to enjoy greater intimacy with the significant people in his life. As a result of his relationship with his therapist, he came to realize that not everyone was his brother and that too often he had expected or seemed to experience others as if they were Francis. He had also found his treatment helpful in enabling him to understand what constituted appropriate and expectable behavior between brothers. He had come to see that in striving so hard to have his boys be kinder and gentler to one another, he might at times expect too much and push too hard, defeating the very purpose he intended. With his therapist's help he was gaining a more realistic understanding of what to expect in his sons' relationship to one another.

In the absence of clinical details from the therapist we cannot know the actual process that led to the gains Dominick made. However, it seems to me that the therapeutic relationship must have been an important component of the treatment. When, for example, I asked Dominick whether he had ever experienced feelings toward his therapist that were similar to those he experienced with Francis, he immediately responded that his therapist was nothing like his brother, though sometimes he saw him erroneously as his brother or expected him to be like Francis. It is by being "nothing like" a troubling figure from the past that therapists can gradually help such individuals as Dominick begin to recognize that not all people are replicas of those who have abused them and to begin to see and respond to others in the here and now as different and unique. It seemed to me that Dominick was also helped in his treatment by developing an understanding of what his brother's motives might have been for abusing him. This helped to relieve him of the feeling that maybe there was something stupid or girlish about him, as his brother had insisted, and to see these insults as motivated by his brother's own problems. As a result he gained a different perspective on his brother that enabled him to come to better terms with Francis's "bad" aspects and to discover or to retrieve some of the "good" experiences they had shared. The integration of these bad and good aspects of his brother paved the way for Dominick to begin to forgive him for his actions in the past.

SIBLICIDE

Information about siblicide is extremely limited, and as far as I have been able to tell little has been learned about the dynamics of fratricide or sororicide. The Bureau of Justice Statistics has put out a special report entitled "Murder in Families" (Dawson and Langan 1994). The report was drawn from a study of a representative sample of all murder cases that were handled in large urban counties in 1988. The researchers found that of the 16 percent of the murder victims that were members of the defendants' families, 1.5 percent were killed by their siblings.

Bourget and Gagne (2006) reviewed the data from coroners' files on ten cases of sibling homicide that were committed over a ten-year period (1994–2003) in Quebec, Canada. The fratricides in this limited study were committed in an impulsive manner with no premeditation. They were unplanned consequences of an impulsive act of violence. In six of the ten homicides, alcohol was used by the offender at the time of the killing. Two of the murderers had schizophrenia or another form of psychosis and one suffered from a depressive disorder. Many of the siblings were "drinking buddies" and close to one another. The small sample size of their study did not, however, allow for any conclusive findings.

Bourget and Gagne did not examine the relationship between these siblings prior to the fratricide. Although their findings did support the need for improved treatment of individuals suffering from alcoholism and serious mental pathology, they did not actually shed light on those psychological circumstances that might contribute to sibling killing sibling. They called for further research in this area.

REMARKS

In an earlier chapter on development I noted how envy, jealousy, and rivalry between siblings can serve to stimulate positive development. In this chapter, we see how under some circumstances a new baby in the family may set the stage for years of discord between a younger child and his older sibling, or serious strife may develop between siblings at any point in the life cycle.

For some individuals envy, jealousy, rivalry, hostility, and the death wishes they have engendered compromise their ability to achieve a sense of self-value and to form meaningful relationships with others. Conflicts with brothers and sisters may be reenacted with love partners, offspring, friends, as well as with one's therapist. Guilt and anxiety related to destructive wishes toward one's brothers and sisters or to one's parents for bringing these siblings into the world may lead to inhibitions of a person's abilities and/or to a lifetime of self punishment.

A psychotherapy that gives a place to brothers and sisters can be helpful in enabling patients to come to terms with their discordant experiences with their siblings. The understanding gained through treatment, as well as a positive relationship with a therapist who may, in some instances, be experienced as a more benign sibling, can help to moderate negative feelings and promote forgiveness of both sibling and self for past hostilities. At best, working through sibling-related conflicts may clear the path for brothers and sisters to form more satisfying, mature adult bonds with each other in the present. In other cases, it may simply take some of the sting out of old conflicts, freeing individuals from their preoccupation with old battles, leaving them better able to move on, even if they do not draw closer to their brothers or sisters.

6

Sibling Sexuality

Sexuality between siblings ranges from those early investigations children make of each other's bodies to satisfy their curiosity, to touching and fondling in ways that provide some sensual pleasure, to more overtly sexual activities such as mutual masturbation and finally to coitus.

Sexual play, sexually tinged activities, and erotic fantasies are thought to be commonplace among siblings (Parens 1988). Their psychological impact may be favorable or harmful and in some instances both, depending upon a variety of factors. The outcome depends, among other things, on whether the exchanges are consensual or forced and whether the relationship between the siblings is positive or discordant. Other influential factors include the nature of the acts, the ages and developmental levels of the children involved, the differences in age between the siblings, the emotional well-being of the family as a whole, the psychological strengths and vulnerabilities of each sibling, the accompanying fantasies, and the way each child subjectively experiences the encounters. Also of consequence are the secrecy with which the acts are carried out, the parents' reactions if they are discovered, and whether the sexual play or activity is occasional or is a regular occurrence spanning a lengthy period of developmental time and occupying a central place in the lives of the siblings.

THE IMPACT OF EARLY SEXUAL PLAY AND SEXUAL ACTIVITIES

In his study of 796 undergraduates at six New England colleges, David Finkelhor (1980), director of the Family Violence Research Program at the University of New Hampshire, found that 10 percent of the males and

15 percent of the females reported some type of sexual experiences with their siblings. Fondling and touching of the genitals were the most common activities reported. The respondents were equally divided between those who considered their experiences negative and those who thought them positive. (Finkelhor believed that there were probably many more students in the study who had sexual experiences with their siblings, but they were reluctant to share this information.)

Several psychoanalysts have suggested that under certain circumstances limited sexual behaviors can, in fact, serve developmental purposes. Melanie Klein (1937), for example, found that such exchanges, when consensual and occurring in the context of a positive relationship, may help to promote capacities for relating and loving. Marie Bonaparte (1953), a French psychoanalyst, observed that in the case of some girls who feared sex as something destructive, limited sexual activities with a caring, supportive brother allayed their concerns and facilitated their move from their oedipal love for a parent to persons of their own generation.

Yet, Bonaparte (1953) also wrote of the deleterious impact of such activities. She pointed, in particular, to the danger of passivity in boys who are seduced by their sisters. Freud provided an example of this in his case of the Wolfman (1918), whose passivity he attributed to his sister's involving him in showing and looking at each other's bottoms, and later his allowing her to touch his penis. Bonaparte was also concerned about the responses of parents to their discovery of their children's sexual involvement. She wrote of a young woman patient who had many lovers but was unable to reach orgasm with any of them. Her sexual inhibitions proved to be partly related to her mother's severe punishments when she discovered the patient and her brother in sexual play. For this woman, each of her adult lovers unconsciously became her brother, and her fear of her mother's discovery was revived.

Henri Parens (1988), in his observational studies, has observed how common sexual activities and fantasies are among young children. He has noted their adaptive as well as their developmentally disruptive potential. According to Parens, they can help transform parental incestuous wishes into age-appropriate ones directed toward peers. On the other hand, there is the danger that the siblings may remain overly attached to each other, making it difficult for one or the other or both to relate to non-familial lovers.

Frank

A man who seems to have used his sexual experiences with his sister as a bridge from his oedipal love for his parents to a lover of his own generation is Frank, a retired lawyer. Now in his seventies, long married, a father and grandfather, Frank regarded his sexual activities with his sister Myra, when he was thirteen and she was nine, as contributing positively to his capacity for loving a woman and to his sexual development.

According to Frank, Myra was an interested and willing partner. Their exchanges consisted of looking at and touching each other's genitals. Frank knew little about sex at the time, but he was aware that he should not go beyond these actions and did not.

In looking back, Frank thought his activities with his sister were motivated both by the urges of his body and a need to know what the mystery of sex was all about. He thought that they helped both of them understand their sexuality better, and believed that they contributed to his capacity for pleasure and for loving a woman in a mature way.

Frank did not know, however, what impact their activities had on his sister. He wondered if she might ever think about or remember them. He never asked her, he claimed, for two reasons. He sensed that she was reluctant to look back at what had happened. He also acknowledged that he experienced some guilt about what he later felt was his having taken advantage of her.

While Frank was speaking of his experiences with his sister during our interview, his thoughts turned to his parents. As a child he was aware that they had a sex life, but he believed he managed in some way to deny it. He had been, he said, engrossed in his own sexual interests which, he claimed, "were totally separate" from the sex lives of his parents and other adults.

Frank's reference to his being "totally separate" from his parents led me to think of Peter Blos's (1979) recognition of adolescence as a second individuation phase during which young people must shed family dependencies, loosen their oedipal ties to their parents, and move to love objects of their own generation. In reflecting on Frank's experience, it seemed to me that his involvement with his sister might partly be regarded as an unconscious effort in the service of accomplishing these adolescent developmental tasks.

Frank's concern about his sister and his guilt with regard to her indicate, however, that his experiences were not without cost. With the exception of those early explorations young children make of each other's bodies out of curiosity, the sexual activities between siblings and the conscious or unconscious fantasies that accompany them are likely to lead to some degree of guilt and/or shame. The secrecy with which these acts are usually carried out and the guilt that very often follows them suggests that the children sense that they are doing something "wrong." Finkelhor (1980) found that regardless of their personal reactions, those students in his study who had had sexual experiences with their siblings had kept them secret. For many respondents, participating in the study was the first time in their lives that they had mentioned them, and they worried about the critical response they might receive.

Whereas initially there is a fear of the reactions of others, with the development of the superego this concern derives from within as well.

On the other hand, according to Juliet Mitchell (2003), many therapists who report the prevalence of adolescent sibling sex comment on what seems to be an absence of guilt or even of a sense of having done wrong on the part of those involved. Mitchell points out that such responses should be considered an indicator of a problem, rather than being accepted at face value.

Margo

Guilt about childhood sexual encounters with a sibling weighed heavily on Margo, a forty-year-old woman who became depressed when her three-year-younger sister, Phoebe, was hospitalized for a severe depression. Phoebe had suffered from periodic depressive episodes since her college years, and Margo had long been troubled by a feeling that she was responsible for her sister's difficulties.

Margo had been very involved in taking care of Phoebe during their childhood. Their parents were rarely home. Their father worked day and night and their mother was preoccupied with civic and social activities. The girls were largely attended to by a succession of maids. Phoebe had looked to Margo for the care and attention that neither of them received from their parents, and as Margo looked back she felt she had failed her sister. She spoke of teasing her, being impatient with her, and sometimes refusing to play with her. However, when she herself was lonely and bored she had been glad for Phoebe's company and felt guilty for having "used her."

It seemed to her therapist that Margo tended to overly focus on her ill treatment of Phoebe and minimized the importance of the many ways in which she had treated her with kindness and caring. It was clear that she had supported Phoebe through many adolescent and adult crises and was for the most part very much there for her. The therapist was puzzled as to why Margo was assuming all of the responsibility for her sister's illness. She wondered if there was something else that had transpired that led to her being so hard on herself. She recalled Margo saying she "used" Phoebe and questioned what she might have meant by that. It took several sessions before Margo responded to that question. When she did, she spoke of how when she was about seven or so and Phoebe about four they shared a room. They were put to bed very early so that the parents could dine alone. In the summer they could hear the other children outdoors playing. It took a long while for them to fall asleep and they made up games such as jumping up and down on their beds to see who could jump the highest. At some point Margo initiated another game in which she would get into the same bed with her sister and rub up against her.

She could still recall the good feeling, and she thought her sister felt good as well. However, she worries now about whether what she did with Phoebe had anything to do with Phoebe's emotional problems.

It proved helpful to Margo to begin to understand that her sexual play with her sister was not that unusual. The therapist helped her to see that as children who received limited attention from their parents and who were left alone together so much of the time, it was not surprising that they had turned to each other for pleasure and comfort and found it in the way they did.

In this short-term treatment the therapist focused on the adaptive aspect of Margo's behavior. This proved of value in so far as it led to Margo's becoming more tolerant and forgiving of herself. However, the therapist did consider other possible determinants of her sexual activities, although she did not raise them. For example, in light of Margo's ambivalent feelings towards Phoebe, as suggested by her teasing and being impatient with her, she wondered whether Margo might have unconsciously wished to inflict harm on Phoebe by involving her in actions that she regarded as "wrong." Or perhaps by playing with Phoebe in a way that she believed her mother would not have approved of, she might have been expressing her anger at her mother for making her go to bed so early with her younger sister while her friends were outdoors playing or for excluding her from the parents' dinner table. Thus, the activities that offered Margo some pleasure and comfort, may also have been a vehicle for expressing her anger at either her mother or her sister or both.

INCEST

Sibling incest has been estimated to occur more frequently than parent child–incest (Bank and Kahn 1997, Hardy 2001, Klagsbrun 1992). Despite the strong taboo against incest, Freud (1916–1917) emphasized how difficult it is for brothers and sisters to resist this attraction to each other.

Although in modern times incest between siblings remains taboo, Glenda Hudson (1999) has noted that the attitudes toward it have varied in different societies at different historical periods. Sibling sexuality, for example, was a persistent theme in eighteenth- and early nineteenth-century literature. Incestuous or near-incestuous encounters were written about as exciting accidents, the siblings generally being the unwitting victims of an error rather than conscious participants. Individuals found themselves attracted to lovers who they later discovered were their siblings. In Daniel Defoe's *Moll Flanders* (1772), for example, Moll learns that her third husband is her own brother. So great is her husband's guilt that he tries to commit suicide twice and eventually dies of consumption. Hudson herself traces in great detail the themes of love and sibling incest that she regards as pervasive in the writings of Jane Austen.

Hudson has understood this interest in incest during that period as rooted in the close, insular familial world of the English upper and middle classes at the time and the strict restrictions governing heterosexual relations with individuals outside of the family. A brother or sister frequently functioned as the center of an individual's world. As a result, unconscious sexual feelings were often enclosed within the family circle.

The definition of incest varies. Bank and Kahn (1997), for example, have defined it as sexual activity between siblings that is heterosexual and that has consisted of "at least one instance of vaginal intercourse and/or oral-genital contact between brother and sister" (p. 166). In the state of New York, where I reside, the New York Penal Law Section 255.25 (http://law.onecle.com/new-york/penal/PEN0255.25_255.25.html) states that "a person is guilty of incest when he or she marries or engages in sexual intercourse or deviate sexual intercourse with a person whom he or she knows to be related to him or her, either legitimately or out of wedlock, as an ancestor, descendant, brother or sister of either the whole or the half blood, uncle, aunt, nephew or niece."

A variety of sexual activities, however, that do not meet legal criteria and erotic fantasies that are not acted upon may be regarded by siblings themselves as incestuous and reacted to psychologically as such. I include in this chapter several case examples of siblings who have responded to their repeated sexual activities with a brother or sister as if they had committed incest, although penetration had not occurred, as far as I could tell.

Family Context

Sibling incest often occurs in troubled families. In the absence of adequate parental care and protection siblings may become involved with each other in a sexual way in order to satisfy unmet needs for closeness and affection, to deal with feelings of loneliness and depression, and as a means of discharging anxiety and tension due to stress (Ascherman and Safier 1990).

More than seventy years ago, Annie Reich (1932) wrote of her psychoanalysis of a young woman who was involved in a sexual relationship with her one-year-older brother. From the patient's sixteenth to her twentieth year the couple had intercourse and she finally became pregnant. Reich understood this incestuous relationship as the outcome of her patient's severe pathology, which she related to her early deprivation, abuse, and constant exposure to sexuality, as well as to the poor socioeconomic conditions facing her family. Reich's description of her young patient reminds us that social factors such as lack of parental supervision, constant exposure to parents' sexual activities, even overcrowded housing in which children are forced to sleep in the same bed, may play a role in excessive sexual activities or actual incest between siblings.

Robin and Jason

The sexual activities between Robin and her brother, Jason, suggest how parental neglect may provide the context for sexual activities (although, as far as I know, their activities did not culminate in penetration). However, Robin responded to the sexual exchanges with her brother as if they had committed incest.

A forty-year-old depressed woman, Robin began treatment about a year after her three-year-older brother, Jason, died. They had been very close all through their growing up years, and as adults they had remained close. When Jason became ill three years ago Robin devoted herself to helping with his care. She felt guilty, however, thinking there was something more that she could have done for him.

As it turned out, her guilt actually had to do with the "heavy petting" they engaged in as adolescents. Robin was convinced that her brother's death was a punishment. She no longer recalled who initiated the sexual activities, which took the form of mutual masturbation, but she knew they both enjoyed the closeness and the good feelings. She blamed herself though. Had she not wanted the exchanges, her brother would not have forced himself on her.

Their mother had worked long hours, and it was their father who was the caretaker. He often left them alone, spending most of his time in a local bar. They were both the recipients of their father's alcoholic rages, and Robin recalled how she and Jason hid when they heard their father coming home. They were very protective of each other and became each other's major source of love and support. Robin believed that their bond was strengthened by the pleasure they found in each other's bodies, despite the guilt she experienced.

Narcissistic Factors

We are reminded that incest was once the prerogatives of the gods of mythology and sister-brother marriages were sanctified among the Egyptian pharaohs. In the case of the pharaohs, such marriages were originally understood as a way of keeping the royal blood pure, but another explanation is that they helped to define the important status of these royal families (Eliade 1987).

A distorted sense of grandiosity seems to lead some modern day siblings to claim the prerogatives once enjoyed by the gods or royalty. Thomas Mann (1912) has written a short story *The Blood of the Walsungs*, which involves an incestuous relationship between twins, Siegmund and Sieglinde, namesakes for the twins who committed incest in Wagner's *Die Walkure.*

The youngest children in the family, Siegmund and Sieglinde grew amidst great wealth, surrounded by luxury, tended by servants, indulged in every way with nothing more expected of them than seeking their own pleasure. They see themselves as of "royal blood," entitled to do the exceptional. One week before Sieglinde is to be married, her fiancé joins the family for dinner. Brother and sister ask him for permission to attend the opera *Die Walkure* together alone before the wedding. When they return that evening, Sieglinde comes to her brother's room and they make love. Later Sieglinde questions what this will mean to her fiancé. Her brother responds, "What about him?" and then goes on to say that "he ought to be grateful to us. He will lead a less trivial existence from now on."

Corinne

Corinne was a patient whose sexual involvement with her two older brothers seemed related to her sense that she was beyond the rules of ordinary life. Corinne had sought treatment out of her concern for her poor relationship with her teenage daughter, Ronda. Motherhood appeared to be the only area of life in which she felt she did not excel. She could not tolerate that and sought from the therapist a "prescription" that would remedy the situation.

During the initial consultation the therapist learned that during her adolescence Corinne began to have occasional intercourse with each of her brothers. One was a year older and the other three years older. She sometimes still slept with them. She showed no concern or guilt about these incestuous activities.

After five months of treatment, Corinne announced that she had purchased a home on the same block as her therapist. When the therapist asked what this move might mean to her, Corinne's response was, "Why not?" She then became irritated and insisted that she had a right to move wherever she wished and that she did not have to explain herself to the therapist. Following the session, Corinne phoned to say that she had decided to stop the treatment, and her therapist's effort to encourage her to come in at least for one session to try to understand what had happened failed. Thus the information about this case is very limited. However, it seemed as if Corinne's sexual involvement with her brothers and her enactment in the treatment of buying a house so close to her therapist, represented her feeling that she was beyond having to observe the rules and that she had the right to cross boundaries.

Lord Byron and His Sister, Augusta

The idea that one has a right to violate taboos brings to mind Freud's ideas about those individuals he referred to as the "exceptions" (1916) who feel they deserve to do as they wish as a result of having suffered greatly early in life. Freud used Richard III, as depicted by Shakespeare, as an example of such a character. He quotes the soliloquy in which Richard attributes his villainy to the fact that he is not able to be a lover because of the deformity he suffered since childhood.

"Nature has done me a grievous wrong in denying me the beauty of form which wins human love. Life owes me reparation for this, and I will see that I get it. I have a right to be an exception, to disregard the scruples by which others let themselves be held back" (pp. 314–315).

One might consider the incestuous relationship between Lord Byron, the famous English poet, and his half sister, Augusta Leigh, as involving Byron's seeing himself as an exception, although their relationship may also be understood as related to the lack of parental care and love that both of them experienced. Reared separately, both Byron and Augusta were abandoned by their father and had difficult childhoods. Augusta Leigh's mother died when she was born. She was raised by a grandmother who died when Augusta was a young girl, and she was passed from one relative or friend to another. Byron's parents had a stormy marriage and his father left the family when Byron was two-and-a-half years of age (Grosskurth 1997). His mother was a deeply troubled woman who struggled to support herself and her son alone.

Brother and sister did not see each other until they met when Augusta was about eighteen and Byron, fourteen. After meeting, they began exchanging letters. Some ten years later, after the death of Byron's mother, their relationship became more intense and within several years became incestuous. That the child Augusta gave birth to was of this union seems to have been confirmed by a letter that Byron wrote when asked if his passion for Augusta and the dangers it entailed were worth it. He replied that it was worthwhile (Marchand 1973–1974). The child, he noted, was not an "ape" and if it was, it was his fault. He indicated that all of his life he had been trying to make someone love him and never received the sort of love he wished for. In Augusta he felt he had found it.

The letter attests to the importance of Byron's relationship with Augusta in providing him with the love he claims to have missed, but Byron may well have felt that he deserved to be an "exception." As some may know, Byron was born with a malformed right foot that was not treatable (Grosskurth1997). His mother was obsessed with making him perfect and subjected him to one painful treatment after another, to which he was said to have submitted stoically. He was very aware that there was something wrong with him and from early on Byron thought of himself as different from other people. Throughout his life he behaved "differently," his incestuous relationship being only one of the many ways he flouted convention.

In some cases of incest, siblings are attracted to each other by their simi-
larity. Their love for one another is essentially self-love, a narcissistic form
of love (Freud 1914). Twins, as in the case of Siegmund and Sieglinde, are
more likely to find a mirror image in each other; however, siblings ordinarily
bear sufficient resemblance to one another that they can find their reflection
in each other.

IMPACT OF INCEST

Bank and Kahn (1997) are convinced that sibling incest, even when it is consensual, always has a profound effect on personality development, because
it represents an attack on social custom and taboo, and frequently involves a
range of feelings that are often contradictory (e.g., caring, fear, guilt, shame,
love). The nature of the impact, they note, depends, in part, on the subjective
emotional significance of the experience. In their study of eighteen patients
they concluded that sibling incest is more likely to have long-term adverse
effects on sisters than on brothers, affecting their view of themselves, their
achievement of a sense of trust, as well as their sexuality, marriage, and work.
There were women whose incestuous experiences appeared to be pleasurable
and orgasmic. A female patient of mine noted that her sexual experiences
with her brother were far more satisfying than her relationships with other
men. The forbidden nature of incestuous sex had for this woman heightened
the excitement and pleasure. However, Bank and Kahn found that a good
number of the women they studied could not have a sexually satisfying experience in a mature, adult relationship. They either chose their partners poorly
or their loving feelings had become split off from their sexual feelings. While
there were two men in Bank and Khan's study, the authors did not discuss
them specifically. However, Bank and Kahn suggest that men are likely to
suffer less from incestuous relationships than women.

   Although these findings are not surprising, these investigators recognize
that their study covered only a small number of individuals who already had
sought treatment for difficulties they were experiencing. We have no idea of
the impact on those many individuals who do not seek treatment. It is also difficult, in evaluating the effect of incest, to determine what is cause and what
is effect. Poor self-esteem, for example, may in some instances be the result
of other factors and lead to incestuous activities. Thus, though the incestuous
experience may exacerbate already present problems, it may not have caused
them. Moreover, though men may suffer less as a result of their incestuous
activities, clinicians generally tend to see fewer men than women, so that
there is less opportunity to study the effect of incest on them.

Henry Roth

Henry Roth, the famous novelist, appears to be a man who was adversely affected by his incestuous experience. His long period of writer's block has been ascribed to his feelings of guilt about having had sexual intercourse with his sister Rose (Pogrebin 1998). At the age of twenty-eight, Roth wrote what many consider to be a literary masterpiece, *Call It Sleep* (1934), and then failed to produce even a short story for the next sixty years. According to Roth's biographer, Steven Kellman (2005) Roth had begun groping his sister when he was twelve and Rose only ten. By the time he was sixteen and she, fourteen, they began to engage in full sexual intercourse. In 1998 Roth's publisher, St. Martin's Press, released a letter that appears to have confirmed the incest. The letter was from Rose who wrote him after she became familiar with his autobiographical novel *Mercy of a Rude Stream* (1994). She chastises Roth for writing about what she referred to as the "revelation" and begs him to delete it from his writing, claiming that it would degrade them both.

It is worth noting that Roth grew up with a very abusive father who favored his sister. His parents had a difficult marriage and his father emotionally abused his mother. In this, his situation was somewhat similar to that of Adam, whose sexual abuse of his sister, I will consider shortly

Roy

Another man who suffered from his sexual activities with his sister was Roy, a thirty-four-year-old, patient. Roy sought treatment several weeks before he was to be married. He had become very anxious and was feeling he could not go through with the marriage, and yet he could not break it off. His wife-to-be was a divorced woman, five years his senior, who had two children. He attributed his anxiety and conflict to being torn between his fiancée and his parents who did not approve of his marrying a woman older than himself who already had a family.

As the initial consultation came to an end and Roy was just about to leave, he stopped and said that there was one more thing he had to tell the therapist which he had never confided in anyone before. With great difficulty, he explained that his sister, Francine, had an out-of-wedlock child fourteen years ago when she was sixteen. He had just begun college. She became pregnant by one of his best friends and surrendered the baby for adoption. As he spoke he became cold and sweaty. He noted that he was very uncomfortable because he had had a very close relationship with his sister.

In the next session, Roy described what he meant by a close relationship. As young children he and Francine began fondling each other in the parental bed when the parents were out for the evening. They undressed, rubbed each other's backs, caressed each other's buttocks, and petted. These activities continued through Roy's adolescence. Roy cried as he related how guilty he felt about their behavior. He knew he was not responsible for his sister's pregnancy, as he had never penetrated her, but he felt as if he fathered her child.

It was not clear whether sharing this information at the start of his treatment played a role or not, but Roy did go ahead with the marriage as planned. Then conflicts about having a child began to preoccupy him. His wife wanted them to have a child together. The thought of impregnating his wife made Roy anxious and he found one reason after another to delay a decision.

Marrying a woman with children had served Roy's unconscious needs well. He had an already-made family and did not have to deal with his own conflicts about becoming a father. To father a child seemed to affirm that he could have impregnated his sister. Moreover, denying himself fatherhood served as a punishment for his "forbidden" sexual activities.

Roy was long accustomed to denying himself. He had a history of "shooting himself in the foot." An excellent athlete, as a young boy he repeatedly injured himself just before a competitive event. When offered a major promotion at work, he did something that caused the company to lose a contract and the offer was rescinded. In his essay "Those Wrecked by Success" (1916), Freud attributed such self-defeating behaviors in certain individuals to guilt over what they experienced as having achieved an oedipal victory. Any success becomes equated with winning the oedipal parent. In Roy's case his incestuous relationship with his sister can be partly understood as making him feel he had won a forbidden person, for which punishment was due.

SIBLING SEXUAL ABUSE

Sibling sexual abuse is thought to occur far more frequently than parent-child sexual abuse (Wiehe 1997). Sexuality may be used to express hostility and power, with one sibling forcing sex on the other. Sibling sexual abuse is generally associated with troubled families in which children have been either deprived or mistreated. This was the case with Tessie's two older brothers, who forced sex on her two older sisters.

An eighteen-year-old young woman, Tessie was referred for treatment after she made a suicidal attempt. She was the next to the youngest of six children in a family of three boys and three girls. Her father was unemployed and drank excessively. A violent man when drunk, he emotionally and physically abused her two oldest brothers and her mother. The children frequently witnessed the father either beating or forcing sex on their mother, whom

Tessie described as a depressed, passive woman who seemed to just "take it." The older brothers, in turn, abused their younger siblings, teasing and beating their youngest brother and sexually forcing themselves on the two older sisters. According to Tessie, her sisters "did not put up much of a fight." Tessie felt that as much as they hated their brothers for what they were doing to them, they nonetheless gained something from the attention they received. Her comment suggested that she was putting herself in the place of her sisters. She might have been glad of the attention, even if at the same time she was repelled by it. At one point Tessie did actually note that though as an adult she felt herself fortunate to have escaped her brothers' sexual advances, when she was younger she often wondered why her brothers did not choose her.

Though I did not meet with Tessie's brothers and can only hypothesize about their abuse of their sisters, it seemed likely to me that these brothers had identified with their abusing father. By identifying with the aggressor, they could experience themselves as the powerful ones rather than the weak victims that they had been when their father was abusing them. At the same time their attacks on their sisters might have provided them with an outlet for expressing their rage at their father and perhaps at their mother, who had failed to protect them, while at the same time providing these brothers with an opportunity for some closeness.

Adam

Ascherman and Safier (1990) have emphasized how multidetermined sibling sexual abuse can be. They have written about a young boy, Adam, who before his sixteenth birthday was tried in juvenile court and convicted of sexually abusing his then nine-year-old sister Laura. While his father treated Laura with love, Adam was the target of his physical and emotional abuse. When younger, Adam had retaliated by destroying his father's valued tools. By abusing Laura, he was harming what he regarded as his father's most precious possession, at the same time as his own abusive actions served as a vehicle for expressing his envy and rage at his sister. According to these investigators, these encounters also afforded him an opportunity to meet some of his needs for closeness, albeit in a sadistic rather than loving way, as perhaps was the case with Tessie's brothers.

IMPACT OF SEXUAL ABUSE

Research suggests that girls who are clearly forced into sex by their brothers experience the same impact as those who have experienced paternal sexual abuse. This may include continued submissiveness in adult relationships, low self-esteem, self-blame, body image problems, the establishment of identity, eating disorders, drug abuse, alcoholism, depression, and symptoms of post traumatic stress disorder (Canavan, Meyer, and Higgs 1992; Hardy 2001). Like parental sexual abuse, sibling sexual abuse may also lead some women to choose abusing partners later in life, in keeping with a compulsion to repeat. Freud (1920) saw this as an effort to master past traumas and Judith Lewis Herman (1992), a well-known expert on trauma today, notes that most theorists agree with that formulation. Repetitive reliving of a traumatic experience can represent an effort at healing and an attempt to integrate the traumatic event. I would add that for a woman who, in the absence of parental care has experienced her brother as the main figure in her life, despite the abusive nature of their relationship, the choice of a pain-inducing partner may serve to preserve an unconscious connection with that brother (Valenstein 1973).

Virginia Woolf

An example of the destructive impact of a brother forcing sex on a sister may be seen in the case of Virginia Woolf, the well-known English writer. Woolf, as many know, suffered from severe bouts of depression and hopelessness throughout her life, culminating in her drowning herself at the age of fifty-nine. Among the traumatic experiences she faced was the sexual abuse by her half brothers, Gerald and George Duckworth (DeSalvo 1989). In trying to understand the deep sense of shame and fear she had about her body, Woolf related it to her abuse at the hands of Gerald. In her autobiography, *Moments of Being* (1976), Woolf recalled how when she was about six Gerald began to explore her body. She does not say that he penetrated her, but she describes his actions in great detail. She writes of how she hoped he would stop and how she disliked and resented his behavior. She also notes how mixed her feelings were and speaks of them as "dumb." That she recalls the experiences as an adult leads Woolf to believe she must have had a strong reaction. "This seems to show," she wrote, "that a feeling about certain parts of the body; how they must not be touched; how it is wrong to allow them to be touched; must be instinctive" (pp. 68–69). The abuse apparently went on for many years.

Louise DeSalvo (1989), who has written a book on the impact of Woolf's childhood sexual abuse on her life and on her writings, has noted how Woolf, in keeping with Victorian ideology that held girls responsible for the morality of their brothers, appears to have held herself responsible for causing the abuse. In our own times, many victims of sexual abuse are also likely to feel responsible for what has happened to them, despite the change in societal attitudes.

Franz and Gunther

Melanie Klein (1937) has written about two brothers, Franz, age five, and Gunther, age six. Gunther, as far back as when he was three years old, forced his brother to perform fellatio and engage in other sexual acts. Klein's analysis of the phantasies accompanying these acts led her to believe that they were largely motivated by Gunther's rage at his brother as well as his rage at his parents, for whom his brother served as a displacement figure.

EROTIC FANTASIES BETWEEN SIBLINGS

One of Freud's major contributions to our understanding of the human psyche was his recognition of the power of unconscious fantasies to generate conflict, to arouse guilt and anxiety, and in some instances to lead to symptom formation. This did not mean that in the case of incest Freud ignored the profound impact of actual sexual experience (Blum 1996).Well after he had questioned the universality of his earlier seduction theory, Freud noted that in those cases in which there has been actual seduction of a child by another child or parent it "invariably disturbs the natural course of the developmental processes, and it often leaves behind extensive and lasting consequences" (Freud 1931, p. 232). Yet, it is striking how powerful an impact fantasies can have. Belief in the power of thought is strong and wishes are often experienced as deeds. Consider the guilt experienced by those mourners who, having entertained death wishes toward the deceased, fear that their thoughts have killed them.

RENEE: A CASE STUDY

In the interest of showing how fantasized erotic longings for a sibling may have long-term consequences, I conclude this chapter with an account of the treatment of one patient, Renee. By providing summaries of the treatment process I hope to show not only the role of erotic fantasies in generating conflict, but also the way sibling issues may emerge in treatment, how understanding can be gained through sibling transferences and countertransferences, and how attention to sibling experiences may contribute to the efficacy of treatment (Edward 2003).

It is important to note that as far as could be ascertained there had never been any actual sexual activities between Renee and her older brother, Neil. During the course of her treatment Renee did recall his hugging her occasionally when she was a little girl and she also remembered one occasion when he took her on his lap. These experiences may have been arousing for both of them, but there appeared to be nothing between them that could be construed as a deliberate sexual act. Of course there is no way to totally rule out such occurrences. In general, distinguishing between historical reality and psychic reality is difficult. When it comes to abusive, incestuous activities there have been cases in which suggestion has played a significant, possibly incorrect role in its reconstruction as well as cases in which actual abuse has gone unrecognized and unaddressed (Good 1996).

Renee, an attractive, very intelligent and articulate thirty-five-year-old, married businesswoman with no children, sought treatment for feelings of anxiety and depression. She grew up in a middle class, intellectual, religiously observant family. Her father was a physician, who, according to her, was rarely home, and when he was he gave his full attention to her seven-year-older brother, Neil.

Her mother, who had died five years before Renee and I began our work together, had been a full-time housekeeper and rarely left the house except to attend church. Renee described her as chronically depressed and frequently physically ill. She kept Renee close, wanted to know everything she was thinking and doing, and was deeply hurt by Renee's efforts to separate.

Her brother, Neil, had been an outstanding student, an excellent athlete, and admired by those who knew him. As an adult he was highly successful and renowned in his field. Renee's envy, jealousy, and resentment of him were palpable. At the same time she longed for his attention and was deeply hurt by what she claimed was his lifelong lack of interest in her.

At the time that Renee began treatment both father and brother lived at a great distance from each other. She maintained weekly telephone contact with her father but rarely spoke with her brother.

Marriage

Renee had been married for five years. She described her husband, Gary, as extremely supportive and encouraging of her. They shared many intellectual interests and worked side by side in maintaining their home. Life was going so well that they were not sure whether they should have a child, lest it upset the balance. Although compatible emotionally, the couple rarely had intercourse. When they did, Renee became anxious and was unable to reach an orgasm. She dismissed this as relatively unimportant. What mattered was that Gary was her "best friend." Unlike her brother, he was interested in what she did and thought and was deeply concerned about her well-being.

Treatment

During the second year of her twice-a-week treatment, Renee and her brother were forced to be in increased contact. Their father's health had begun to deteriorate and they needed to make plans for his care. During this period Renee's relationship with her brother took center stage. What follows are summaries of a series of sessions during this period.

Session I

Renee began this hour telling her therapist how unhappy she had been since their last meeting, during which the therapist had advised her of the dates of her vacation. She had been thinking of how the therapist would probably be engaged in exciting activities on her holiday, enjoying interesting people and having a wonderful time. She, however, would be home pursing her "ordinary, dull" routines. She started to weep, saying that she was such a boring and uninteresting person in comparison to the therapist. Gradually her crying ceased and she began to talk about a work assignment. She then turned to thoughts of her brother taking off on his bicycle trips during school vacations while she was stuck at home. She expressed her resentment of his freedom and the pleasures he could have. She spoke of him as the interesting person in the family. He was exciting, attractive, and successful. She could see why he was uninterested in her. She knew he saw her as boring. It was the same today. They rarely speak but when they do he never inquires about her or her work. She began to cry again but composed herself as the end of the session drew near. The therapist said it seemed that she was experiencing her as if she were her brother and her anger at her for her vacation appeared similar to what she had felt about him as she was growing up. She was helping them see how painful that had been for her. She made no response but when she rose to leave, she offhandedly commented that Neil had recently sent her a very expensive birthday gift. For a moment she sounded pleased. However by the time she reached the door she angrily noted that it had arrived late.

Session II

This was the first session after the therapist's vacation. While she was away Renee had sustained a minor physical injury and she began to describe the fall she had taken. The therapist listened, wondering what connection there might be between her accident and the therapist's being away. Thoughts about her accident led Renee to the memory of a time when she had been ill as a child and her mother left her for a few moments to purchase some food at a small grocery down the street. Her brother returned from school and found her in great discomfort. She recalled with great pleasure his solicitousness, kindness, and attention. However, as soon as their mother returned he left and joined his friends. She became very angry at this point, noting that he left her for his friends. She hadn't really mattered to him. The therapist said that she could appreciate how unhappy it had made her to have him leave when she had so enjoyed his attention. Yet, wasn't it surprising, given her feeling that her brother was totally indifferent to her, to discover that there was at least one time when he had been more caring? "Well," she said," it didn't last." The therapist appreciated that that had been hard for her and yet, she said, "it seems that it's important for you to stay with the feeling of his being indifferent to you. I am reminded of your telling me about the birthday gift he sent you and then somehow undoing all the good feeling you had by focusing on its arriving late, which left you angry."

Session III

In the next session Renee recalled her brother visiting her in an apartment she had rented after graduation from college. One night he went off to a dinner to which only men were invited. When he returned they stayed up most of the night speaking of politics, philosophy, literature, and then, she noted rather sheepishly, premarital sexuality. He had treated her as an equal and she had felt as smart as he was. However, she had found it strange to be talking about sex with him, and then she made a slip, using her husband's name instead of her brother's. She seemed aware of the slip, but when the therapist encouraged her to reflect on it she quickly launched into a long tirade against male organizations that excluded women and continued for the rest of the hour to complain about men in general and her brother in particular.

When she seemed to have exhausted the topic, the therapist said that she thought their recent sessions, including today's, suggested that despite her anger and resentment towards her brother, she actually loved him dearly and that he had not been as indifferent to her as she needed to think he was. To the therapist, her slip suggested that she had wished he would make love to her and be her husband. These were uncomfortable ideas and she avoided them by always keeping in mind a picture of her brother as an arrogant male with special privileges and herself as an envious woman who was enraged at him. After some moments of silence she said, "You're right. I did admire my brother. When he was home there was joy and though I was envious and jealous of him, I enjoyed the happier atmosphere he created." After a rather long silence, Renee said she wondered if her brother might have had similar feelings toward her. Perhaps his distancing from her was protective. She then recalled a time when she was a little girl when he seemed to like to hug her. Once he took her on his lap and she remembered the good feeling she had, but at the same time she thought it was not right. Even as she recalled this time, she felt pleased. The idea of his wanting to be close to her made her feel attractive. However, as soon as these words were out of her mouth she began to criticize her brother for being inappropriate. She also expressed anger at her mother who, when she told her about this, seemed not to have taken the matter seriously. The therapist drew her attention to the fact that she had again become angry with her brother right after she expressed good feelings about him and about herself, feelings that were both affectionate and sexual. Perhaps seeing herself as unattractive and undesirable protected her against any wishes that she or her brother might have for sexual intimacy.

Session IV

Following the previous session, Renee received a phone call from her brother. They were having trouble planning for their father long distance, and he offered to visit him. She pointed out that she realized that despite the fact that he lived closer to her father than she did, it was still a long trip and meant interrupting an important project he was working on. In the past she would have seen his effort on behalf of their parents as an attempt to ingratiate himself with them and make her look less attentive. She was surprised that she viewed his offer now as an attempt to spare her. She felt grateful to him and thanked him for his help, something she had never done before. This made her feel good about him and about herself.

Session V

In the next session, Renee reported that her mood had been fluctuating. She was warmed by the exchange with her brother, but was concerned about how inept she was becoming at work. She was making many mistakes and one of her fellow employees had complained about her. She feared she would be demoted. She referred to herself as "hopeless." She was wondering whether she was somehow reacting to their recent talks about her brother. After her last session she had sent a holiday card to him. Last night she had felt tormented and worthless. She is beginning to recognize that she needs to be hard on herself, to beat up on herself, so to speak. When she woke this morning she felt no one liked her. She is starting to feel as if she creates these bad feelings in herself. "You were right when you said that as soon as I feel good, I start to get down on myself and end up feeing badly."

A few moments after that comment Renee suddenly became visibly troubled. There was a long pause and then she said that a fantasy had come to mind. She had it sometimes as a child. She noted how difficult it was for her to speak of the fantasy. She began to cry, but went on to say that the fantasy was painful but pleasurable and sexually arousing. In it she is tied up and a man is forcing himself on her. Her associations to the man in the fantasy pointed to his being her brother and the therapist noted that it seemed as if she could allow herself to enjoy forbidden sexual pleasure with him, provided she was forced to submit and tolerate pain.

After another long silence, Renee began to speak of a book she had read during her adolescence. She could not recall its title but went on to recount what she remembered of the story. It told of a girl who deeply admired and loved her older brother though he constantly put her down, castigated her, and hurt her. She stoically endured his ill treatment. When they grew up, brother and sister became increasingly estranged. Ultimately the brother refused to see his sister at all for he erroneously believed she was involved in a scandalous love relationship. At the end of the book there was a catastrophic flood. Renee was not clear whether the sister tried to rescue the brother or he tried to rescue her. However, they both drowned. Renee concluded her account of the book saying that finally the sister claimed her brother in death.

The reader may recognize that the book Renee was referring to was *The Mill on the Floss* (1860) by George Eliot. Eliot writes that "brother and sister had gone down in an embrace never to be parted: living through again in one supreme moment the days when they had clasped their little hands in love and roamed the daisied fields together" (p. 557). The book concludes with the inscription written on their tombstone: "In their death they were not divided."

The Mill on the Floss deals with at least two common unconscious fantasies: the wish to rescue a loved one and the wish to die with him or her. Ernest Jones (1911) has suggested that the wish to die with another can equal the wish to sleep and lie together. When there is a belief in an afterlife, this fantasy contains the hope that after death, a wish not permitted in life will be granted. According to Freud (1910), the rescue fantasy can signify the giving of a child to a loved one.

Therapeutic Action

It is always difficult to accurately identify just which threads have been responsible for the therapeutic action of a treatment, but I believe the work done around Renee's relationship with her brother was of considerable value to her. She began to understand how her guilt over her unconscious longings for her brother had led her to overly focus on her envy and resentment of him as a defense and how her desire for him had affected her sexuality. She began to understand how she punished herself for what she regarded as her incestuous wishes by compromising her successes and how she "beat up" on herself and sometimes played a role in getting others to hurt her emotionally. She was able to understand how she displaced her feelings for her brother onto others, which facilitated her being able to establish more satisfying social relationships. It also became clear that by not allowing herself to "take in" whatever positive things her brother had to offer, as in the case of the gift, she had deprived herself of the opportunity to gain from whatever recognition he gave her over the years at a cost to her sense of self-worth.

Renee also began to consider that her brother might have had his own difficulties that determined his reactions to her. Life in their family had not been easy. Perhaps, too, his distancing himself from her might have partly represented an effort to protect himself against some desire he had to be closer to her.

It is important to note that as much as Renee's fantasies about her brother had complicated her development, he had in some ways facilitated it. Without him her mother's intense need for Renee might have been even more onerous and Renee's efforts to separate even more difficult. At the same time both her love for him and her envy had led her to make certain valuable identifications with him. Her love of travel and of literature and her interest in politics all owed something to him.

Among the changes that occurred in the treatment was Renee's increased sexual desire and a wish to have a more mature sexual relationship with her husband. Unfortunately, her husband was not prepared to engage with her sexually. Before the treatment concluded he had sought therapy for himself at her urging.

Toward the end of her treatment Renee's father died. Her brother spent a week or so with her after the funeral. They were of comfort to each other despite the fact that he remained at a distance. Renee had begun to recognize that this was his way with everyone. She seemed to be coming to terms with the fact that they would never be the close companions she had hoped they would be. However, she appreciated that he was there for her and would be in the future, in his way. Now that her father was dead, he was, after all, her only relative.

Discussion

This case helps to demonstrate the power that unconscious erotic fantasies may assume as well as affirming the fact that siblings may be attracted to each other sexually, even as they may also serve as displacement figures for their parents. It also shows how siblings may form an "oedipal-like" relationship with one another (Sharpe and Rosenblatt 1994) and that the romantic love of a sibling and the sexual fantasies it may evoke, can assume a powerful and long-lasting significance in the lives of certain individuals (Abend 1984). For some siblings, their relationship helps to pave the way for their love of persons outside of the family. For others, as with Renee, the conflicts created by such a "sibling love affair" may prove detrimental and be among the issues that bring them into treatment, whether they are conscious of that or not.

REMARKS

Suggesting that sibling sexual contact may have a positive impact is sometimes misunderstood as recommending it (Finkelhor 1980). Years ago I was given the opportunity to read an extremely thoughtful paper by a well-respected clinician who found that in the case of certain of her women patients, erotic contact with their brothers appeared to favor their sexual development, in part, by easing their oedipal struggle with their parents. When presented, the paper was interpreted by some attendees at the meeting as advocating sex between siblings. It aroused such anger among some in the audience that as far as I know, the speaker never submitted it for publication.

It is clear, however, that sexual play, sexual activities, and erotic fantasies among children are ubiquitous and, when consensual and occasional and occurring within an affectionate relationship, they may contribute to development in some ways, even as they may complicate it.

At the same time it is essential that we appreciate the damage that can be done when sexual exchanges are forced and express hostility and wish for power over the other person. Unfortunately, all too frequently sibling sexual abuse has been regarded as less harmful than parental abuse and therefore has received less attention. Each situation is unique, and the impact of whatever sexual attraction or activities or fantasies siblings experience with each other will depend upon their unconscious as well as their conscious responses.

7

Siblings with Special Needs

Johnnie was about fourteen when we became neighbors. His home was behind mine, and his parents and I occasionally exchanged greetings over the back fence. I knew little about Johnnie other than that he had been born with cerebral palsy and was confined to a wheelchair. Most of the year I rarely saw him, however, as soon as spring arrived his four siblings would sometimes push him around the block in his chair at great speed, laughing and loudly calling out, "Here we come!" Johnnie was full of smiles and waved at everyone they passed. As I waved back, I thought how fortunate he was to have brothers and sisters to share moments of fun with him. What a help it must have been to his parents to have other children who could be there for him now and in the future! At the same time I wondered how they cared for their large, closely spaced family while coping with Johnnie's needs. What was it like when Johnnie's brothers and sisters were not having fun with him or when they found their efforts to help him burdensome? And what was it like for Johnnie to be confined to a wheelchair while his siblings were running freely and able to do so many things that he was unable to do?

During the time that I lived behind Johnnie, I was employed as a social worker in a school for severely emotionally disturbed children, most of whom had been diagnosed as autistic. I worked with the parents and gained some familiarity with the challenges they faced. I learned how demanding the daily care of their children could be, how much effort they had to make to secure the assistance and programs that they and their children needed, and how concerned they were about the future. I left my meetings with those families filled with deep respect and admiration for them, knowing that the days and years ahead would demand much of them.

This was at a time when little attention was being paid to the relationships between siblings in those families. This has changed, and helping professionals are far more aware today of the challenges that all members of a family face when one of them has special needs, whether they are temporary or lifelong, or whether they are life threatening or chronically incapacitating.

In this chapter I will review some of the ways individuals with emotional, cognitive, or physical impairments and their healthier siblings may affect each other's development and lives. Consideration will be given to those situations in which a brother or sister was born with disabilities, and to those families in which a sibling became physically or mentally ill or severely injured later. I will not only consider the impact that a special needs sibling may have on their well brothers or sisters, but also the impact that healthier brothers and sisters may have on their sibling with disabilities, to which we have paid less attention.

I have drawn on clinical examples, my own and those of colleagues, as well as biographies and memoirs, clinical literature, and interviews with individuals who were not patients. Most of these interviewees were clinicians whose assistance I solicited through various professional organizations I am affiliated with. Although I had expected these helping professionals to share their work with patients whose siblings were impaired, almost all of them shared their own personal experiences with their special needs brothers or sisters.

Some of the siblings to be considered in this chapter have played a significant role in caring for their physically or emotionally disabled brother or sister. Some have helped with their daily care and assumed responsibility for them when their parents could no longer do so. Some have tried to save their brother's or sister's life by donating a part of their body to him or her. Some have devoted themselves to assisting and emotionally supporting their parents. Some have performed all of these functions and more.

I begin with those families in which a child is developmentally disabled from birth, who may be brain injured or autistic, or who suffers from some other severe developmental disturbance.

Let me offer one caveat before proceeding. I use the term *special needs* here interchangeably with such words as atypical, challenged, disabled, impaired, or handicapped in referring to individuals who manifest serious cognitive, emotional, or physical problems. I also use the words *neurotypical, healthy,* and *normal* when I refer to siblings who do not share their brother's or sister's problems. Given the stigmatization this group of individuals has experienced, I appreciate that they and their families are rightly sensitive to the terms used to refer to them. Yet the acceptability of one term or another varies from time to time and from group to group, and so I have chosen to use a variety of terms that are to be found in existent literature.

DEVELOPMENTALLY DISABLED SIBLINGS

Parents

How parents react to their child with disabilities plays a critical role in how their other children respond to their atypical brother or sister. Although the disappointment and heartache of bearing a child with serious developmental impairments are universal, parents deal with the challenges they face differently. Their responses depend on their own strengths and vulnerabilities, the nature and extent of their child's disabilities, the amount of support they receive from family and friends, and the resources available to help their child and themselves through the difficult journey ahead. How each parent understands having an atypical child may also affect reactions. In some religious families, for example, the birth of a child with severe developmental problems may be experienced as having some special purpose, and parents are able to find their faith in the God they worship a source of strength and support. Others may regard it as a matter of chance, a random act that could happen in any family but unfortunately has happened in theirs. Still others may view it as a punishment for some past transgression, either actual or fantasized.

Even under the most favorable of circumstances, the birth of a cognitively, physically, or emotionally impaired child is a painful experience. Simon Olshansky (1962), drawing on his personal and professional experiences in counseling parents who have a severely cognitively impaired child, suggests that the sorrow these parents face is something they will bear throughout their lives, although the intensity of the experience varies from parent to parent and from time to time.

Peter Gombosi (1998), a psychoanalyst and father of an autistic son, has written about the impact on parents when their child is diagnosed as autistic, a diagnosis that is frequently not made until a child is around the age of two (there is considerable variability in this). Having thought their child to be healthy, the diagnosis violates their expectations. Parents must then face the loss of the healthy child they expected, and begin to care for and love the child they actually have at a time when their inner resources are severely overtaxed. Fortunately most parents do manage to mourn their loss and to develop an attachment to the child they have. Nonetheless, Gombosi emphasizes that it is important for helping professionals to bear in mind that the trauma these parents experience is "enduring, ongoing, and doesn't fade with time" (p. 273). This is to be regarded as a normal and not a pathological response.

At the same time that parents are trying to deal with their feelings, they must contend with the day-to-day care of their disabled child; secure medical, educational, as well as other services; and face their worries about the future. If they have other children they must find ways to maintain their attachment to them and provide them with the love and care they need. Among other things this means providing them with the information they require to understand the nature of their brother's or sister's problems, tolerating their concerns, and helping them to contain the feelings their sibling with disabilities are likely to arouse.

While acknowledging the difficulties involved, Lee Whitman-Raymond, (2005), a social worker who has studied how parents cope with having a child with special needs, has found that what was significant in her particular qualitative study of parents of atypical children was the way the parents she interviewed rose to the occasion and found the psychic and physical energy to deal with and advocate for their children. Her research has led Whitman-Raymond to question the idea that the sorrow of these parents is chronic. Instead, she sees them as experiencing "cyclic sorrow" when milestones are supposed to be reached but are not, such as going to college, getting married, or having children.

Meeting the Challenges

Kenzaburō Ōe, the 1994 Nobel Prize winner for literature, has written about the way he and his family sought to meet the challenges raised by the birth of his brain-injured son, Hikari. He has made his family's experiences with Hikari a central theme in some of his writings. In his novel *A Personal Matter* (1969), which is thought to be based on Ōe's own personal experience, Ōe writes of a father who wishes to flee when he sees his deformed son, but who, over time, makes him an important part of his life. In his nonfiction book *A Healing Family* (1996), which is about his own family, Ōe goes on to show how important his son, Hikari, became to him and to his wife and two other children.

Ōe and his wife began their life with Hikari by acknowledging to each other, as he thought most parents of children with disabilities do, that they had no choice and just needed to "get on with it." (Ōe 1965, p. 59). Ōe does not deny their suffering, but he writes of the joy they found in Hikari and points to the growth that each member of the family made as a result of their efforts to help him over the years.

The personal strengths that Ōe and his wife brought to their efforts and the devotion that they gave to each of their children are impressive. They also enjoyed certain advantages in raising a disabled child that many other such families do not have, including access to needed medical care and special educational programs, as well as support from other parents of children like Hikari and from friends and professional colleagues. I have the impression, too, that Ōe as the writer and his wife as the artist who illustrated *A Healing Family*, found an opportunity for sublimating some of their feelings in their creative endeavors. Ōe's writings also provided the family with an opportunity to enlist others in "bearing witness" to what they had experienced in raising a child with disabilities. Their challenges were also made somewhat easier by the fact that Hikari himself had a congenial nature and a special talent that brought pleasure and pride to Hikari himself and to the entire family. From early on, he showed a remarkable musical aptitude and as an adult composer he has had two recordings to his credit.

These parents' adaptations to Hikari and their efforts to meet the needs of their other two children, as well as the advantages that the family had, were very important, I believe, in enabling Hikari's brother and sister to develop the positive feelings they have had for him. Ōe writes in particular of the close relationship Hikari enjoyed with his sister, and it seems likely that the favorable brother-sister relationship he described in his novel *A Quiet Life* (1990) was modeled on the relationship between Hikari and his sister. In that book a young adult sister is left in charge of her four-year-older neurologically impaired brother. She is depicted as extremely caring and protective of him and at the same time she appears to genuinely enjoy him. In turn the brother in the book keeps a careful watch over his sister and at one point saves her from harm.

Such a reciprocal relationship is often difficult to achieve between individuals with developmental disabilities and their neurotypical siblings. The lack of equality and mutuality in their relationship with their atypical sibling is a source of pain for many healthy brothers and sisters. Some readers may recall Peter in an earlier chapter who sought in his therapist the "good enough" brother that his sibling with cognitive limitations had been unable to be.

Christopher Knowles

The experience of the Knowles family in meeting the needs of their son, Christopher, as well as those of his sisters, provides another example of a family that has "gotten on with it," in a way that has helped to foster positive relationships between their special needs son and his siblings. Brain injured due to prenatal toxoplasmosis, Knowles was also later diagnosed as autistic. His parents, a graphic designer and an architect, provided him with the encouragement and the materials that enabled him to become the artist he is today.

When Knowles was fourteen, theater director and playwright Robert Wilson heard his poetic sound recordings and arranged for him to make an impromptu onstage appearance in *The Life and Times of Joseph Stalin*. Since then, Knowles has continued to collaborate with Wilson, and his texts have been used in many of Wilson's operas. His art, represented by a well-known New York City gallery, has traveled to venues all over Europe (most recently at the IV/AM museum in Valencia, Spain). Today Knowles lives in his own apartment and has a serious relationship with a woman. He works part time in his father's architectural office and produces his art there as well.

Knowles, who was fifty years old at the time of this writing, has three sisters, two of whom I interviewed (Roslyn, a year younger than Christopher, and Mariah, five years his junior). All of the children and their parents in this family are involved in creative pursuits.

Like Ōe's son Hikari, Christopher was fortunate in receiving the medical and educational attention he needed and is endowed with unusual talents that his family has encouraged and supported. Until the age of six he was involved in an intensive home treatment program offered by the Institute for the Achievement of Human Potential (Doman 2005) and had the advantage of the special schooling he required.

Knowles's sisters pointed out how during their earliest years that their parents had impressed upon them how important it was to respect their brother and to help him secure a place in the world. Both women seemed to have gained from the prodigious efforts their mother and father made to help Christopher, as well as from the support and encouragement they themselves received from each parent.

The projects that were created to further Christopher's development had great appeal for his sisters as they were growing up. They were intrigued with and enjoyed using the interesting equipment that was designed to help him with his motor activities and the art materials that were made available to him.

Roslyn grew up to be a designer, and believes that she was influenced in her career by Christopher. His creative uniqueness, his being different from other people, and the family's involvement with unique and creative artists and people led her, she explained, to becoming open to novel ideas and to people who are different. She sometimes wonders what it might have been like if she had grown up with a brother like Christopher in a more conventional family.

Yet all was not easy with Christopher. One of the sisters noted that it was difficult to understand why it was all right when Christopher drew on a piece of furniture, but when she did the same thing she was admonished. There were times when both sisters were embarrassed by their brother. Mariah recalled his having a tantrum on the street and pinching him to make him stop. It only made him scream louder. Roslyn also recalled being ashamed when Christopher would begin screaming or laughing inappropriately or yelling curse words out in public. If he did this at home their parents would reprimand him and he would stop. However, there was little that could be done when he lost control outside of the house. She was amazed that her two-year-younger sister was able to stand up and admonish people who made fun of him when they could see he had problems. As a teenager, when one of the sisters brought a friend to watch a theater piece of Christopher's, she was somewhat embarrassed. On one hand she was very proud of him and on the other hand she felt his differences were on display.

As Christopher grew older, his sisters found their brother easier. He learned many social skills, though he was not actually very social and tended to keep very much to himself. He could still be annoying, sometimes jogging in place and twirling his arms while looking at his shadow. This continued for several decades.

In her twenties Mariah shared an apartment with Christopher for awhile. She found this a positive experience although Christopher sometimes became upset when unexpected things happened and when his routines were interrupted. She took pride in the fact that she was often able to anticipate what might upset him, sometimes mitigate the situation, or when he became anxious, find ways of calming him.

Today, Mariah noted, not only the family but outsiders as well respond to Christopher's warmth and friendliness, and he seems to bring out the warmth in others. He is extremely thoughtful, remembering, for example, everyone's birthday with cards and congratulatory phone calls. Mariah felt fortunate in having Christopher for a brother and would not, she noted, have wanted any other. Not only did he influence her artistically but she believes she is a more non-judgmental, open-minded, patient person as a result of growing up with him. It was not enough to say she learned tolerance, she added, for actually she learned to celebrate differences.

Aware that children like Christopher can cause a family far more trouble than she had experienced, Mariah thought that the positive experience she had with Christopher was due to the fact that she was the youngest in the family. She did not have any responsibility for him and never had to restrict him or say no to him, which minimized any tension between them.

While acknowledging that there were difficulties, both sisters emphasized the positive aspects of their experience with their brother. This raises the question of what role defenses may have played in their attitudes toward him.

In any sibling relationship there is considerable ambivalence and children ordinarily depend on defenses to deal with their hostility. Negative feelings are likely to be intensified when a brother or sister is disabled. However, although defensive efforts can be deleterious, they may also enable an individual to more effectively face challenges, and, as Hartmann (1939) pointed out, through a change in function, what was once defensive may become adaptive. It is my impression that in many families in which there is a developmentally handicapped child, an emphasis on that child's positive attributes may make the negative features more tolerable and facilitate a more positive relationship, provided the difficulties are acknowledged and not denied.

When It Is Difficult to "Get On with It"

For some parents the challenges associated with rearing a child with a severe disability and attending to their other children make it very difficult to "get on" with the tasks ahead. Some of the adult siblings I interviewed, grew up before the medical advances available today were made, before the disability organizations were formed that now offer services and advocate on behalf of those with disabilities, and before the passage of the Americans with Disabilities Act in 1990, which provides special services and protection for special needs children and adults. Those parents were on their own caring for their disabled children at a time when they also bore the stigma of having an "atypical" child. It was not that long ago when the terms "moron" or "imbecile" or "feeble-minded" were used by the psychological community to refer to children with serious cognitive impairments.

Even with the availability of more community services, few families have the advantages that Hikari Ōe's and Christopher Knowles's families had. Both of them had the economic means to avail themselves of the professional services their children required, and were in a position to hire help or to secure the assistance of friends so that they could get some time off from their responsibilities. Each of them had children with unusual talents that these parents could nourish and that eventually enabled their sons to find a place in the world. They could see their efforts on behalf of their children bearing fruit. The parents themselves had talents that provided them with satisfaction and feelings of success, helping to support their own positive feelings of self.

There are parents who are so overwhelmed by the birth of a child with serious developmental disabilities that, even with support and resources, their ability to deal with the problems they face is compromised. In the case of some parents, emotional or physical problems that preceded the birth of their special needs child have left them ill equipped to contend with the responsibilities they face and overly strains their inner resources. There are also families in which the challenges associated with raising their atypical child lead to or exacerbate tensions between the parents, leaving them without the support they so much need from each other. It is worth noting that the incidence of divorce among this group is significant enough to have led the National Autism Association (www.nationalautismassociation.org/familyfirst.php) to launch a special program to try to keep these marriages together.

The Flynns

Mr. Flynn, the father of Myrna, a woman in her sixties, and Lorraine, her year-younger sister, found it extremely difficult to face the limitations of his son, Foster, who suffered from a rare genetic syndrome involving physical deformities, cognitive limitations, and emotional difficulties. As Foster was growing up Mr. Flynn expected him to perform like a normal child and treated him as such. His denial of Foster's limitations not only proved disturbing to his son, but was upsetting to both sisters.

Myrna was born when Foster was three and Lorraine was born less than a year later. During the girls' early years their parents were frequently away from home, traveling from doctor to doctor in an effort to secure treatment for Foster. Several unsuccessful attempts were made to repair his physical deformity. While the parents remained with Foster in the hospital during these procedures, Myrna and Lorraine were left in the care of a housekeeper or relatives. Even when the parents were home, the girls were mostly tended to by housekeepers, for Foster's need for their mother either kept her too busy or made her too exhausted to tend to her daughters.

Despite Foster's obvious difficulties, their father expected him to perform up to his age level and became frustrated and angry when he failed to do so. Lorraine could still recall the sadness she experienced seeing her brother mounting the stairs with his head down after one of their father's many outburst of anger at him. Myrna remembered how the pleasure she had in bringing home a report card with all As evaporated as she watched her father berate her brother for his poor marks.

Both Lorraine and Myrna remembered Foster as a good-natured child who had been kind to them when they were small. They spoke of playing with him when they were little. He used to bring them something to eat on Sunday mornings when their parents were sleeping late. As the girls grew older, however, his socially inappropriate behavior made him hard to live with, and along with his disfigurement, he increasingly became a source of embarrassment to them. They were very confused about him. They realized that their brother was not normal, but then they wondered why their father was always angry at him for not doing what normal children could do. Following their father, they too sometimes tried to get him to perform beyond his capacities, which led them to feel guilty when it became clear that he was unable to meet their expectations.

Despite his father's prodding, the provision of tutors, lessons in a foreign language and music, which he greatly enjoyed and for which he showed considerable ability, Foster was forced to drop out of regular school in the tenth grade. After some vocational training their father secured him a low-skill, low-wage job (which he held until he was fifty-five years of age, never missing a day of work). At some sacrifice to himself, their father arose early every day to take him to the train. He watched over Foster's earnings and eventually helped him secure an apartment of his own. For the last twenty-five years his parents' support and assistance has enabled Foster to live independently. His father makes his decisions and manages his life. Both sisters admire their father for the care and support he has provided their brother but remain troubled by what went on in the past.

Each of them felt their mother's unavailability keenly, but they each responded differently. Myrna sought to garner her mother's attention through being needy. Her frequent illnesses and bed-wetting brought her mother to her. When she had a toilet accident at school, during the fourth grade, her mother became very concerned and arranged for her to see a therapist. Myrna valued the therapy for it meant having her mother all to herself on the days of her appointments.

Myrna eventually came to understand her bed-wetting as serving several purposes. By identifying with her brother who wet the bed, she not only gained her mother's attention, but her enuresis served as a vehicle for expressing her rage at her mother who had to clean up the mess. Further evidence of the hostility associated with her bed-wetting was the fact that she used to think that if her parents were dead she would not wet any more.

Myrna had urged her parents to send Foster away. At one point her parents did decide to place him in a boarding school, but changed their minds when he became upset and admonished them for wanting to get rid of him. Myrna was very disappointed.

Myrna had several therapeutic experiences over the years, both group and individual. She found one therapist particularly helpful. He had confirmed that Foster was severely handicapped. Due to the way her father treated Foster, Myrna had grown up very confused about her brother. Was he a normal boy who refused to perform, or was he disabled, as she was quite certain he was? It was a relief to have her therapist validate her perceptions. He also helped to relieve some of the guilt she felt about her wish to be rid of Foster, by recognizing how hard it had been to have a brother like him and how understandable it was that she wished to be free of him. At the same time he enabled her to attach more importance to the positive exchanges she had over the years with her brother and still has. Recognizing that she loved him as well as resented him helped her to feel better about herself.

Unlike her sister, Lorraine dealt with her mother's lack of availability by trying to become as independent as possible. Aware from an early age of how overwhelmed her mother was by her brother's constant needs and demands, Lorraine was determined not to call upon her. She tried to relieve her mother of some of the burdens of Foster's care, reasoning that perhaps then there would be a little of her mother left over for her. When it was her birthday, for example, and Foster asked her what she wanted as a present, she advised him that the best gift he could give her would be to leave their mother alone for a while each day. She tried to teach him to do things for himself so that her mother would need to do less for him. The youngest in the family, she grew up feeling as if she were the eldest and recalled wishing that she had an older brother who would help her.

Although Lorraine saw her determination to be independent as a way of gaining more from her mother, the fact was that she was more or less forced to be on her own. Of all the children in the family, she appeared to receive the least care and attention. She felt required to be the "problem-free child" in the family.

Until she went away to college Lorraine was able to maintain this façade, but once she left home she developed anorexia. At one point her condition was so serious that she was hospitalized. Her parents paid for her medical and psychological treatment, but kept their distance. They did not even pick her up from the hospital when she was discharged. With the help of her therapist, she came to understand her eating disorder as a cry for help—a way of showing her parents that she, too, had needs—as well as a way of expressing her rage for their failure to pay attention to her.

When we spoke together, Lorraine pointed out that she had paid a price for the independence she developed early in life. Though she can give to others, she cannot accept what others wish to give to her. She must do everything for herself, which does not allow for the development of the reciprocal relationships with others that she desires.

Yet, despite the difficulties, Lorraine felt she had gained something from her relationship with Foster. She attributed her capacity to be empathic with people who are different from her and her efforts to stand up for people who are being mistreated to her experiences growing up with her brother. Like Emily and Sarah, and many other siblings of special needs individuals, finding the good in their experiences with their disabled siblings is especially meaningful.

It was not clear how growing up with Foster might have affected the relationship between the two sisters. According to Myrna, she and Lorraine were close as children and adolescents. She believed that because they needed each other so much they were afraid to be competitive. Today they are friendly but they live at a great distance and see each other only infrequently. Myrna expressed her concern that by being so far away, she has left her sister to shoulder the responsibility for Foster and for their now aging parents. Although Foster has come a long way, she knows he is not easy to be with. I sensed her discomfort with this arrangement, but it sounded as if it was settled that her sister would carry the ongoing responsibilities in the family.

As a result of their brother's limitations, both of these women experienced interruptions in their attachment to their mother and were forced to separate prematurely. They each found Foster's behaviors troublesome and embarrassing and felt angry at him and at their parents. They were also both troubled by their father's treatment of their brother and yet they reacted differently, reminding us of the importance of not generalizing with regard to the impact of a developmentally handicapped sibling on their brothers or sisters.

The different responses of these women to having a brother with special needs may reflect dissimilarities in their temperaments or other inborn factors, as well as the different treatment they each received from their parents. Myrna's difficulties were noted and responded to by the parents more fully, whereas Lorraine was left to struggle on her own. One can imagine that Lorraine's premature independence was welcomed by this overtaxed mother and father. It is also likely that with one child with severe disabilities and another with emotional problems, these parents did have a strong need to see their third child as healthy. Yet, it is important to bear in mind that other unknown factors may have contributed to the different ways these two sisters responded to having a brother with disabilities. It is important not to assume that the difficulties faced by children growing up with siblings with special needs are solely related to that experience.

Wynona

In Wynona's case, both parents appear to have denied that Wynona's sister had profound developmental disabilities. Shirley was born when Wynona, who was thirty-six when I interviewed her, was eight years old. She never was able to learn to speak, feed, or toilet herself. Yet, their mother always acted as if Shirley were a normal child, minimizing her problems, and behaving as if she were no burden. When Wynona sought her first psychotherapy at the age of twenty-four, she did not even tell the therapist that her sister was disabled. Instead she described her as a lovely young girl.

Wynona was married at twenty-five but separated from her husband after six months. At the time I interviewed her, she was considering marriage to a young man whose employment would necessitate her moving to another area of the country. Her parents strongly objected to her leaving them and she was deeply conflicted.

Wynona began to help care for Shirley when she was about ten while her mother was at work. Except for the hours when she attended a special program, and Wynona was in school, Wynona was in charge of her sister. Wynona claimed she had not found this responsibility difficult except when she took Shirley out of the house and people stared at them. She was confused by their responses for she had been brought up to feel there was nothing wrong with her sister.

Today, her parents don't leave home except for a few hours a day during the week when an aide cares for Shirley. They want Wynona to move back home and help them. She feels bad about not acceding to their wishes, not only for their sake but for her sister's sake as well. She knows that her sister is happier when she is at home. So far Wynona has been able to resist their urging. She knows that living apart from her family is essential if she is to have any life of her own.

When people ask about her siblings, Wynona often claims that she has none. This makes her ashamed but sometimes she just doesn't want to talk about Shirley. She is aware that her shame and her guilt have prevented her from moving forward. Long before she felt guilty about moving out of the household, she felt guilty about having things and doing things that Shirley was unable to have or do. As she was growing up she tried to limit her accomplishments so that she would not have or do more than her sister. She convinced herself, for example, that she was not smart and actually developed a learning disability during her early years in school. Being different from Shirley also made Wynona feel as if something was being "torn away" from her.

Wynona grew up determined she would never marry or have children for fear they would be handicapped. Her husband, however, loved her sister and promised that he would take care of her in the future if the need arose. This was what attracted her to him. As it turned out he was not ready for marriage, and the marriage did not work out.

Wynona has always felt the need to make up to her parents for her sister. She is the only positive thing in their lives. She resents being in this position and tries to move on but always gets derailed. Now that they are growing older they need her help even more. Things have also worsened. Her sister has begun to have seizures and is more difficult to care for. She can't abandon them. She worries about what life will be like when her parents die and she has to assume full responsibility for her sister.

When Wynona's first therapist suggested that her marriage represented her effort to get away from the family, she was very upset, for she values the strong bond she has with her family. They are very good to her. If she needed her mother in the middle of the night, she would be there. It would be easier if they were "rotten" parents. Telling me about her difficulties only made her feel guiltier. She felt as if she were betraying them. She wanted to be sure I would not give her real name in my book. Yet on the other hand, she wished her parents would read what she was saying. Perhaps they would begin to think about what she was dealing with. They have no idea what life has been like for her. She cannot tell them for they simply could not understand. They need to feel that all is well with her. Since she was a child they hadn't wanted to hear about anything being wrong with her. She recalled being ill one day during her elementary school years. Her mother minimized the importance of her symptoms and insisted that she get up and go to school. She kept throwing up in school and later in the day the school nurse called her mother to come and take her home.

Wynona was concerned that even with the help of her therapist, she might not be able to free herself sufficiently to marry and leave the area. However, the fact that their work together has enabled her to maintain her own residence gives her some hope that the treatment may in time make it possible for her to move on with her life.

Wynona's experience is that of many young people in her situation who have had to assume responsibilities beyond their years for the daily care of a sister or brother; who have had to join parents in denying that anything was wrong with their sibling, even as they can observe that this is not the case; and who have been called upon to fulfill the role of the healthy, problem-free child. The guilt that Wynona experienced is a burden that many siblings of individuals with disabilities face. Guilt about their normalcy, which resembles the survivor's guilt described by Niederland (1968), guilt about their anger toward both their siblings and parents, and guilt over the wish to separate (Modell 1965) are not uncommon among this group of siblings, and may lead them to inhibit their own abilities and limit their lives. As I listened to Wynona, I wondered whether guilt over her hostile wishes, which she had so strongly defended against, played some part in her unconscious choice of an unsuitable marriage partner and perhaps even in her decision not to have a child, as if she were not entitled to the happiness of a successful marriage and parenthood.

When Wynona spoke of her shame in not wanting to tell people she had a sister, I was reminded of a young man I once treated who felt guilty that he never mentioned his schizophrenic brother to others. He told those who asked that he had no siblings. He saw this as a way of avoiding the pain he experienced in having to talk about his brother. Though that was true, we eventually discovered that not acknowledging his brother also expressed an unconscious wish to get rid of him. It was this wish to destroy his brother that led to the crippling guilt he experienced and prevented him from living a satisfying life. Recognizing his destructive wishes and understanding the reasons for them enabled him to eventually forgive himself and helped free him from the need to punish himself.

In Wynona's case, it was not only difficult for her to separate from her parents, but it was also hard to separate from her sister. She suggested this when she noted that being different from Shirley felt like being "torn away" from her. Despite Shirley's limitations, it appears that Wynona was very close to her. It seems reasonable to imagine that Shirley was company for Wynona during the long hours that both parents were away from the home, easing any feelings of loneliness she might have experienced. The intimate bodily care she provided Shirley and the role she played as her auxiliary ego are also likely to have favored the development of a symbiotic-like tie to her sister.

Perhaps we have not sufficiently appreciated the difficulties that some caretaking siblings in these families may have in separating from their disabled brothers or sisters, not only because of their guilt over their anger toward them and their desire to separate from them, but also because they have forged a bond that has become vital to them as well.

CHILDREN'S RESPONSES TO THEIR ATYPICAL SIBLING

In addition to their parents' attitudes toward their developmentally disabled offspring, there are other factors that are likely to influence the responses of neurotypical children to their special needs brothers and sisters. These would include their age and developmental level at the time they become aware of their sibling's difficulties, the nature of their brother or sister's disability, their own and their sibling's personalities, the availability of resources for the sibling and for the family (e.g., medical care, educational resources, counseling, support groups, respite care, etc.) and the economic, social, physical, and emotional circumstances of the family. Like all families, these families are faced with illness, losses, divorces, and other adverse events that add to the difficulties in caring for a child with special needs and their other children.

The Personality of the Special Needs Sibling

Often, it is the personality of the sibling with special needs that helps to determine his impact on the other children in the family. Lois, a woman I interviewed, spoke of the positive role her brother Larry, who had Down syndrome, had played in her life. Despite his cognitive limitations, he was always easy for her to love. Although there were times as a child when she was embarrassed by him and worried about bringing friends home lest they would no longer want to be her friend once they saw her brother, Lois found in him the warmth which she felt was lacking in the other members of the family. It was Larry who welcomed her home from school each day with a big hug.

When I interviewed Lois, Larry, now fifty-five years old, was living with her and her husband and their three teenage sons. Her father, who had cared for Larry alone since the death of her mother six years before, had died that year. Larry was staying with Lois during the week and on the weekends he alternated visiting two of his brothers who lived close by. Lois spoke of how easy it was to be with Larry. He was helpful to her around the house and her sons and friends all warmed to him. She was amazed at Larry's sensitivity. He seemed to sense that her husband wanted more privacy, and when her husband returned from work, Larry would retire to his room. She thought she could continue having him live with her, but agreed with her brothers that Larry would have a fuller life in a group home, and they had applied to one for him.

Several months after I first spoke with Lois, Larry had moved into a group facility. She contacted me to say that he was very happy there. She visited him weekly and he continued to spend some weekends with her or their brothers. Many times, though, he preferred to remain with his "buddies." She noted that she had probably found the move more difficult than he did. She missed him. He always made her feel deeply loved. She enjoyed him and she also gained satisfaction from the closeness she felt with her parents while she was caring for him. She had admired their devotion to her brother, and she felt a sense of pride in carrying on in the way they had. Her parents had been very careful not to burden her and her brothers with Larry's care and assumed that responsibility all of their lives. After having children herself, she could not understand how they had managed to care for him and the rest of the children in the family so well. It helped that Larry had been such a sweet-natured person and did not present the difficulties that she knew many atypical youngsters do.

It was clear that Lois had formed a strong attachment to her brother and that he met some very important needs of hers. With our recognition of some of the difficulties that individuals with special needs siblings encounter, it is important to appreciate that they and their healthy brothers and sisters can still form meaningful attachments, and, despite their handicaps, siblings with special needs can play a positive role in their normal brothers' and sisters' lives.

WHEN SIBLINGS GROW UP

How they will manage their siblings with special needs when their parents can no longer do so (and when they may need to care for their aging parents as well) is a worry shared by many of these brothers and sisters. Not all are as fortunate as Lois in having a special needs sibling who is easy to get along with, brothers to share the responsibility, and a good facility like the one Lois found for Larry. Some brothers and sisters are concerned about finding a mate who will accept their siblings. Indeed, as in the case of Wynona, the willingness of a partner to include the sibling in their lives and in some situations their homes, becomes a criterion for some individuals in selecting a partner. Wynona's concern about having a biological child is also shared by many neurotypical siblings. Joyce Carol Oates (Johnson 1998), for example, whose eighteen-year-younger sister is autistic, decided not to have a child partly as a result of her fear that the disorder might be genetic.

The full emotional impact of having a brother or sister with special needs may not be recognized until a person reaches adulthood and assumes the responsibilities of marriage and parenthood. This was the case with Caryl Fisher who along with her husband, Fred, sought marital therapy when their little son, Joey, was two. Married for five years, they had begun fighting and were finding it impossible to communicate with each other. Caryl felt that Joey was the cause of their difficulties. He had interrupted the once strong bond they had had with each other, and Fred was focusing a good deal of attention on Joey. She was feeling left out.

Caryl was the older of two children. Her brother, Harold, was four years younger than she. He had never been diagnosed but she thought he must have been schizophrenic. Her parents were unable to control him. He set fires, was a danger to himself and others, and tyrannized the entire family. She pleaded with her parents to send him away to a program for troubled youngsters, but they insisted on keeping him home. As she saw it, her brother ruined their family life. At the age of twenty-four Harold died of a drug overdose.

Fred had an older sister and a younger brother and sister. He described his family as "close knit" but gave very little specific information about his siblings and his parents or of his relationship with them.

Caryl complained that Joey was becoming difficult. He was very active and was beginning to refuse to comply with her wishes. She had begun to think of what her therapist believed to be the age-appropriate behavior of a toddler as a sign that her little son was growing up to be just like her brother. At the same time she appeared to be experiencing her husband as one of her parents who was giving all of his time to her brother and neglecting her needs.

In her treatment, the opportunity to express the fear and anger she had experienced as a child in relation to her brother and her rage at her parents for their preoccupation with him and their failure to protect her proved helpful to Caryl. She began to see how she was misperceiving her son and husband and reacting to them as if they were members of her childhood family. Encouraged in her treatment to begin to read something about two-year-old children, she began to realize that Joey was behaving like most children his age.

As his wife began to work through some of her issues, it became easier for Fred. Understanding where some of Caryl's difficulties came from relieved him of the feelings of failure that he had been experiencing. Her complaints that he did not understand her had shaken his own sense of self-value and led to his withdrawal out of a fear he would do or say the wrong thing.

The relationship between husband and wife began to improve. However, Caryl continued to complain about the restrictions that motherhood imposed on her life. She never went anyplace. She had no friends. Actually it was she who was limiting her life. Fred was eager for her to engage a baby sitter so that they might go to the theater or dinner, but she never felt the time was right. In one session, when Caryl referred to her home as a "prison," an exploration of this led to the realization that *she* was making her home a jail. It was her punishment for her fantasy that her wishes had killed her brother. With an acceptance by her therapist of how Caryl's fear and anger at her brother could make her wish to be rid of him and with a better understanding of how she confused wishes with deeds, she began to identify with her therapist's more benign attitude toward her destructive fantasies. This helped to modify her punitive superego, which insisted she pay for her imaginary crime, and in time enabled her to take advantage of her husband's efforts to make their life more enjoyable.

SERVICES

Increased awareness of the challenges that siblings of developmentally disabled brothers and sisters face has begun to lead to a variety of services for this population. Organizations such as the Association for the Help of Retarded Children, United Cerebral Palsy, the National Alliance on Mental Illness and others are offering programs for siblings (a list of such organizations can be found in an online directory, Disabled Online (www.disabledonline .com/link-director.organizations).

As an example of such a program, Dr. Ruby Phillips (1999), an assistant professor at Lehman College, has reported on a service for brothers and sisters of siblings with special needs connected with an East Coast inner city school for economically disadvantaged children. The program was developed partly as a response to the concerns of a group of parents whose special needs children were attending a program at a community center.

The fifteen-week after-school program was designed to support this group of siblings and included group discussions, recreational activities, and homework help. The children were divided into groups of fifteen for the group discussions, which were intended to offer the children an opportunity to discuss their feelings. The discussions began with the leader asking each child if anything "important" or "troubling" had occurred that day and the children were encouraged to discuss any concerns they had regarding school, family, or friends. In addition to the open-ended group discussions, specific subjects were addressed each week relevant to the experiences of having an atypical sibling. These included such topics as "What are disabilities?" and "Why do people stare?"

The children who participated in these groups showed a decrease in sibling-related stress, suggesting that the interventions were providing a buffer to the pressures of having a sibling with a disability. Even when the children experienced stressful incidents they seemed to be less affected. They clearly gained from the support they received from the other children and from the adults. One girl commented that though she had friends at school, none of them had a brother like hers. It was good to be with people who knew what she was experiencing. There was also evidence that the program contributed to a lessening of depression and anxiety and to the development of self-esteem. The children gained even when there was no direct work with the parents or the family as a whole. Although the program recognized that interventions involving the whole family were desirable, frequently parents were unavailable and even when they were, they often were too busy with their special needs children to participate.

David Strauss (personal communication 2010), a social work psychotherapist who works with such groups, has also found that they afford the children an opportunity to express feelings that they are often uncomfortable sharing with their parents. Even if they do share they find that their parents often have a difficult time hearing them. Many of these children are keenly aware of how important it is to their parents that they not be negatively affected by their atypical brothers or sisters and try to spare them an awareness of the difficulties they are facing. It is helpful to them to be able to speak freely to a leader who can listen to, validate, and contain their feelings, and to find that there are other children like themselves who have similar fears and feelings. For many children the group experience is reassuring and normalizing, helping to reduce whatever feelings of guilt and shame they may have.

One of the largest supportive programs for siblings of children and adults with disabilities is the Sibling Support Project (www.siblingsupport.org).

This organization helps agencies develop peer support and education programs that are referred to as Sib shops. When the Project published their most recent book, *Thicker Than Water* (Meyer 2009), there were more than 225 Sib shops in eight countries. This organization also developed the first Listserv on the Web that provides participants with the opportunity to exchange information and experiences. Like the groups described by Dr. Phillips, these Sib shops and the online exchange offer siblings an opportunity to express their feelings and concerns and to have them validated.

THE IMPACT OF HEALTHY SIBLINGS ON THEIR DEVELOPMENTALLY DISABLED SIBLINGS

Less attention has been paid to the impact of their healthier siblings on individuals with developmental disorders than the other way around. I was struck several years ago by a letter to the editor of the *New York Times* from an autistic individual who was responding to an article that had appeared earlier in that newspaper regarding the difficulties of growing up with an autistic sibling. The writer pointed out that normal siblings were not easy to live with either and wrote of the bullying that he had occasionally experienced at the hands of other children, including his own siblings, who sometimes denied being related to him. The writer complained that no one ever asks what it is like for autistic children to deal with their brothers and sisters, and suggested it was time that individuals with disabilities were accorded equal time to complain.

The bullying that the writer speaks about and the direct expressions of resentment and hostility toward siblings with disabilities probably occurs more frequently than is known. One study (Sullivan and Knutson 2000) has shown that developmentally handicapped children are 3.44 times more likely to be maltreated than non-disabled youngsters. Given the high incidence of sibling abuse (Straus and Gelles 1990), it is likely that some of these children have been maltreated by their siblings.

I did not learn of any cases of physical or sexual abuse in my interviews with parents or siblings, but several parents expressed concern about how critical their healthier children were of their impaired siblings, and how they often teased or made fun of them. One mother noted how pained she was to hear her two older, athletically competent sons deride their cognitively and physically impaired younger brother for his physical awkwardness. When he was attending the same school as they, they were so embarrassed by his obvious physical deformities that they avoided him and acted as if he were not related to them. Today, as adults, they no longer mistreat him but they have little to do with him. A ninety-year-old woman I met with, whose autistic son lives independently and helps her with chores in her apartment, spoke of her sadness in hearing her adult daughter refer to her brother as a "loser." She won't visit her mother when her brother is present. Another mother spoke of discovering her daughter, when she was little, pushing her two-year-older sister with cerebral palsy down on the floor and then laughing when her sister could not get up. This mother understood how humiliating that was for her older child, especially because it was her little sister who had overpowered her.

Being disabled often upsets the natural age order, with older children being treated as if they were the youngest in the family. The reader may recall from an earlier chapter the bitter resentment a sibling with epilepsy had against her younger sister who was caring for her. As the older one, she insisted she should be in charge even though she couldn't be.

Diane Leamy (personal communication 2008), a social work psychoanalyst who treats children with developmental disabilities, sometimes sees her young patients with their siblings. She often finds them able to stimulate growth in each other. The opportunity for both to process their feelings about each other and understand the basis of their differences can be freeing for each of them. Each has an opportunity to learn what life is like for the other. It often surprises the siblings with special needs to learn that their healthy brothers or sisters do not always have an easy life either.

Dr. Leamy found that many of her child patients admired or even idealized their healthier siblings but at the same time they were frequently envious and resentful and could be very hurtful to them. One can imagine how difficult it must be for children who are aware of their healthier sibling's abilities and achievements to contend with their own limitations. At the same time they are often dependent upon their siblings for help, support, and companionship, which makes it difficult to deal with whatever envy or anger they may feel.

A preliminary study of information from 238 previously completed parent interviews conducted at the Cody Center for Autism and Developmental Disabilities (Van Sise 2007) supports the idea that children with developmental disabilities can gain from their relationship with their neurotypical siblings. For example, this study has shown that children with autism are less likely to have speech problems and more likely to get along with others when they grow up with siblings. They are also less likely be teased by other children, to interrupt others' activities, and to talk excessively.

In general, counseling of individuals with special needs has focused largely on helping them develop self-help and social skills and to control any troubling behaviors. As essential as these educational interventions are, addressing their emotional needs, including their feelings about their relationships with their healthy brothers and sisters, is very important. A group of therapists in England, for example, have demonstrated the value of the "talking therapies" with developmentally disabled individuals in a book titled *Psychotherapy and Mental Handicap* (De Groef and Heineman 1999).

In addition to the services offered by the established organizations for individuals with special requirements, the members of the disability community have themselves begun to develop organizations to serve their needs and advocate on their behalf. There is, for example, the American Association of People with Disabilities (www.aapd.com/site/c.pvI1IkNWJqE/b.5406299/ k.FBCC/Spotlight.htm) which helped achieve the passage of the Americans with Disabilities Act of 1990, which was amended in 2008. Another organization is the Autism Network International (www.autreat.com) which was created by autistic people and brings autistic individuals together for a variety of activities.

WHEN PROBLEMS DEVELOP LATER IN LIFE

Up to now I have been considering situations in which children were born with disabilities. Mental illness, accidents, life-threatening physical illnesses, the development of a chronic illness, loss of sight or hearing or other functions can strike at any time. Brooke Ellison (Ellison and Ellison 2001) was eleven years old when she was struck by a car, leaving her a quadriplegic. Her sister was thirteen and her brother was nine at the time. Elizabeth De Vita-Raeburn's brother Ted, whom she has written about (2004), was nine when he developed aplastic anemia and she was six.

Author, Jay Neugeboren's (1997) brother Robert was nineteen when he had his first schizophrenic episode and Jay was twenty-one. Melinda, whose treatment I will describe later, was eight when her five-year-old brother developed cancer.

Siblings in these circumstances face many of the same challenges that confront those whose brother or sister was born with a developmental disorder. As children and adolescents, they must deal with overburdened parents who are forced to focus much of their attention on their disabled sibling. They are often called upon to assist in their sibling's care, and family activities may be restricted. Guilt over negative feelings toward their ill or injured brother or sister can be difficult to bear. How can one resent a sister who is suffering so or a worried, overburdened parent who is forced to attend to her? One of the differences between this group of siblings and the siblings of atypical children, however, is that they have already established a relationship with their siblings and parents before their brother's or sister's illness or accident occurred, for better or worse.

For however long their sibling is ill or incapacitated, healthy brothers and sisters must face the loss of their sibling as they have known and related to him as well as the loss of their parents as they once experienced them. When the relationship has been positive, feelings of loss may predominate. When it has been highly conflicted, anxiety and guilt about hostile wishes may become a major source of concern.

Jay Neugeboren (1997), who has been a devoted advocate for the mentally ill, has written a moving account of what it was like for him when his brother, Robert, developed schizophrenia as a young adult. Over the years Jay has supported his brother through crisis after crisis, through a lifetime of hospitalizations and group home placements, and a variety of interventions and treatments.

As boys, the brothers were very close. They took great pride in concluding that of all the siblings they knew, they got along the best—this despite the fact that Robert was their mother's favorite and Jay envied him.

Jay recalls his brother's first hospitalization. He watched as Robert tried to chew his own tongue, and he remembered how he wished he could trade places with him or that he could do something to make him the brother he had once been. He also feared that his brother's fate would be his own or that he, too, would wind up mentally ill. He worried about how much of his brother's condition might be due to him. Jay saw himself and Robert as bound to each other and believed that any success or happiness he achieved had been earned at the price of Jay's suffering and failure.

Jay had full responsibility for his brother. He struggled with this responsibility and acknowledged that although he wanted to cure and comfort his brother, at the same time he wanted to run from him and never see him again. When people asked him about how he dealt with his brother and his feelings about him, Jay replied that though he still broke down after a visit to Robert and worried whether he had said or done the right thing when they were together, he got through his visits by acting as if he had two brothers—one the brother he grew up with who had died, and another brother who had taken his place. That brother looked like his first brother and shared their history, a great sense of humor, a love of literature, and a generous spirit; the other brother was a very different person who lived a harder, narrower life.

After years of struggling on his brother's behalf, Jay finally succeeded in having his brother placed in a small facility that has met his needs and in which he has done well (Neugeboren 1999). Were it not for his brother, it is likely that Robert's condition would have continued to deteriorate.

Brooke Ellison

After Brooke Ellison's accident her mother, Jean, remained with her during her hospitalization, went with her to high school each day, and later accompanied her to Harvard University until she graduated. Over the years she has been Brooke's constant companion and nurse. The book that Brooke and her mother wrote, *Miracles Happen* (2001), does not consider the impact that her accident and her disabilities might have had on her brother and sister. Brooke, however, expresses her understanding of how hard the years since her accident have been for her siblings and her father, and her recognition that she was not the only person in the family who experienced a profound loss. She was well aware that the attention she received was taken from the rest of the family. She expresses her appreciation for the help her brother, Reed, gave her through the years, noting among his other kindnesses the special meaning it had when he took her to her senior prom.

Elizabeth De Vita-Raeburn

Before his death, Elizabeth De Vita-Raeburn's brother Ted, who was diagnosed with aplastic anemia, was hospitalized for eight and a half years in a laminar airflow room to protect him from infection. In her book *The Empty Room* (2004), De Vita-Raeburn tells what it meant to her to be the healthy one, the lucky one in the family. The travails of her life were too small to merit consideration. Nothing that happened in her life approximated what had happened to her brother. There was never a time when she felt entitled to feel bad or to cry. Her depression as a child went unnoticed, not only by her parents but even by her physician. Times when she was sick were frightening, because they often made her mother angry. Perhaps it was the extra stress or the fact that her complaints were so minor compared to the problems her brother was having that annoyed her mother, or perhaps her mother became frightened that she too might become seriously ill.

De Vita-Raeburn writes about how, prior to her brother's illness, they had fought, helped each other, played together, and been allies. When he was hospitalized, they were rarely alone, but when they were they talked and found interests to share such as books, model making, and music. There were times when she knew her brother wanted no part of her and she made herself quiet. As he grew older, it was her brother who voiced concern about the effects of his illness upon her.

De Vita-Raeburn claimed that whatever normal competition she might have experienced with her brother, had he been well, was inhibited. She learned not to compete. When she was assigned a teacher in school who had taught her brother as well, she "shrank," partly because she was afraid of competing with her brother. Once a child whom her mother described as "the social one," she became a person who was not seen or heard after her brother's illness.

In 1972, when her brother was diagnosed, the only hope of a cure was a bone marrow transplant, and De Vita-Raeburn proved to be the best match in the family. As an adult, she could still recall fighting feelings of panic as her arm was held down and the technicians drew her blood for the tests. In the end her bone marrow was not a proper match, which led to her feeling like a failure. Adding to her discomfort was the guilt she experienced at being relieved that she no longer had to experience the needles. This was on top of her belief that she had caused her brother's illness by wishing that something bad would happen to him when she was angry at him.

Melinda, a Child in Treatment

Melinda's brother, Phillip, was diagnosed with cancer when she was eight years old. A year later her mother, Ms. Frank, sought treatment for Melinda at a community clinic. She was concerned about Melinda's intense envy and hostility towards Phillip. She had resented him from the day Ms. Frank brought him home, but since he became ill her negative feelings had increased dramatically. Ms. Frank was also bewildered and annoyed by the fact that Melinda had begun crying frequently for no apparent reason.

When Ms. Frank brought up the crying in an initial family interview the therapist asked Melinda if she could share why she was crying. She did not answer but immediately began to cry and leaned into her mother for comfort. Ms. Frank responded with a disgruntled look on her face and pulled away from her daughter, noting with annoyance that Melinda always did that.

Melinda's longing for her mother and Ms. Frank's difficulty in responding to her were apparent from that first session. Although Melinda had a positive relationship with her father, it was clear that it was her mother she wanted to be close to. In one treatment hour, she complained tearfully that since her brother became ill her father had begun to take her shopping, but he did not know what girls needed. She wished her mother would take her because "she is a girl."

She also spoke of her dislike of shopping with her father because he took her brother with them in his wheelchair. She did not want to be seen with her brother. Even in school, she did not speak to Phillip for she didn't want people knowing she has a "sick" brother.

In one session, Melinda drew a picture of the layout of their house, noting the location of each family member's bedroom. Phillip's room was near the parents' bedroom, whereas hers was at the end of the hall. There was no light coming into her room and she complained that her mother would not arrange for a hall lamp, lest it disturb her brother. The distant parental bedroom suggests oedipal issues, but at that moment the therapist felt that Melinda was expressing her feelings about the distance that had increased between her and her parents since Phillip was ill. Seeking to be responsive to Melinda's needs, her therapist wondered if it might help to have a night light in her room. Melinda thought it might. However when Ms. Frank was approached about this, she became very annoyed. She was tired of Melinda wanting to be in charge of things and found her "bossiness" troubling. Some moments later, she remarked that Melinda always pushes her buttons. She wondered why. It feels, she noted, as if she is jealous of her own daughter. When she is with Melinda she realizes she acts as if she were a nine-year-old.

Ms. Frank's relationship with Melinda had apparently been troubled before Phillip became ill. Her fears and worry about her son and the burdens associated with caring for him exacerbated the conflict between them. Ms. Frank had no patience with Melinda's discomfort and seemed unaware that Phillip's illness and her own understandable preoccupation with him might have anything to do with Melinda's greater need for her attention and her increased hostility toward her brother.

It is unfortunate that Ms. Frank could not become involved in Melinda's treatment, particularly as she seemed to be aware that there was something Melinda was stirring up in her that was interfering with their relationship. However, at that particular time, it was not feasible. Her therapist therefore concentrated on trying to help Melinda as much as possible without her mother's involvement.

In the eight sessions available in that clinic, Melinda's therapist sought to provide her with an opportunity to express her feelings about her brother and her mother and to offer her a relationship with someone who was interested in and accepting of her. When Melinda noted that the worst thing that ever happened to her was her brother getting cancer, the therapist accepted her negative feelings and encouraged her to talk about how his illness had been the worst thing in her life. Melinda was able to express her resentment that he was taking her mother away from her. She spoke of her feelings of embarrassment when she was seen with him and of her worry that she might "catch" her brother's illness and perhaps die. The therapist explained to her the nature of Phillip's illness and assured her that cancer was not contagious. She also suggested that children with a sick brother like hers were likely to have feelings very similar to hers. In a more intensive treatment, Melinda's concerns about her parents' bedroom being so far from hers might have been explored more fully at some other point. In this short-term treatment, however, the therapist deemed it important to show Melinda her understanding of how hard it was for her to have her parents seem farther away from her and how sad and angry it made her when they had to give so much of their time and attention to Phillip.

The fact that her therapist could listen and hear Melinda's negative feelings and fears and contain them, which neither parent was able to do at the time, proved to be of value. In one of her stories Melinda wrote about how much she loved her therapist. She spoke of admiring her just as she was, which suggested that she felt her therapist accepted her "just as she was," with all of her angry feelings and thoughts.

John S. Murray (2000), a nurse with the U.S. Air Force, has written about children who have siblings with cancer. He has focused on how the needs of such an ill sibling interrupt the healthy child's attachment with their parents. He points to the important role a clinician can play as an attachment figure for these siblings and has noted the value healthy siblings can derive from the therapist's responding to the questions they have about their brother or sister's illness, and the opportunity to express their feelings and concerns, and the chance to feel listened to and heard.

South Nassau Communities Hospital in Oceanside, New York, has developed a prevention and support program, SIBS Place (www.sibsplace.org), for children between the ages of five and seventeen who have a brother or sister who has cancer or another serious or life-threatening illness. The program offers therapeutic support through individual and group counseling, paying attention to the fears, the sadness, the isolation, and the abandonment that children often experience as a result of their parents' need to spend much of their time in the hospital with their ill sibling, as well as the jealousy, guilt, and loss of power and control that are common concerns among this population.

SIBLINGS AS ORGAN DONORS

De Vita-Raeburn (2004), whom I mentioned earlier, reminds us that in some cases in which siblings have a life threatening illness like cancer, sisters or brothers are called upon to try to save their siblings' lives by donating a part of their body to them.

Organ donation is a complicated and controversial medical intervention, whether the donor is a family member, a friend, or someone unknown to the recipient. It has both physical and psychological consequences for both donor and recipient and raises serious ethical questions. The offering is not without cost to the donor. Although blood, skin, and bone marrow are replaceable, the procedures involve some temporary discomfort and pain. The donation of a kidney means more extensive and painful surgery and greater risk.

Having children serve as organ donors is particularly controversial; especially the idea that parents may conceive a child specifically for that purpose (Fox and Swayze 1992). However, a sibling frequently proves to be the best match for transplantation and in many cases is actually the only person available to donate.

In 2000, a group of one hundred representatives of the transplant community met, under the sponsorship of the National Kidney Foundation and the American Society of Transplantation, to recommend practice guidelines for transplant physicians, health care planners, primary care providers, and all those concerned about the well-being of live organ donors (Authors for the Live Organ Donor Consensus Group 2000). According to that group, minors may donate when the potential donor and recipient are both likely to benefit, when the risk for the donor is extremely low, when all other opportunities for transplantation have been exhausted, and when the minor freely agrees to donate without coercion (established by an independent donor advocate). In the case of very young children, intellectually impaired, or mentally ill siblings, parents are recognized as the decision makers for the health care of their offspring unless it can be shown that their actions will cause them neglect or harm. Such cases then usually find their way into court.

The justification for children in a family serving as organ donors generally rests on the idea that in preserving the life of a brother or sister the donor enhances the welfare of the family as a whole, even if the donor's individual well-being is diminished by the temporary discomfort. This is based on the premise that the loss of the sibling would be a loss to the entire family as well as to the donating child. By promoting the well-being of the family, the child is therefore thought to promote his or her own well-being (Ross 1993).

Jodi Picoult has written a novel, *Her Sister's Keeper* (2004), which has also been made into a film, about a thirteen-year-old girl, Anna, who was conceived to keep her then three-year-older sister Kate alive. When she was two, Kate was diagnosed with acute promyeloctic leukemia. Anna's role began at her birth when her cord blood helped put her sister into remission. Over time Anna was called upon to donate lymphocytes, granulocytes, and peripheral blood marrow. Each procedure imposed some degree of physical discomfort and her role as her sister's lifesaver placed significant limitations on her. She always had to be on call.

The relationship between the sisters is depicted as positive. They are competitive but loyal, resentful of each other at times, and at other times find great comfort and pleasure in each other. They are actually each other's only friends as Kate's illness restricts her exchanges with her peers, and her need for her sister severely restricts Anna's opportunities for socialization with friends. It is hard, Anna points out, to have friends to your house when your sister needs to rest or to visit their houses for sleepovers when your mother needs to pick you up in the middle of the night to go to the hospital to help your sister.

At age thirteen, when Anna is asked to donate a kidney, she decides she has given enough of her body (there is more involved in this but I don't want to give the story away). Although she realizes this will be a death sentence for her sister and will cause conflict with her parents, she seeks a lawyer to help her lay claim to her own body.

Although this is a work of fiction, Picoult has provided us with a picture of some of the agonies, the dilemmas, the anxieties, the conflicts, and the challenges that parents and siblings experience in such situations. She depicts the plight of a critically ill teenager who requires an organ donation, of parents who struggle to keep one of their children alive and are forced to do so at the expense of another, and of the siblings of a child with a life-threatening illness who often must forfeit their parents' attention and who may see themselves as valued primarily for their capacity to save their sibling's life.

The reader is given an opportunity to see how a sibling's role as organ donor can intensify her attachment to her ill sister, even as it may simultaneously evoke greater hatred and resentment of her. When Anna recalls her wish when she was about three to kill her sister, we can understand that wish. When she has a nightmare in which she is cut into so many pieces that there is not enough of her to put her back together again, we recognize how donating a part of their body can evoke deep concerns in children about the intactness of their bodies and arouse fears of losing body parts. Gaddini (2005) has pointed out that young boys and girls tend to think of themselves as enclosed in a balloon-like structure. Skin penetration may therefore be associated with bodily disintegration. These are childhood fears but they retain power in the unconscious long after childhood.

In an article on bone marrow donation in childhood (Parmar, Wu, and Chan 2003), a first-year medical student reflects on his actual experience as a bone marrow donor for his younger brother. He felt overwhelmed and fearful at the prospect. When he had to have his blood tested, he felt that he was shouldering an unfair burden. As the day of the transplant came closer he became more nervous and frightened but kept his emotions to himself. He knew that what he was going through was far less difficult than what his brother was enduring, and was aware that the life of his brother depended on his bone marrow. He found strength, he writes, in the fact that his parents recognized how helpful he was being to his brother. After the transplant his parents stayed at the hospital with his brother and he and his sister were cared for by friends and relatives. The loss of attention from his parents, particularly after what he had gone through, made him feel neglected and abandoned.

Years later, as he reflected on the experience, he felt somewhat ashamed that he had had such selfish thoughts, even though he was aware that they were understandable and probably common among others in the same situation. He also realized that his parents had to remain with his brother after the transplant.

In recognition of the complex emotional aspects of transplantation, the authors of this article emphasize how important it is that both donor and recipient receive counseling during the time they are making the decision for transplantation, during the process itself, and after the procedure has taken place.

Both the decision to ask a sibling for a donation and the decision of the donor to offer a body part to a brother or sister are emotionally demanding. To ask for a donation means putting a sibling at risk. It is especially difficult to ask when the relationship between the siblings has been strained or more seriously conflicted. Yet not asking means forfeiting a chance for life.

To refuse to try to save a sibling's life often means opprobrium not only from the ill sibling but from other members of the family as well. Most importantly, to refuse is to feel as if one is causing the sibling's death. Yet to accede is to risk compromising one's own well-being. Unless one has other siblings who prove to be matches, who will there be to help that sibling if he needs an organ to save his life? Again, what about those situations in which the sibling relationship has been discordant or in which a sibling has abused her own body? Randy Cohen (2005), who writes a column for the *New York Times* titled "The Ethicist," received a letter from a woman who shared her conflict over whether to donate a portion of her liver to a sister who had been an alcoholic and with whom she had been on bad terms for years. Cohen responded by noting that whatever this woman did she would suffer. If she donated she would feel taken advantage of and if she declined she would feel like a "cur."

Unconscious and conscious factors affect these decisions. Laurie Rosen (2002), a social work psychotherapist, has written about a patient suffering from end-stage renal disease who was unable to convey his urgent need for a transplant to his sister. In the course of his treatment for a severe depression, he came to realize that the guilt he felt over the death of a younger sister when he was a child had led him to feel that he was not entitled to a transplant. He saw his illness and the discomfort he experienced undergoing dialysis along with certain complications as a fitting punishment for his imaginary crime. Working through this understanding finally enabled him to be more open about his suffering and his dire need for a transplant, and when his sister understood what he was facing, she agreed to donate one of her kidneys to him.

For Paul, a thirty-five-year-old man, the decision to donate his kidney to a brother with whom he had a very poor relationship, was determined on the surface by a wish to please his parents and to be a "good" brother. Paul was unaware, however, that his decision was primarily based on an unconscious desire to get closer to his distant, critical brother. His expectation was that after the donation his brother would be grateful, apologetic for his past disregard of Paul, and eager that they become friends. However, after a successful transplantation, his brother simply offered his thanks and then withdrew from him again. Paul became bitter and depressed and sought treatment. Perhaps if he had had the opportunity to explore more fully his motives for wishing to donate prior to doing so, Paul might have anticipated or have been prepared for such an outcome, or perhaps he might have thought differently about donating.

Many clinics do offer counseling to prospective sibling donors and in some cases make it possible for siblings who do not wish to donate to find a way to decline (sometimes by finding a medical reason why their donating is not advisable). However, I was unable to ascertain how available such services are and if they are, how much attention is paid to helping donors get in touch with whatever unconscious fantasies may be affecting their decision. I also was unable to assess how much attention is given to helping both donor and recipient through the process and afterwards.

What happens if an ill sibling dies despite a transplant or if the donating sibling incurs a serious medical problem as a result of the efforts to save the life of a brother or sister? Even when the consequences are not so extreme, counseling before, during, and following a transplant process is essential.

Abraham Freedman (1983) has written an account of the impact on one of his patients of receiving a kidney from his brother that describes the aftereffects of his receiving the donation. His patient was the sixth in a family of eight siblings. He had developed nephritis at about age five. During his treatment it became clear that he thought that his illness had been a punishment for certain misdeeds toward his siblings in the past, one of which had to do with the brother who was giving him the kidney.

After the transplant he felt responsible to his brother for the donation. He believed that if the transplanted kidney were to be injured it would be like harming a part of his brother. He sometimes thought of killing himself, but rejected the idea, partly because he needed to protect his brother's kidney.

During his analysis, he realized how deep his love for his brother was and he thought of the kidney as a bond between them. As the treatment proceeded, warmth toward his brother continued, but he became able to accept his brother's kidney as a part of himself.

We have much to learn about the psychological consequences of organ transplantation between siblings. We must pay attention to the emotional as well as the medical factors involved and recognize the importance of considering and dealing with the unconscious and conscious issues that these procedures raise for both the sibling who donates the organ and the one who receives it.

REMARKS

Whether a person's siblings are born with developmental disabilities or are handicapped later in life by mental or physical illnesses or crippling injuries, they all face significant challenges. During their growing up years, healthier or neurotypical children are likely to receive less parental attention, bear increased responsibilities for themselves and often for their siblings, face certain restrictions on family life, and deal with troubling feelings. Special needs brother or sister, on the other hand, must deal with their limitations while watching their healthier brothers and sisters do many of the things they wish to do but cannot. Siblings may therefore become the recipients of each other's anger and frustration resulting from the plight each faces. They may act out these negative feelings or may develop defenses against them that may sometimes prove adaptive, but may on the other hand interfere with their development.

Children whose siblings are born with developmental disabilities must deal with their parents' reactions to having an atypical child. Some healthy children devote themselves to easing their parents' pain. Some develop an overwhelming sense of responsibility for their parents' well being (Safer 2002) and deny their own needs. Some develop a precocious or pseudo form of independence and a compelling need to succeed that prove costly to them over the years.

Ordinary sibling rivalry may also be increased as healthy children experience their parents' attention to their atypical brother or sister and their tolerance for behaviors in them that they themselves would be disciplined for. For the handicapped child there is the envy of all that the healthy sibling can have and do. Yet the hostility and resentment that they may feel toward each other are likely to be more difficult to tolerate in themselves or to express outwardly. How can one envy and hate or be embarrassed by or wish to be rid of a brother who is confined to a wheelchair or a sister whose life is threatened by cancer? Such negative attitudes leave their mark in feelings of guilt and shame and a sense of self as "bad" that leads some siblings to develop self-defeating or self-punitive patterns of behavior that shadow their adult lives. Children with disabilities may also find it difficult to experience their resentment directly or express it, insofar as they are limited by their conditions or because of their dependence upon their healthy siblings for care and support.

On the other hand, difficulties in self-control may lead them to lash out in ways that make family life very difficult.

In some of the cases cited in this chapter, we have seen how a child or an adult may fear becoming like a disabled brother, or experience guilt over his or her own good fortune. In the case of those individuals whose siblings will require care for the rest of their lives, there is concern about how they will manage when their parents can no longer care for their brother or sister. Whether they will find mates who will accept their sibling and help in their care, if that becomes necessary, and whether they should have biological children, lest they develop disabilities, can also be pressing issues.

On the other hand, many individuals, including some of those referred to above, without denying the difficulties of having a sibling with disabilities, see the traits they most value in themselves as having been fostered by their relationship with their brother or sister with special needs. In *Thicker Than Water* (Meyer 2009), a compilation of essays written by a group of adult brothers and sisters, many of the contributors have written about the positive influence their physically, mentally, or emotionally challenged siblings have had on their development and lives. Kim Keprios, for example, who has worked on behalf of people with developmental disabilities and their families and has been honored for her leadership excellence in that field, has shared her experiences with her brother Mike. One of five children, Mike was born without eyes and was cognitively impaired. Kim describes him as affectionate, funny, patient, tolerant, and the provider of unconditional love. Now living in a group home, employed in a fast food restaurant, as well as serving as a volunteer at a thrift store for a program for the disabled, Mike brings their family together, serving as an anchor for them all. Kim writes that he has brought meaning and purpose to her life and has been the inspiration for her work in advocating for people with disabilities and their family. At the same time she acknowledges her worries about him. How will he handle the death of their parents, and how will she care for him in the future? If he dies before she dies, who will provide her with the unconditional love that he has given her that has meant so much to her?

How members of these families react to and deal with the physical and emotional tasks that arise when one member is impaired from birth or develops a physical or mental illness or meets with a crippling accident at any point in life will vary in accord with myriad factors, some of which have been considered in this chapter. However, it is clear that they all share in common a need for what Donald Winnicott (1965) referred to as a "holding environment" by which I believe he meant an environment in which a mother meets her child's basic physical and psychological needs in an attuned way. A holding environment for the families whose offspring have special needs means adequate economic and social resources; educational, medical, and psycho-therapeutic services; and the support of friends and family. The availability of counseling or psychotherapy is also important not only for parents and the siblings of children with special needs, but also for their disabled brothers and sisters. In addition to enabling family members to obtain whatever concrete services they require, many parents and children in these families find their burdens lighter when they have the support of a clinician who can tolerate their pain, accept their negative feelings, bear witness to their difficulties, validate their feelings, appreciate their strengths, and help them explore and work through whatever unconscious issues may be complicating their efforts to deal with the challenges they face.

8

The Death of a Sibling

As I began this chapter, I found myself recalling two photographs that sat on my mother's bureau when I was a child. One was of a sweet looking little girl with a large bow in her hair, and the other of a beautiful young woman dressed in an evening gown. I was aware from early on that they were my mother's deceased sisters. The younger was Stella and the elder, Rosa. I do not recall any conversations about them over the years, but I grew up with an impression of Rosa as having been a beautiful, talented, and gentle young woman who meant a great deal to my mother. I had no idea what Stella might have been like. After my mother's death, an elderly relative explained that Stella had died at the age of two from a childhood disease, two years before my mother was born, and Rosa's death had been due to a kidney disease when she was eighteen years old. My mother was sixteen at the time.

I don't know whether those photographs remained in my mother's room after I left home. However, in their later years when she and my Aunt Janette, the youngest in the family, reminisced, as they often did, about their childhoods, it does not seem to me that they ever spoke of their deceased sisters, nor do I recall ever asking about them. As a member of a profession in which loss is well recognized as a critical event in the lives of families it now seems strange that I've given no thought to what these deceased sisters might have meant to my mother or to how their deaths might have affected her until I embarked on this chapter. Only now do I wonder what my mother and aunt's silence represented. Were these two surviving sisters continuing a pattern of not speaking about their lost siblings that began in their childhoods? Had my grandparents decided that there was no need for my mother to know about a child who had died before she was born? Might I have refrained from inquiring about those sisters for fear it would be too

155

painful for my mother to talk about them or did I perhaps attach too little importance to the loss of a sibling?

SIBLINGS AS UNRECOGNIZED MOURNERS

The latter is unfortunately frequently the case. The death of a sibling is often not regarded as a major loss. Brothers and sisters are apt to be what Ken Doka (Doka and Davidson 1998) has referred to as "disenfranchised" grievers, whose loss is not publically or socially recognized.

When Elizabeth De Vita-Raeburn's only brother Ted, whom I considered in the preceding chapter, died at the age of seventeen after his eight-year illness, De Vita-Raeburn, who was fourteen at the time, found that her relationship with him and her grief were ignored by those around her. Instead of seeking to console her, friends and relatives tended to stress the importance of her being good and the need for her to support her grief stricken parents, as well as pointing out how lucky she was to be the healthy child in the family.

T. J. Wray in her book *Surviving the Death of a Sibling* (2003) writes of the "dismissive condolences" that adults often receive on the death of a sibling such as "thank goodness it wasn't your husband or one of your children" or "Your brother died? How awful! How are your parents?" Wray found that such comments led her to wonder if her grief over her brother's death was somehow inappropriate. Yet, as she noted, she had never lost anyone so close to her before.

Flomenhaft (2006), in his study of thirteen siblings who lost brothers in the World Trade Center bombing, also found that they were not recognized as prominent grievers. They were excluded from the legal circle of those entitled to privileged information regarding death notification and financial settlements. The media on the whole did not recognize the depth of their loss. Friends and relatives often seemed unaware of the pain they were experiencing. One of the respondents in Flomenhaft's study, Stacey, in describing what it was like for her when her brother died in the bombing, explained that people would ask her how her sister-in-law or her parents were doing, not how she was. She found that her loss went unnoticed despite the fact that she considered her brother to be one of the closest persons in her life. He knew more about her, she noted, than even her parents.

Stacey attests to a lack of appreciation of the importance and uniqueness of the sibling relationship and a failure, in many instances, to understand how profound such a loss is. This lack of recognition of the gravity of the death of a brother or sister deprives siblings of the support of concerned and involved others that is so necessary if the complex and difficult tasks of mourning are to be accomplished.

In the case of children, failure to appreciate the impact of their loss is of great concern. Although their grieving parents may appreciate their suffering, it is often extremely difficult for them to meet their remaining children's basic needs, let alone provide them with the understanding and emotional support they require. Thus it is essential that other family members or friends recognize the importance of the loss that the siblings have sustained and that someone be available to help them understand what has happened and to offer them the support they need

This chapter demonstrates how significant the loss of a sibling can be; how it can affect the development and lives of the surviving brother or sister, sometimes serving as a pathogenic force; and how such a loss can become a central issue in an individual's psychotherapy.

I shall not review the psychodynamics of mourning here. Let me say, though, that I follow Bowlby (1980) in his conclusion that even very young children can grieve the loss of loved ones and yearn for them. I also follow Freud in his recognition that the acceptance of a loss does not mean the end of mourning. Freud affirmed this in a letter he wrote to Ludwig Binswanger on the death of his daughter, Sophie, who had died nine years earlier at the age of twenty-seven. "Although we know," he wrote, "that after such a loss the acute state of mourning will subside, we also know we shall remain inconsolable and will never find a substitute. No matter what may fill the gap, even if it be filled completely, it nevertheless remains something else. And actually, this is how it should be. It is the only way of perpetuating that love which we do not want to relinquish" (E. Freud 1960, p. 386).

PARENTAL REACTIONS

The impact of the death of a brother or sister on surviving siblings is influenced by a variety of factors such as the age of each of the siblings, whether the surviving siblings have formed a more or less stable inner representation of their lost brother or sister, the nature of their relationship with each other, the cause of the sibling's death, and the degree to which loving feelings have helped to neutralize hateful feelings. Of particular importance, in the case of developing children and adolescents, are the reactions of their parents to the death of their brother or sister.

The death of a child is probably the most painful of all losses. It reverses the natural order of things, violating our most basic expectations. We expect parents to die before their children. Having given them life, parents are supposed to protect them and keep them alive. The death of a son or daughter means a loss of a part of a parent's self, both biologically and emotionally. Dreams of the future are dashed. The dead child can no longer fulfill parents' hopes and assure some continuation of their own life when they are gone. Parents lose the love, the pleasures, and the satisfactions that children ordinarily provide. Feelings of helplessness and powerlessness threaten their sense of efficacy and self-worth and tend to arouse feelings of shame and guilt, no matter that they have done everything possible to protect and care for their child.

I am familiar with a woman who, after losing her son to a fatal illness, responded with a sense of relief when she learned that a well-respected member of her profession had also lost a child. If such a competent, caring person as that mother had lost a child, then she reasoned that she could not be so "bad." It did not matter that she and her husband had been devoted parents who had done everything possible keep their beloved son alive. Failure to do so left her with the feeling she was a "bad" mother.

So profound is the grief of parents at the loss of a child that it is often impossible for them to maintain their usual attitudes and connection with their remaining children and to help them deal with their grief. Their surviving children may absorb their pain and in some instances identify with their affective state in an effort to connect with them in their mourning. Andre Green (1999) has written about the depression in some children whose mothers become totally immersed in their bereavement. While they continue to care for their other children they distance themselves emotionally. Green refers to such a mother as a "dead mother." Although she remains alive she is detached from her offspring. Green has observed that very often these are mothers who have lost young children.

A father or other substitute person may help to compensate for the inability of a mother to engage with her surviving children until she can once again relate to them. However, in some families the loss of a connection between a surviving child and the bereaved mother may be forever!

James Barrie

This was so in the case of James Barrie, who created that remarkable character Peter Pan (1860–1937), the boy who never grew up (Bank and Kahn 1997, Kulish 1989, Pollock 1978). Barrie's mother never recovered from the death of her son David who died in a skating accident the night before he turned fourteen. Barrie was six at the time. David, an athletic, handsome, and charming young boy, had been his mother's favorite. James, on the other hand, was said to have been something of a disappointment to her (Birkin 1979).

In his book about his mother Barrie (1913) described how she became ill after David's death and lay in bed with his brother's christening robe beside her. On one occasion his teenage sister told Barrie to go to his mother and remind her that she still had another son. When he approached her he found her crying. When she asked him, "Is that you?" he realized she thought he was his dead brother. Young Barrie replied in what he referred to as a "little lonely voice," "No, it's not him, it's just me" (p. 12). Then he saw her turn away from him.

Barrie frequently sat at his mother's bedside and tried to amuse her by recounting funny experiences in the hope that he might help her forget his brother. At some point his sister suggested that he attempt to get their mother to speak about David. Though reluctant to do so he sometimes did. At first he wrote that he was jealous and tried to stop her fond memories. At one point he asked, "Do you mind nothing about me?" (p. 14).

Barrie tried to become as much like his brother as he could so that his mother might not see the difference between them. Recalling that his brother had a cheerful way of whistling that had pleased his mother, one day he put on a suit of his brother's clothes and went into her sick room and whistled. Instead of pleasing her, as he had hoped, he realized that his efforts had actually caused her pain.

When Barrie's mother died, twenty-nine years after David's death, Barrie wrote, "I had not made her forget. . . . In those nine and twenty years he was not removed one day further from her" (p. 16).

James tried to be the boy his brother was when he died. We may conjecture that he not only sought to keep David alive in this way, but also by being like David he was trying to be the son his mother favored. It is of interest that as a man Barrie actually did give the appearance of a much younger person, being only about five feet tall. Although he married, his marriage is thought to have been unconsummated. With no children of his own he became deeply involved with the five children of another family, the Davieses, and when their father died he supported the family emotionally and financially. Bowlby (1980) has suggested that Barrie's attentions to the Davies family were in keeping with a compulsion to care for others that he had developed as a result of his efforts to care for his mother.

Although Barrie's mother's grief cast a pall over his growing up years, his efforts to woo her from her depression and to win her love have been understood as playing an important role in his later success as an author and playwright. According to George Pollock (1978), what began as Barrie's effort to amuse his mother became an independent creative endeavor. Pollock has studied other talented individuals, such as Jack Kerouac, Thomas De Quincy, and Kathe Kollwitz, who also lost siblings, and has concluded that the death of a brother or sister, although not accounting for creative potential, can stimulate or direct creativity. At times such creative efforts may be restitutive or reparative.

SORROW WITHOUT WORDS

"Give sorrow words: the grief that does not speak Whispers the o'er-fraught heart and bids it break," wrote Shakespeare in *Macbeth*, act IV, scene III (2005, p. 138). Unfortunately, all too often families discourage or even prohibit speaking about the deceased sibling in an effort to avoid actively confronting their grief. Aware of their parents' distress and fearful of upsetting them, many siblings feel compelled to avoid any mention of their lost brother or sister, to hold back their tears, and to suppress their own feelings. In so doing they are deprived of the opportunity to deal with their grief. Their parents' unwillingness to talk about their dead sibling also creates or adds to the distance between parents and child at a time when a child has a great need for parental attention and support.

Elizabeth De Vita-Raeburn (2004) writes about how her parents didn't talk about her brother Ted or his death. To talk, she notes was to risk seeing each other's pain and to risk "falling apart" (p. 25). Her grief remained unexpressed, unrecognized, and "frozen." She developed a way of detaching from her feelings and in her struggles to cope, she turned to drugs and alcohol in her teens and later developed an eating disorder. She formed relationships in which her needs were overlooked, which eventually triggered tremendous anger in her. This pattern of relating appears to have had its roots in her earlier anger when she was forced to inhibit her feelings and when her sorrow went unrecognized. At twenty-six, more than ten years after her brother's death, DeVita-Raeburn sought treatment. In her first session when her therapist asked what she wanted to say, she responded, "I am my brother's death" (p. 27).

WHEN FANTASY HOLDS SWAY

In the absence of discussion, particularly about the realities of what has happened to their siblings, children often fill in the unknown with their own fantasies. These may include the fantasy that their negative feelings toward their sibling were responsible for his or her demise.

Consider Meredith, a thirty-two-year-old patient, who was unable to let herself succeed in her marriage, her work, and in her several therapies. When she was three years old, Meredith lost her six-month-old sister, Amy. Meredith recalled hearing a noise in the room the night that Amy died, but went back to sleep. In the morning her mother found her sister dead as a result of Sudden Infant Death Syndrome. Meredith became convinced that by not responding to the noise her sister made she had been responsible for Amy's death.

Her mother began to drink after Amy died and distanced herself from Meredith. Her father withdrew into his work, remaining away from home as much as possible. Her mother never mentioned Amy's name and became enraged when Meredith asked questions about her. In the absence of any explanation about what had happened to Amy, Meredith's fantasy of having killed her sister gained power.

At the age of twenty-six, Meredith sought treatment. She began to access her resentment of the little sister she thought she had only loved and to understand the way her hostile wishes had led her to the fantasy that she was responsible for her death. According to her magical way of thinking, the wish had been equal to the deed.

Although the wish for the death of a sibling is commonplace, it is a wish that was never meant to be granted (Charles 1999). When siblings actually die, individuals may conclude that it is their destructive wishes that destroyed them. The inability of parents to listen to their children's feelings and fears and to offer explanations of what actually happened may leave a child more prone to the development of explanatory fantasies.

Meredith's parents' refusal to talk to her about her sister's death also made her feel disconnected from them and alone. How painful this was for her became clearer through an experience in the treatment. During the second year of treatment, Meredith's therapist lost a close member of her family and had to miss several sessions. Meredith learned of the death in the therapist's family from a person in the community. When the sessions resumed, Meredith insisted that the therapist tell her how she was. Aware of what had transpired when Meredith's sister died, the therapist deemed it important to be direct and open in her response to her patient. She told her that the loss was difficult and that she was sad and fatigued, but that she felt ready to continue their work together. Later, Meredith spoke of the relief she had experienced at that moment. She had been so afraid that her therapist would be silent like her mother, and that she would lose her as she had lost her mother. By being able to ask the question she also felt as if she had shown the therapist that she was interested in and concerned about her and that by answering, the therapist had indicated she understood and accepted her concern. It felt as if they were connected rather than separated by the therapist's loss. How she wished she had been able to have had a similar experience with her mother!

WHEN SOMEONE LISTENS

I was reminded once again how important it is for bereaved siblings to be able to express their feelings by a colleague of mine who recently led a small group of young people ranging in age from nine to seventeen who had lost a brother or sister. Holding back their feelings at home in order not to upset their parents, the members of the group found that the opportunity to speak freely about their feelings was the most valuable part of the group experience. Not only was it a relief to be able to verbalize their sorrow at the loss of their sibling, but they found it useful to be able to speak about the pain they were experiencing as a result of watching and worrying about their parents. Some expressed their fears that their families were falling apart. Some wondered if they would ever again have a good life. Many expressed the conviction that they would never be as good as their deceased sibling and never as pleasing to their parents. The relief these siblings showed in being able to talk together and to recognize their common concerns suggested how difficult it must have been for them to suppress their concerns and feelings in their efforts to protect their parents.

THE "GOOD CHILD"

In order to protect their parents, some surviving siblings not only hold back their grief, but feel impelled to avoid giving their parents any difficulty and to severely limit their demands upon them in order to compensate them for their suffering. Unfortunately, their parents are often too preoccupied with their loss and too immersed in their sorrow to notice these efforts, leaving these young people with the feeling that they don't count, that it is only the deceased sibling who matters. Sadly, some parents, having lost a favorite youngster, do convey to the surviving child their feeling that the wrong child has died (Bank and Kahn 1997).

The need to be the good child is often experienced by those children who are aware that they were conceived in order to help their parents deal with the loss of a sibling whose death preceded their birth. Such children are often referred to as replacement children, a topic to be considered later in the chapter. Suffice to say here that these children often feel not only the need to make up to their parents for their sorrow by being good, but in some instances being good means earning the right to live and not to die like their brother or sister.

CHANGING ROLES

When a sibling dies the roles of the remaining siblings are likely to alter. New roles may threaten a child's sense of identity. In some families the surviving child now becomes the only child. When the youngest dies, the next in line may become the baby of the family, or when the eldest dies the next in line may face new expectations and responsibilities and receive different treatment from younger siblings and parents. Marcy, age ten, for example, who was five years younger than her brother when he was killed in an accident, found herself expected to do the things that he had done as the elder, many of which proved beyond her developmental capacities. At the same time she lost her place as the "baby" in the family and no longer could enjoy certain emotional advantages that that position had once afforded her.

In some families the attention that had been given to a sibling during illness is shifted to the surviving brother or sister. After years of being almost totally preoccupied with the care of her brother, De Vita-Raeburn's mother (2004) turned to Elizabeth for solace and companionship. Fearful of losing her only remaining child, she became overly concerned with Elizabeth's health and well-being. At twelve years of age, Elizabeth's developmental need was to gain her independence and establish her own identity. Her mother's need was to keep her close and have her remain a child.

One can understand parents' increased concern for and preoccupation with their surviving children after their loss and their wish to get close to them and to seek comfort from them. Unfortunately these reactions are frequently at their children's expense.

SIBLINGS AS SUBSTITUTES FOR THEIR LOST SIBLING

In putting her energies and time into her remaining child, De-Vita Raeburn's mother may also be seen as trying to substitute her daughter for her lost son. Replacing a lost child with another child in the family is not uncommon. Parents may turn their attention to one or another child or they may actually try to make another child into their lost daughter or son. Some may emphasize whatever similarities existed between one of their living children and the deceased child or they may attempt to foster those physical or character traits or interests that will make one child better resemble their lost offspring. Other parents deliberately conceive another child to replace the deceased one.

Albert and Barbara Cain (1964) studied six disturbed children seen in a child guidance clinic who were conceived to replace a deceased child in the family. They noted the burden that these children experienced by having depressed, withdrawn parents who were frequently preoccupied with their lost child. Some of the parents tended to compare the living child with the lost sibling, to the disadvantage of their surviving child. At least two of the mothers came to feel that by taking the place of their lost child, their substitute child was "responsible" for the death of their son or daughter. The Cains were careful to emphasize that their observations of this small group of clinic patients did not mean that children in such families could not grow up as intact and well-functioning individuals. Rather, by studying this small sample of children they sought to alert parents and professionals to the fact that there are potential dangers in bearing a child to replace a deceased child.

These "replacement" children often feel they are living for two people (Bank and Kahn 1997). They may find themselves compared with their deceased brother or sister, sometimes favorably and to their parents' satisfaction and sometimes unfavorably, to the disappointment of both parent and child. Too often such children feel they are not accepted for themselves but only as substitutes for their more favored and frequently idealized dead brother or sister. Some children strive to become like the image their parents have of their brother or sister whereas others may fight to be different and achieve their own sense of a unique self.

Some replacement children believe that their existence is at the expense of their lost brother or sister, leaving them guilty and yet glad they are alive. Like the only child described by Jacob Arlow (1972) who gains satisfaction from not having a rival but who then develops a fantasy that he has deprived his would-be sibling of life, the replacement child who feels he would not have been born had his sibling lived may also entertain a fantasy of having been responsible for his brother or sister's death.

Theresa, who was born a year and a half after her two-day-old brother died, believed she would never have been born if he had lived. She was convinced that her mother preferred boys and that had her brother survived, her mother would never have had another child. She therefore felt she owed her life to his death. In her unconscious, this equated with having destroyed him and led to a fantasy that if she conceived a child, the fetus within her, which she thought of as her brother, would destroy her in retaliation.

Millie

One of the contributors to this book, Millie, wrote to me of her experience as a replacement child. She did not actually find out until she was eight years old that prior to her birth, her mother had given birth to a baby girl who died at one month. Millie was born about a year later. This was told to her by an aunt. When she asked her mother why she had not told her about her sister, her mother said she feared it would upset her and she would be as devastated as she, the mother, had been.

Although her parents never spoke of the baby all those years, Millie always sensed that they had suffered in some way. From early on, prior to her knowledge of her sister's death, Millie felt that she needed to make her parents happy. She decided that the way to do that would be to be successful in school. If she were not, it would hurt her parents. She felt that she had to succeed in order to deserve to live. Even as a little girl she knew that there was something strange about her need to succeed and her anxiety about failure.

Learning about the baby was actually a relief. It explained why her parents seemed so unhappy all the time and why she might have gotten the idea that she was born to make up to them for some suffering they had endured.

The need to justify her existence continued to burden her. She was naturally very bright and did very well at school. However, this did not bring her the satisfaction she expected it would. She felt that it was not fair that she did so well because she did not have to work hard to accomplish what she did. She felt too that, despite her efforts, she was a great disappointment to her father. She believed that he had wanted her to be like the baby they had lost, who, she had been told, was blond haired and blue eyed. Millie was dark haired and dark eyed. She was convinced that she never measured up to her dead sister and that whatever she achieved was not fair, just as it was not fair that she had lived and her sister had died.

As an adult, with the help of her analyst, Millie, began to understand more fully what was behind the demands she made upon herself, her feeling she had no right to a life of her own, her need to compensate her parents for their loss and to win their love by being like her idealized sibling. It took many years of analysis for Millie to finally accept the idea that she had a right to her own life and that what she was able to do in life was enough.

Salvador Dali

There are numerous accounts of well-known individuals who have been replacement children. Among them is Salvador Dali. Dali was born nine months and ten days after his brother died at the age of twenty-one months. His brother was also named Salvador. According to one of Dali's biographers (Parinaud 1976), the parents never recovered from their loss. They spoke of their dead son constantly. Dali is said to have carried a lifelong burden of guilt for having stolen his elder brother's existence while at the same time actively striving to achieve his own sense of identity.

Dali attributed both his problems and his triumphs to the loss of the first Salvador. "All the eccentricities which I commit, all the incoherent displays are the tragic fixity of my life. I wish to prove to myself that I am not the dead brother, but the living one" (Dali 1942, p. 23). He went on to write that in killing his brother he gained immortality for himself. Like some other replacement children, Dali believed that because he gained life as a result of his brother's death he was responsible for the death. Perhaps his preoccupation with time may have been related to his conflict over having survived his brother and having so much more time than he.

Vincent van Gogh

Earlier in the book I referred to Vincent van Gogh and his symbiotic-like relationship with his brother Theodore. Vincent also had another brother, born just a year before Vincent, who died shortly after birth and whose death had a significant impact on the artist's development and life. Vincent was born on the same day as his brother and was given the same name and the same number in the birth records. His parents idealized their dead son. Nagera (1967), in his psychoanalytic study of van Gogh, has hypothesized that it was the idealized image that they offered to Vincent for emulation that accounted for the high ego ideals Vincent set for himself and the fear of failure that this brought with it. According to Nagera, Vincent feared competing with the idealized dead Vincent. Success meant an attack on his brother and an attempt to take his place in the affection of his parents. This fantasy seemed likely to have been coupled with the fantasy that he was in some way responsible for his brother's death. Nagera has further hypothesized that van Gogh came to associate death with success. If he were to be thought as good as his brother, it would be necessary for him to be dead like him. It is for such unconscious reasons that Nagera understands Vincent's compromising his own success.

Nagera has also postulated that van Gogh's concerns about competing with his dead brother played a role in his fear of success. Whether a sibling is a replacement child or not, competing with a dead brother or sister is likely to be more conflictual and generate more intense guilt than vying with a live brother or sister. The surviving child is very often competing with an idealized brother or sister who is remembered as being more than he might have been in life and who generally is thought of as without flaws. Like James Barrie, there is no winning against such a rival. How can one wish to vanquish a foe who is already dead and unable to stand up for himself? What kind of person engages in such a competition? In the end, the actual death of the sibling may seem to surviving sisters or brothers to be the outcome of their competitive wishes, leaving them feeling responsible and guilty.

WHEN SIBLINGS MOURN

Although the response of parents has a profound impact on the way a sibling reacts to the death of a brother or sister, individuals face their loss in ways that are separate from their parents. In addition to the pain caused by the death of a sibling, such a loss confronts children and adolescents with realities that are difficult to bear and deal with. Irrespective of their parents' responses, the loss of a child in a family forces the surviving children to recognize that death is not only for the old. They, too, may die. Parents cannot keep their children alive no matter how hard they try. Neither child nor parent is omnipotent. Whereas coming to terms with one's lack of omnipotence is an important developmental achievement and a requisite for a reality-based view of the self, premature disillusionment may threaten the development of confidence in oneself and others as well as a sense of optimism about life in general. The awareness of the fragility of life may also contribute to increased anxiety on the part of surviving children with regard to their own well-being, leading some to cling more closely to their parents, which in turn makes separation more difficult. On the other hand, there are other children who engage in risky behavior as a way of asserting their independence or as a counterphobic response to their fears.

The Catcher in the Rye: A Tale of Mourning

Although the ways a child faces and deals with the loss of a brother and sister are unique and determined by a multitude of factors, there are certain reactions and adaptations that are relatively common. As a way of highlighting some of these commonalities, I draw on the experiences of J. D. Salinger's adolescent folk hero Holden Caulfield. Although the central theme of *The Catcher in the Rye* (Salinger 1951) is generally regarded as the conflict between an adolescent and adult society, the novel can also be understood as a sensitive account of how one adolescent boy struggles to come to terms with the loss of his brother. That *The Catcher in the Rye* is rarely considered as a tale of mourning may reflect the general lack of appreciation of the significance of sibling loss (although others have referred to the novel in their consideration of siblings, e.g., Bank & Kahn 1997, Rowe 2007). The only person, as far as I have been able to tell, who has considered it as such is the now deceased, distinguished scholar of American literature Edwin Haviland Miller, Professor Emeritus of English at New York University (1982). Yet Salinger has provided us with a rich picture of some of the dynamics of mourning that many individuals share. We find in his writing the sorrow and yearning for the lost object, the anger and envy and guilt that are so often associated with loss, the continuation of the bond to the lost person, the use of objects to connect the mourner with the deceased, and the rescue fantasies that mourners sometimes entertain as a way of undoing their loss.

The reader may recall that Allie, Holden's brother, died of leukemia at the age of eleven when Holden was thirteen. Holden recalls Allie as "fifty times" more intelligent than him and the "nicest member of the family." The night that Allie died, Holden slept in the garage and broke all the windows with his fist. It was, he says, a stupid thing to do, but he hardly knew he was doing it. His hand continued to hurt him once in awhile and as a result of his actions he lost the ability to make a fist.

According to Bowlby (1980), anger is very much a part of normal mourning and outbursts such as Holden's are frequent after the death of a loved one. The anger may be understood in different ways. E. H. Miller (1982) has proposed that Holden's behavior reflected his anger at himself for wishing Allie dead and at his brother for leaving him alone and burdened by guilt. His anger might also, I would suggest, have helped him to defend against his feelings of sadness and helplessness which are more difficult to tolerate, especially for an adolescent. It is also possible that his self- destructive behavior represented a way of externalizing his inner pain or of punishing himself for whatever guilt he felt related to Allie.

Bowlby (1980) has proposed another explanation for anger and outbursts in the face of the death of a loved one. He likens such responses to the protests of an infant when he feels he has lost his mother and seeks to summon her by crying and thrashing about. Explosive behaviors on the part of the bereaved during the early weeks and months after a loss, when the urge to search for and recover the lost person is likely to be intense, may similarly represent an attempt to recover the lost person.

Envy and Guilt

At one point Holden imagines himself getting pneumonia and dying. He thinks about all the people who attended Allie's funeral. He notes that everyone was there. His envy of his brother for receiving so much attention when he died is clear. It is likely that he also envied his brother during his illness, when his parents must have been preoccupied with their concerns about his ill brother and deeply involved in his care.

Guilt over his anger and rivalry with his brother are seen in Holden's efforts to repair a previous hurt he had inflicted on his brother. When he was feeling depressed, Holden notes that he sometimes talks out loud to Allie. He keeps telling him to go get his bike and meet him at a friend's house. It happens that years ago he and that friend were going someplace and Allie heard them making plans and wanted to be included. Holden wouldn't let him join them. He explains that it wasn't that he never took his brother with him. It was just that one day that he didn't. He claims his brother did not get angry at him. In fact he describes Allie as never getting angry, but Holden says he keeps thinking of that incident anyway, when he gets depressed.

Although one may wonder to what extent Holden's view of his brother as the "nicest" person in the world might have been an idealized picture of Allie serving to defend against his negative feelings toward him, in my reading of the book I felt that this young adolescent had lost a beloved brother for whom he yearned. Even as Holden may have entertained guilt over his past rivalry, I believe that a therapist seeking to help this young boy would find it essential to connect with this side of Holden's relationship to his brother as well. Too often in the past there was a tendency on the part of therapists to overly focus on the rivalry and guilt in treating sibling mourners without giving sufficient recognition to the loving side of their relationship.

Connecting Objects

At one point in the novel Holden is asked to write a paper for another student in his class and he writes about Allie's baseball mitt, which he keeps with him. The mitt had poems written in green ink all over the fingers and the pockets. Like many other mourners, Holden found in Allie's baseball mitt an object that helped to connect him with his brother. Margaret Gibson (2004) refers to such things as "melancholy objects." According to Salman Akhtar (2005), such objects play an important role in helping a mourner establish a meaningful continuity between the living and the dead. They become "bridges across the chasm of time and generations and ultimately serve life-enhancing purposes" (p. 64). It should be noted that Vamık Volkan (1972) who was one of the first to write about such objects, referring to them as linking objects, has described how they may also play a part in pathological mourning.

A Continuing Bond

In *The Catcher in the Rye*, Holden's bond with his brother continues. He carries him with him in his mind, and at times calls upon him for help and support. For example, when Holden walks to the end of the block and steps off the curb he fears he may not get to the other side but instead may disappear. To reduce his anxiety he pretends he is talking to Allie, asking him not to let him disappear. Then when he reaches the other side of the street safely he thanks Allie for his help.

While death ends a life, it does not end a relationship (Bank and Kahn 1997). It is now generally accepted that despite the permanence of physical separation, the bereaved can be emotionally supported through such a continuing bond to the deceased (Packman, Horsley, Davies, and Kramer 2006) in a way that is ordinarily adaptive and that favors a positive adjustment to the loss. On the other hand, for those who have had extremely conflictual or abusive relationships with their deceased sibling, a continuing connection may be problematical, and one of the tasks of therapy may be to help such individuals loosen their destructive bond with a sibling.

There is the question of why Holden fears crossing the street. Might he fear that he, too, will die like his brother? Concern about their own well-being is frequently heightened in siblings who have lost a brother or sister. Or does he fear he will be punished for negative feelings toward Allie, and so he calls upon him in the hope he will be forgiven? Whatever accounts for his fear, Holden seems to gain comfort from thinking of Allie as someone who would help him survive.

Rescue Fantasies

At one point in the book Holden shares a wish to act as a rescuer He tells his sister Phoebe how he pictures little kids playing a game in a big field of rye and nobody's around except him. He is standing on the edge of a cliff and what he has to do is to catch everybody if they start to go over the cliff. He knows that it's crazy, but it's the only thing he'd really like to do. While speaking of his fantasy Holden misquotes Robert Burns's poem "Catcher in the Rye," referring to a passage as "If a body catch a body coming through the rye." Phoebe points out that the actual line is, "If a body meets a body coming through the rye."

Rescue fantasies were first described by Freud (1910b) in connection with children's wishes to give back to their parents the life they owe to them by rescuing them from danger and death. The concept has been extended over time (Akhtar 2005). We may hypothesize that Holden's wish to rescue others represented his wish to restore his dead brother to life.

Complicating Factors

Unfortunately, as the reader learns, four years after his brother's death Holden is hospitalized for what Salinger refers to as a "nervous breakdown." Prior to his hospitalization he was expelled from several schools, had continuously alienated people, provoked fights in which he was beaten, and made sexual advances that he never carried out. Whatever efforts he made to deal with Allie's death were not sufficient.

The Catcher in the Rye is, of course, not a case study, and there is a great deal we do not know about Holden, such as his early relationship with his parents and siblings and what his development and personality had been before he lost his brother. We do know, however, that he was very much alone with his grief. He does not reach out to his parents, nor do they to him. He realizes that his mother has never gotten over his brother's death and he does not want to burden her. His father is depicted as distant and unavailable. If Holden's self-destructive behaviors represented an unconscious cry for help, his efforts seem to have gone unheeded until they apparently could not be ignored.

Holden's treatment took place several years after the loss of his brother. We do not know how he might have fared had he received help when Allie died, perhaps even during Allie's illness. We do know that it is extremely important that there be someone available to grieving siblings—a relative or a family friend or in some families a therapist—someone they can count on to be there for them as long as necessary when a parent cannot assume that role.

Sharon

For Sharon, who at the age of eight lost her one-year-older sister, it was a psychotherapist who filled this role. Sharon lost her sister, Nora, in a tragic accident. The children were riding their bikes on a quiet country road, bordering a farm, and a tractor crossed the road, crashing into them. Nora died immediately and Sharon was very badly hurt. After a period in intensive care and several surgeries, Sharon recovered but the family was devastated. The parents felt unequal to helping Sharon. They sought the help of a therapist, Mrs. Lent.

Sharon and Nora were not biological sisters but had been adopted at the same time from the same orphanage in China when Sharon was four and Nora was five. The family had consulted Mrs. Lent on an as-needed basis following the adoption, so she was known to them and to the children.

Sharon's loss was profound. She had lost her beloved playmate. Nora had been her constant companion ever since they left the orphanage where they had shared their infancy. As they moved to their new home in a strange country with its unfamiliar language and unfamiliar people, food, habits, sights, and sounds, they had had each other to help weather the strangeness of their new life. The bond they had formed was a strong one.

Sharon recognized that her parents were overwhelmed and absorbed in their own grief. She tried to protect them by not sharing her painful feelings and by being as undemanding as possible. When her therapist noticed one day that Sharon's clothes were much too tight, Sharon explained that she hadn't wanted to tell her parents for fear of bothering them. As much as possible she sought to be invisible.

In a safe atmosphere where she could speak her mind to an adult who could tolerate and hold her pain, Sharon was able to express her feelings about her loss, about her loneliness without her sister, and her perception of her parents as fragile and inaccessible.

At the same time her parents were relieved that Sharon had someone to provide her with what they could not. With the passage of time, they did regain some of their former strength but their ability as caregivers remained compromised. It was as if in the face of their loss they were reluctant to invest as fully in Sharon as they had originally in both girls.

In time Sharon began to develop more confidence and to regain a sense of fun and playfulness. She became better able to make demands when they were appropriate. In her play she began to imitate many of the activities that her sister had excelled at and that she had previously shied away from. She felt freer to identify with her sister, whereas earlier she felt that doing things that Nora did was like competing with her, something that exacerbated the guilt she experienced over having survived the accident.

More Than One Loss

Unfortunately, one tragedy does not preclude another. A family may lose more than one child. A parent may die before or after the loss of a sibling. One or more children in a family or one or both parents may die at the same time in an accident or catastrophe, leaving surviving siblings. Virginia Woolf, writing about the death of her older sister Stella who had been a surrogate mother to her after their mother died when Virginia was thirteen and Stella was twenty-six, noted that her mother's death had been a "latent sorrow," which at the time she could not deal with. When Stella died two years later, Woolf wrote that beneath her response to the loss of her sister "lay sunk the other death" (Woolf 1976, p. 124). She recalls at the time, saying to herself, "But this is impossible; things aren't, can't be, like this." The second death weighed more heavily as a result of the first.

Scott

Scott, a fifty-five-year-old man, married with two children, lost two siblings. At the age of twelve, he lost his six-year-old sister Jessica, one of a set of twins. Several years before we spoke together his four-year-younger brother Glenn, with whom he had been very close, died of AIDS. Both parents were deceased by then. Still surviving was Jessica's twin, Monica.

Jessica, the first child to die in the family, passed away unexpectedly three days after she became ill with what was thought to be spinal meningitis. The family was overwhelmed. The twins had been seen as a special blessing. They were beautiful children and attracted a great deal of positive attention from friends and relatives. After Jessica died, they were no longer a "special" family.

Scott's mother became severely depressed after her little daughter's death and their father shut down emotionally, focusing all of his efforts on keeping the family going. Although a devoted parent, he had been a difficult person to get close to even prior to the loss of his daughter. After Jessica's death he withdrew even further. Scott felt that he had lost both of his parents when his sister died.

Scott noted that previous to Jessica's death they had been a happy, fun-loving family. His mother was a joyful person, very accepting and attentive to all of her children, and understanding of her sometimes rambunctious sons.

Following his sister's death they became trapped in their grief. From a house of fun, theirs became a house of gloom. No one in the family spoke about Jessica or their feelings about her death. Their mother would begin to cry when her name was mentioned and his father made it clear that he needed to avoid speaking of her. During their weekly visits to the cemetery where Jessica was buried, they prayed silently as they tended her grave, but no one spoke.

At the same time, he and his sister and brother were taught that they must never forget their sister. They were to keep her alive by remembering her. When they did enjoy themselves, they felt guilty that they were not thinking of her at those moments, and they also felt sad that she was not there to share in the enjoyment. They not only absorbed the grief and suffering of their parents but they felt compelled to match their parents' sad moods and mute any pleasure they might enjoy.

In time, their mother was able to resume her mothering of the rest of her children. When she began to become alive they also began to do the same. There were parties once again and life became "lighter." Scott's father, however, continued to repress his feelings and though he remained devoted to his family, he kept his distance.

Scott believed that the guilt his parents experienced over not being able to keep Jessica alive was transmitted to each of the children. For his mother and father the job of parents was to protect their children from harm and in this they saw themselves as having failed. Their guilt was reinforced by their religious outlook. Having regarded the twins as a special gift from God, the family viewed her being taken away as a punishment for some reason that they could not fathom.

Scott's relationship with Jessica before her death, as well as with Monica, was like that of most siblings, a mix of love and envy and resentment. Before they were born Scott had enjoyed a special status in the family as the older brother and had been very close to his mother. Because he could not compete with the twins, he dealt with his envy and jealousy of them by becoming very helpful to his mother, and in this way he remained close to her. Scott traced what he referred to as his "crazy" sense of responsibility to this effort. As the girls grew up, Scott enjoyed his position as older brother and recalled being a bit bossy with them. Monica was very compliant, but Jessica was more assertive and so at times there had been some friction between them.

Scott began to experience serious anxiety symptoms in his early twenties and sought treatment. With the help of his therapist, he began to express many of the feelings he had repressed. Scott had identified with his father, who kept his feelings to himself. He believed that that was the manly thing to do. Unlike his father, his therapist was a man who was at ease with his feelings and he offered Scott a different model of masculinity. Scott also found in his therapist someone who could tolerate hearing about his pain and who could bear witness to the tragedy he and his family had experienced, someone who could appreciate his love of his sister and yet understand and accept his anger at her as well as at his parents for the way they dealt with her loss. That he could express his feelings without fear of hurting someone, and the realization that his therapist would stay with him as long as he needed him helped him, he said, engage in the treatment. His confidence in the therapist's willingness to work with him as long as necessary, seemed particularly important to Scott, for he mentioned it several times. I wondered whether there had been some push on the part of others that he or the family "get over" their sorrow more quickly. An intolerance for the length of time mourning takes is not unusual.

As Scott described his treatment, it seemed to me that his therapist had provided him with a sound holding environment (Winnicott 1965). According to Clare Winnicott (1955), cited by Kanter (2004, pp. 151–152), by recognizing the importance of a client's experiences and not turning away from them, by staying with him as he recounts them, a therapist provides an individual with an opportunity to relive the experiences. This can give him the courage to feel their full impact. Only, Claire Winnicott suggests, when he can do that can an individual's own healing processes be freed. She adds that she deliberately used the word "hold," because it involves "acceptance" of the client and what he shares with his therapist but also includes what the therapist does with what he accepts.

Although Scott gained much from that early treatment, he noted that his sister's death left its mark. It remains something of a struggle for him to get close to others, out of a fear he will lose them. When his daughter was born he was aware of some tentativeness in relating to her. His father seemed to understand his anxiety and advised him to not let what happened to his sister interfere with his enjoyment of his lovely little girl. His father's response may suggest that he, too, grew over time.

A Second Loss

Scott only learned of his brother's illness shortly before his death, when Glenn could no longer conceal that he had AIDS and needed more help. As close as the brothers were, Glenn had never told him how he contracted the illness. During his last months, Scott visited Glenn almost every day, and helped his sister-in-law care for him.

To Scott the loss of a second sibling not only revived for him feelings associated with his earlier loss, but led to doubts about the fairness of life itself. After burying their sister, the family had thought that the other members would be spared to live to an old age. The sense of helplessness and feelings of anxiety associated with his sister's death returned. However Scott was in a different place than when his sister died. He was older, more mature, and had a supportive family of his own. He also was in therapy when Glenn died and had his therapist's support, as well as the advantage of the help he had received earlier around Jessica's death. The fact that his parents were both dead and were spared the agony of losing still another child also made the loss of his brother easier. He and his sister had only their own grief to deal with.

Yet, a death from AIDS, like suicide or any other deaths that are stigmatized by society, places an extra burden on a surviving family. Both Scott and his sister found it difficult to explain Glenn's death to their relatives, and while they did so they both had to struggle with feelings of confusion and shame. They also had to face the fact that there was much about their brother that they did not know.

It was clear that sharing this information with me was very painful for Scott, and I greatly appreciated his generosity in doing so. In speaking with me about what it was like for him during our conversations, he noted that though difficult, he has found that speaking about his lost siblings generally has a positive effect. It is as if each time he shares his experience with someone he works something else through.

As in my other interviews with brothers and sisters who lost siblings, I frequently found listening to what Scott had to share painful. The experience gave me a new appreciation for what it means to "bear witness" and to "hold" another's distress.

THE IMPACT OF SIBLING LOSS LATER IN LIFE

For some individuals who have lost a sibling in childhood, the full impact may only be experienced later in life. They may have attached little or no importance to their loss, sometimes not even mentioning it when they initially seek treatment. Such was the case with Mrs. King, a seventy-five-year-old woman who sought treatment three years after her husband's death. She felt that something was wrong in the way she was mourning. She did not expect mourning to come to an end, but she could not understand why she couldn't free herself of the feeling that she had failed him while he was alive. In reality she knew she had been a good partner. Why this vague and unsettling feeling of failure?

This was the second marriage for both Mrs. King and her husband. He had lost his first wife six years prior to their ten-year marriage and she had been widowed for four year before they wed. Mrs. King spoke warmly of her husband and of their relationship. Their life together sounded rich and rewarding. They each brought married children and grandchildren to their union and were both close to each other's families. Over time their respective children became very attached to each other. After Mr. King died, both her own children and her stepchildren were very attentive and supportive of her.

As Mrs. King spoke of her relationship with Mr. King and as I experienced her in our sessions, it was hard to understand her feeling of having failed her husband. The differences between them seemed minimal. Sometimes she found him a bit slow and he found her a bit too much on the go. There were some political differences, and they could become somewhat heated in their arguments. What became increasingly apparent, though, was that the feeling she failed someone was not limited to seeing herself as a disappointing wife. She generally had a low regard for herself. She felt she failed to live up to the expectations others had of her. It didn't matter that she attracted many friends, had achieved distinction in her career, and was evidently much admired and loved by her family.

It was not, however, until Mrs. King offhandedly referred to herself as a "replacement" wife that we began to gain a clearer understanding of her feelings of not measuring up. She was aware that she had always had a certain amount of discomfort about being the second wife, but was surprised at using the word *replacement*. In the following session Mrs. King reported a dream in which she was out buying a vase to replace one she had broken, but she could not find one as beautiful. In associating to this dream she wondered whether her feeling of failing her husband had to do with a feeling that she had not been as satisfying a partner as his first wife, that she had been a disappointment to him. Yet she consciously believed that she had made her husband happy in her own way.

As she explored this idea she informed me for the first time that when she was two years old her eight-year-old brother had died in an accident. She had no memories of him, but she had heard much about him from her father. He was apparently outstanding in every way and her father was immensely proud of him. She didn't believe he had ever gotten over his death. As much as her father loved her she was certain he never derived the satisfaction from her that he had gotten from her brother. In time it became clear that her idea of being a disappointing second wife drew on her having been a disappointing replacement for her lost brother.

There were other factors that were complicating Mrs. King's mourning, which were taken up over time, such as her rivalry with and anger at the first Mrs. King, which seemed a displacement of her envy and anger toward her brother, as well as anger at her husband for loving his first wife, which partly represented a displacement of her resentment of her father for his preference of her deceased brother. Although oedipal issues are likely to have played a role in generating Mrs. King's concerns, they did not emerge in the limited number of sessions we worked together. Following our consideration of the way in which issues with her deceased brother were affecting her mourning, Mrs. King decided that she had gained enough from the work and decided to terminate. In a holiday card written six months after we last met, she reported that she feeling much better and was "getting on" with her life.

Mrs. Brown

Another patient, Mrs. Brown, became extremely anxious during her only daughter's pregnancy. She herself had been one of three children. She spoke of a three-year-older brother who was retarded. He was institutionalized when he was fourteen and died when he was a young adult. She vaguely mentioned a third sibling, a sister, who had died many years ago. She was too young, she said, to know anything about her. After this one reference to her sister, she never mentioned her again.

Much of the early therapeutic work with Mrs. Brown centered on the impact her retarded brother had had on her. She was very concerned, in the light of his disability, as to whether her own daughter would be normal and now whether her grandchild would be healthy.

During one session about five months into the treatment, when Mrs. Brown became extremely anxious after mentioning the coming grandchild, the therapist found herself thinking about the infant sister who had died and who had never been talked of in the treatment. She shared her thoughts with Mrs. Brown, who couldn't understand why the therapist would think of her sister. She insisted that she was too young to know anything about her or to have her death matter. Perhaps, the therapist replied, it had meant more to her than she thought it did.

The therapist encouraged Mrs. Brown to try to find out more about what had happened. Her parents were deceased, but she did have an aunt she could consult. When she somewhat reluctantly did, she learned, much to her surprise, that she was eleven years old when her sister was born. The baby had several serious birth defects and died at nine months of age. Mrs. Brown apparently had repressed all memory of what had happened. Yet, after talking with her aunt she noted that she was vaguely aware that she once had a strange feeling that her mother had killed an infant.

Mrs. Brown's anxiety subsided as soon as her healthy, intact little granddaughter was born, but this fantasy became a starting point for several years of work during which she developed a deeper understanding of the profound impact that her sister's and her brother's deaths had on her development and personality.

WHEN A SIBLING COMMITS SUICIDE

The suicide of a loved one is one of the most difficult deaths to cope with. The fact that a brother or sister has chosen to die tends to intensify feelings of rejection, abandonment, and anger. Given the ambivalence inherent in the sibling relationship, guilt over death wishes and over not having been able to prevent the suicide can be very difficult to bear, and sometimes leads surviving siblings to compromise their successes in life. Judith Rappaport (1994) for example, has written about two women whose conflicts about having a child were in part determined by their unconscious guilt over their brothers having taken their lives.

A friend and colleague of mine, whom I shall refer to as Dr. Long, shared with me something of her treatment experience with Rona, a young woman in her late forties. Rona's three-year-younger sister, Morgan, committed suicide at the age of twenty-five, a tragedy that Rona did not share with Dr. Long until a year after the treatment began. At about the time she graduated from college, Dr, Long had also faced the suicide of her several-years-younger sister.

Rona, the patient, was a talented, accomplished professional writer who had written several novels. Nonetheless, whenever a promising career opportunity arose, she failed to take advantage of it. She entered psychoanalysis, determined to uncover the reasons for her self-defeating behaviors.

In the early days of her treatment, Rona briefly mentioned that she had a three-year-younger sister, Morgan. She noted that once Morgan was born, her father, with whom Rona had been very close, "deserted" her in favor of her sister. She described Morgan as someone who just attracted people to her, whereas Rona was shy and retreated from relationships.

It was following a dream that Rona referred to as a "nightmare of the utmost" that she finally told Dr. Long of her sister's suicide. In the dream, Rona saw herself as a lion who was about to attack an unsuspecting lamb. When the lamb started bleating pathetically the lion moved in for the slaughter. Suddenly, the lamb looked up at the lion and screamed, "Only your feelings can kill me." At that point Rona cried out as if pleading her own case in a courtroom, "She killed herself, I didn't kill her. She killed herself!" She then abruptly ceased talking and asked the therapist if she had ever told her about her sister's suicide.

Dr. Long was startled by the omission of such an important piece of history. She was also deeply shaken, and, uncharacteristically, wanted the session to be over. She was taken by surprise at the intensity of her reaction. She quickly recognized that it was a reminder of her own sister's suicide. She thought she had worked through those painful buried feelings long ago.

Her own responses, which she did not share with Rona, led Dr. Long to a careful consideration of her countertransference reactions that enabled her to separate her own experience from Rona's. At the same time she felt a deeper connection with her patient because of their shared experience.

In the analytic work that followed, Rona began to see that her sister's suicide was an important organizing force in her life. She came to recognize how her guilt led to her need to compromise her success and punish herself. She believed she could have prevented her sister's death and felt complicit in the suicide. She, Rona, did not deserve a fulfilling life. Like many survivors of sibling suicide, Rona felt she had not helped her sister enough, not been there enough for her. Her atonement for her guilt drove her to "shoot herself in the foot" at every turn. She could travel the road but she had to sabotage reaching her destination.

Rona's dream, which they returned to time and again in the treatment, helped her face her jealousy of her sister's close relationship with their father. Over and over, it was pointed out that though Rona harbored jealous feelings, these feelings did not kill her sister. Gradually, her self-blame lessened. Her therapist was able to remind her, as her therapist's analyst had once reminded her, that Rona's actual actions had often reflected a willingness to help Morgan, which for some reason her sister had rebuffed. For both therapist and analyst, the determination to remove their sisters' pain was far greater than their ability to instill the will to live in them.

It was no coincidence that as Rona continued to more deeply explore and unravel the feelings inside that had become such a barrier to her success, her last few interviews for a job had been successful and one of the companies had offered her a position.

WHEN OLDER ADULT SIBLINGS DIE

The loss of an older adult sibling ordinarily does not have the same impact on the development of an individual's character and personality as when the loss occurs during childhood, adolescence, or even young adulthood. Parental reactions to the loss are likely to play a less significant role in determining the impact, although until bereaved parents die, their sorrow remains a deep concern for their children. The reactions of older siblings to the deaths of their brothers or sisters are ordinarily determined by their relationship with them over the years and the roles they have played in each other's lives. For those siblings who have been close, the loss is likely to mean losing a companion, a supportive figure, and a person with whom one's past has been closely intertwined. Even when the relationship has been a troubled one, a sibling loses the person who knew him the longest and who through shared memories often helps them maintain their ties with their parents. As one former patient of mine wrote to me following her brother's death at the age of sixty-five, a brother who had badly mistreated her during their childhood: "Regardless of the past, I feel a loss. Something about just being a unit for so many years has left me with an attachment to him." She went on to say she will miss being able to reminisce about their parents and family life during the years to come.

When the relationship has been positive the loss often means pain and yearning and sorrow, and when it has been troubled it frequently means guilt and regret that it had not been more loving.

Raymond

A seventy-two-year-old friend of mine, Raymond, whom I have known since he and his two-year-younger brother, John, were boys, wrote in response to my condolence note what it meant to him when John died: "He was more than a brother to me. We were neighbors; we shared the experience of sitting on a board; we were golf partners, confidants, and most of all, we were best friends. I know of so many instances where brothers barely communicate. That was never the case with us. In the past ten years that we have been living a block apart, there was rarely a day when we did not either talk on the phone or in person at least once. My life has changed considerably since losing my best friend."

I was not surprised at Raymond's reactions for I recalled the brothers as very close while growing up. Following their graduation from college they started a business together. Years later they took jobs in different localities, but once they retired they and their wives moved to the same community and, as Raymond said, became "best friends."

Genevieve

At the age of seventy-seven, when Genevieve lost her seventy-nine-year-old brother, Jeff, she lost not only a valued companion but someone who encouraged and took pride in her accomplishments. Sister and brother had been separated as young children, but were reunited as adults. Their mother had been sick throughout their early years and several times, while she was hospitalized, they were placed together in temporary foster homes. They became extremely close during these placements. When their mother died, Genevieve was five and Jeff was seven. Jeff was placed in an orphanage and Genevieve in the home of an aunt in another state. The separation was difficult for both of them.

When they were adults and had families of their own they finally relocated near each other. Jeff then began to play an important role in his sister's life. He encouraged her interest in returning to school to become a teacher and applauded her accomplishments. He knew the obstacles she had had to overcome in order to achieve, and was generous in his praise and support of her efforts. Genevieve felt that he provided her with the acknowledgment and affirmation that she had failed to receive as a child and she thrived as a result.

He was also very generous to her. She treasures the jewelry that he gave her as well as a piece of sculpture he made. They afford her a feeling of closeness. She knows her brother would be happy to know the pleasure his gifts continue to give her.

As it turned out, my interview with Genevieve took place around the time of the third anniversary of Jeff's death. Genevieve noted that she was finding his loss more difficult as the years went by. She missed his companionship and his acknowledgment of her. She also found herself regretting that she had not sought more information from him about those years when they were still living with their mother and father. She has forgotten what it was like and knows he would remember. It would help each of them to share their history together. He was such a fine teacher. His interests were so broad and there were no subjects that he could not illuminate with his good ideas.

As we spoke, Genevieve recalled a day she and Jeff had spent together at a museum viewing the work of an artist that neither of them was familiar with and whom they immediately both loved. Thinking about that day reminded her of how little time one often gets to spend with siblings, especially if one is a girl with brothers. A girl, she added, is more likely to go shopping or have lunch with a sister than with a brother.

Genevieve valued what time she did spend with her brother. They had missed so much of each other while they were growing up. She had lost a precious part of her life when he died and feels cheated by his death. Both of their old ages would have been enriched by each other's presence.

Kay

Unlike Genevieve, Kay, who was in her fifties when I spoke with her, had had an extremely difficult life with her brother, Stanley, before he died at the age of fifty of an alcohol-related illness. Although, she loved him dearly, she experienced relief as well as sorrow when he died.

There were three children in Kay's family, each born two years apart. Kay was the eldest, Stanley the middle child, and Lynn the youngest. Their father was a disturbed, alcoholic, abusive man, and their mother was severely depressed. The parents fought constantly and finally separated when Kay was fourteen. Her mother moved the family to a new home and at that point Kay assumed the role of caretaker for her siblings.

As they moved into their teens, the three children also became alcoholics. Kay stopped drinking with the help of AA at the age of forty-six. Six years later Lynn stopped when she discovered she had hepatitis C. Stanley, however, continued to drink heavily.

Although they lived separately after their parents died, the siblings remained close and supported each other. Only Lynn married. They created a family together, sharing holidays and other family times. However, Stanley's drinking was a constant problem and the sisters were unsuccessful in their attempts to help him stop.

When he died after falling down a flight of stairs during an alcoholic delirium, Kay noted that she and her sister, though deeply saddened, were relieved. They no longer had to worry every day about his getting into trouble or having a car accident or harming someone. They were no longer constantly enraged at him for destroying himself, nor were they fruitlessly seeking ways to get him to stop his drinking.

According to Kay, he is always in their thoughts. They speak of him all the time. He was a very witty person and they joke a lot together, feeling that through laughter they can try to keep the best of their brother alive. They try hard to hold on to the good times they shared with him. She and her sister count themselves fortunate in having each other to share these good moments with.

It is not surprising that Stanley's death, though painful, was experienced as a relief by his sisters. There are many situations in which the death of a loved one, troubling as it may be, is a relief. Studies suggest, for example, that, in the case of widows or widowers who have been the primary caretakers for their ill spouses and watched them suffer, their deaths may be experienced as a relief (Bonanno et al. 2002; Carr, Wortman, and Wolff 2006) and their grief may be more muted.

Myrtle

Myrtle, a seventy-four-year-old woman, lost her sixty-nine-old sister, Sandra, three years before we spoke. Myrtle noted that at the time of her sister's death, she had not been particularly upset. Her sister had been ill for three years before she died. Prior to her illness the siblings had had a strained relationship, although they had been close as young children. They continued to be in contact, but they were frequently at odds with each other. Nonetheless, when Sandra became ill, Myrtle put their differences aside and helped to take care of her.

Although she was saddened by her sister's death, Myrtle did not feel her loss as strongly as she would have expected. It was only now, six years later, that she was feeling more troubled. She thought it might be because many of her friends were getting older and falling ill or dying. As an unmarried woman without children, she was feeling very much alone. Were Sandra still alive, perhaps they might have put old hurts aside and become better companions to each other.

While she was speaking with me, Myrtle recalled Sandra's funeral. She had not wanted to speak at it. However, before the rabbi began the prayers at the gravesite, she asked him to wait a minute and she began to sing the beginning of a Brahms lullaby. It was a song their mother sang to Sandra when she was a baby. Singing it was like bringing their mother close to Sandra and to her. It also brought back the days when she loved taking care of her baby sister, including singing to her. Thinking about the lullaby seemed to restore the feelings of love and closeness the two sisters had once experienced before they moved further apart. Perhaps, she said, she felt more than she realized upon Sandra's death, but had warded off the feelings until more recently. Did this mean that she was beginning to mourn Sandra now?

REMARKS

In this chapter I have tried to show how significant the loss of a sibling is, how profoundly the death of a brother or sister can affect the development and lives of surviving siblings, and to highlight some of the multiple determinants that help shape the impact of this loss. In some situations the emotional consequences of this life-altering event may be recognized at the time or soon after the loss. In others it may lie dormant for many years before emerging into full consciousness.

I have tried to show how critical it is that individuals who have lost a sibling have the opportunity to share their feelings and to be listened to, to be given accurate information about their brother's or sister's death, and to have their pain understood and tolerated. When, as is often the case, bereaved parents cannot provide the support their surviving children need, then it is imperative that there be someone else who can do so on a consistent basis. Sometimes a member of the family or a close friend may play this role. Many times the role falls to a therapist. George Hagman (1996) has termed such support during mourning as "environmental involvement" and emphasizes how its availability provides a necessary context for the difficult and complex process that mourning is and at the same time affirms the worth of the mourner himself.

In many situations, however, environmental support may not be sufficient. Several case vignettes have been offered to show the role that psychotherapy can play in helping an individual deal with the death of a sibling.

Only when we recognize the vital role that siblings can play in each other's development and lives can we can fully appreciate what a complex and unique impact the loss of a brother or sister can have on those siblings who survive. When we do, we shall recognize siblings as the true mourners they are.

Afterword

When I began this book in 2004, it was not unusual for psychoanalysts who wrote or spoke about siblings to begin their remarks by expressing surprise and regret over the dearth of attention being paid to the sibling relationship. These writers or speakers seemed to think of themselves as the first to explore the topic. This sense that the importance of siblings had been overlooked by psychoanalysts was reflected in the titles of at least two psychoanalytic conferences. In 2003 the Washington Square Institute for Psychotherapy and Mental Health in New York City titled their conference on siblings "Siblings: A Neglected Chapter in Psychoanalysis." In 2008, the Association for Psychoanalytic Medicine and the Academic Society of the Columbia University Center for Psychoanalytic Training and Research held an international symposium on siblings and titled it "Missing: Siblings in Psychoanalysis."

That siblings have frequently been neglected in psychoanalytic treatments seems to be borne out by many of the therapists who, following one of my presentations on the topic, have indicated how little attention their siblings received in their own treatment and how little attention they themselves accorded their patients' sibling experiences.

This book is a testimony, however, to the fact that siblings have received more attention than we have been led to believe. Clearly, they have been the subject of interest and study by members of a variety of fields and disciplines, including psychoanalysts. Yet, it appears that the information that has been gained has failed to give a prominent place to siblings in the psychoanalytic situation.

Psychoanalysts' lack of attention to the sibling relationship can be understood partly as a result of the central role that the parental Oedipus complex has held in psychoanalytic theory. This has sometimes made it difficult for therapists to recognize the role that sibling-related desires and animosities play in an individual's conflicts. Instead of viewing siblings as persons in their own right the tendency has been to see them primarily as displacement figures for their parents.

At a deeper level, Prophecy Coles (2003) has suggested that a neglect of siblings in psychoanalysis may represent an unconscious wish on the part of therapists to be the only child. By ignoring the importance of brothers and sisters, we may, I would suggest, be ridding ourselves of those siblings who have stood in the way of our being an only child.

If therapists' own unconscious sibling conflicts may play a role in their failure to give their patients' siblings a place in their treatment efforts, one wonders whether they may also partly account for the way members of the profession have often behaved toward each other. I refer here to the hostility and competition that has been relatively common in the past among psychoanalysts of different persuasions and how new theories are sometimes met with derision, not unlike the way older siblings scorn the arrival of their new brothers and sisters.

Yet the fact that an international conference was held by two traditional psychoanalytic organizations and that at least three books have been published on the topic by psychoanalytic publishers (Coles 2003, Lewin and Sharp 2009, Rowe 2007) during this decade suggest that siblings are beginning to gain greater attention among psychoanalysts.

This interest in siblings may be partly attributable to the influence object relations theories have had on psychoanalysis in general. A greater appreciation of the child's need to relate to others and the elaboration of the role of the relationship between the developing child and his or her partners as delineated in attachment theory, self psychology, developmental ego psychology, and other object-related theoretical perspectives have not only increased our understanding of the parent-child relationship, but have led to a greater interest in the roles that other important figures play in an individual's development. I think here of the recognition of the contributions marriage partners (Blanck and Blanck 1994) may make to each other's ongoing development or the role that children play in fostering their parents' development (Benedek 1959).

The challenge for clinicians is to determine how we can best apply the knowledge we are gaining about siblings in our clinical work. Through case examples, I have tried to show in this volume some of the ways we may draw on what we are learning in our treatment efforts. However, just as it took time to more fully apply our understandings of the mother-child relationship and the father-child relationship in the therapeutic situation, it is likely to take time for us to draw on our knowledge of the sibling relationship. For some of us, it may take more knowledge and experience in order that we may recognize sibling transferences and countertransferences as distinguished from parental transferences and countertransferences. What is important is that we recognize that the attachment to and love of a brother or sister can be a sustaining force and lead to identifications that can help to promote a sound sense of self, or may lead to a binding tie that compromises healthy individuation; that erotic fantasies and sexual play with a sibling may help pave the way for mature sexuality or seriously interfere with healthy sexual development; that rivalry and hostility between siblings may help foster individuation or lead to a lifetime of enmity; that abuse by a brother or sister may be as harmful as abuse by a parent; that siblings with special needs may have a profound effect on the development of their brothers and sisters and vice versa; that siblings in today's non-traditional families may face challenges that were unknown to the more traditional families that prevailed in the past; that cultural differences can influence the way siblings relate to each other; and that the loss of a sibling is a major loss and needs to be recognized as such by their families and by society as a whole.

Bibliography

Abarbanel, J. (1983). The revival of the sibling experience during the mother's second pregnancy. *The Psychoanalytic Study of the Child.* Eds. A. J. Solnit, R. Eissler, R. S. Neubauer. New Haven: Yale University Press. 38: 353–379.

Abend, S. M. (1984). Sibling love and object choice. *Psychoanalytic Quarterly* 53: 425–430.

Adler, A. (1928). Characteristics of the first, second and third child. *Children* 31: 14–25.

Agger, E. M. (1988). Psychoanalytic perspectives on sibling relationships. *Psychoanalytic Inquiry* 8: 3–30.

Ainslie, R. (1999). Twinship and twinning reactions in siblings. Pp. 55–68 in *Brothers and Sisters,* ed. S. Akhtar and S. Kramer. Northvale, N.J.: Jason Aronson.

Akhtar, S. (1995). A third individuation: Immigration, identity, and the psychoanalytic process. *Journal of the American Psychoanalytic Association* 43: 1051–108.

———. (2005). *Objects of Our Desire.* New York: Harmony Books.

Alcott, L. (1868–1869). *Little Women.* London: Roberts Brothers.

American Association of People with Disabilities. (nd). http://www.aapd.com/site/c .pvI1IkNWJqE/b.5406299/k.FBCC/Spotlight.htm (August 25, 2010).

American Society for Reproductive Medicine Ethics Committee. (2003). *Fertility and Sterility* 80: 1124–1130.

Apter, T. (2007). *The Sister Knot.* New York: Norton.

Arlow, J. (1972). The only child. *The Psychoanalytic Quarterly* 41: 507–534.

Ascherman, L. I,, and Safier, E. J. (1990). Sibling incest: A consequence of individual and family dysfunction. *Bulletin of the Menninger Clinic* 54: 311–322.

Austen, J. (1814). *Mansfield Park.* New York: Modern Library Paperback Edition, 2001.

Authors for the Live Organ Donor Consensus Group. (2000). Consensus statement on the live organ donor. *Journal of the American Medical Association* 284: 1–11.

Autism Network International. (n d). http://www. autreat. com/ (April 21, 2010).

Balsam, R. H. (1988). On being good: Internalized siblings with examples from late adolescent analyses. *Psychoanalytic Inquiry* 8: 66–81.

Bank, S. P. (1995). Before the last leaves fall: Sibling connections among the elderly. *Journal of Geriatric Psychiatry* 28: 183–295.

Bank, S. P., and Kahn, M. D. (1997). *The Sibling Bond.* New York: Basic Books.

Barbell, K. (1995). Is our family focus wide enough to include siblings? *Children's Voice* (Winter): 4–5, 24. http://www.casey.org/cnc/policy_issues/sibings.htm (June 8, 2006).

Barrie, J. M. (1916). *Peter Pan.* Kensington Gardens: Hodder and Stoughton.

———. (1913). *Margaret Ogilvy.* New York: London: Hodder and Stoughton.

Bell, Q. (1972). *Virginia Woolf: A Biography.* New York. Harcourt Brace Jovanovich.

Benedek, T. (1966). Toward the biology of the Depressive Constellation. Pp. 356–376 in *Psychoanalytic Investigations Selected Papers.* New York: Quadrangle/The New York Times Book Co., 1973.

———. (1959). Parenthood as a developmental phase: A contribution to the libido theory. *Journal of the American Psychoanalytic Association* 7:387–417.

Berzoff, J., Flanagan, L. M., and Hertz, P., eds. (1996). *Inside Out and Outside In.* Northvale, N.J: Jason Aronson,

Birkin, A. (1979). *J. M. Barrie and the Lost Boys.* New York: Clarkson N. Potter.

Blanck, G., and Blanck, R. (1968) *Marriage and Personal Development.* New York: Columbia University Press.

———. (1994). *Ego Psychology: Theory and Practice*, 2nd ed. New York: Columbia University Press.

Blos, P. (1979) *The Adolescent Passage.* New York: International Universities Press.

Blum, H. (1996). Seduction trauma and pathogenesis. *Journal of the American Psychoanalytic Association* 44: 1147–1164.

———. (2007). Little Hans: A centennial review and reconsideration. *Journal of the American Psychoanalytic Association* 55: 749–765.

Bonanno, G. A., Wortman, C. B., Lehman, D. R., et al. (2002). Resilience to loss and chronic grief: A prospective study from pre-loss to 18-months post-loss. *Journal of Personality and Social Psychology* 83: 1150–1164.

Bonaparte, M. (1953). *Female Sexuality.* New York: International Universities Press.

Bourget, D., and Gagne, P. (2006). Fratricide: A forensic psychiatric perspective. *Journal of the American Academy of Psychiatry and the Law* 34: 529–523.

Bowlby, J. (1980). *Attachment and Loss*, vol. 3, Loss, Sadness and Depression. New York: Basic Books.

Brinich, P. M. (1990). Adoption from the inside out: A psychoanalytic perspective. Pp. 42–63 in *The Psychology of Adoption*, ed. D. M. Brodzinsky and M. D. Schechter. New York: Oxford University Press.

Brodzinsky, D., and Brodzinksy, A. (1992). The impact of family structure on the adjustment of adopted children. *Child Welfare Journal* 71:1 (Jan–Feb): 69–76.

Brodzinsky, D. M., and Schechter, M., eds. (1990). *The Psychology of Adoption.* New York: Oxford University Press.

Brodzinsky, D. M., Lang, R., and Smith, D. W. (1995). Status and social conditions of parenting. Pp. 209–232 in *Handbook of Parenting*, vol. 3, ed. M. H. Bornstein. Hillsdale, N.J.: Lawrence Erlbaum.

Brown, J. R., Donelan-McCall, N., and Dunn, J. (1996). Why talk about mental states? The significance of children's conversations with friends, siblings, and mothers. *Child Development* 67: 836–849.

Bryant, B. (1992). Sibling caretaking: Providing emotional support during middle childhood. Pp. 55–69 in *Children's Sibling Relationships: Developmental and Clinical Issues*, ed. F. Boer and J. Dunn. Hillsdale, N.J.: *Publisher name.*

Burt, A., ed. (2006). *My Father Married Your Mother.* New York: W. W. Norton.

Buxbaum, E. (1949). *Your Child Makes Sense.* New York: International Universities Press.

Cain, A., and Cain, B. (1964). On replacing a child. *Journal of the American Academy of Child Psychiatry* 3: 443–456.

California Cryobank. (n.d.). http://www.sibling-registry.com/why.cfm (August 4, 2010).

Camp to Belong. (2004). Newsletter "*Belong.*" http://www.camptobelong.org (October 30, 2008).

Canavan, M. M., Meyer, W. J., and Higgs, D. C. (1992). The female experience of sibling incest. *Journal of Marital Therapy* 18: 129–142.

Carr D., Wortman, C. B., and Wolff, K. (2006). How older Americans die today. Pp. 49–78 in *Spousal Bereavement in Late Life*, ed. D. Carr, R. M. Nesse, and C. B. Wortman. New York: Springer.

Case Family Programs, http://www.casey.org (accessed October 30, 2008).

Charles, M. (1999). Sibling mysteries: Enactments of unconscious fears and fantasies. *Psychoanalytic Review* 86: 877–901.

Chomsky, N. (1982). *Language and Problems of Knowledge.* Cambridge, Mass.: M. I. T. Press.

Chung, I. (1999). Cultural competence in the clinical situation. *Psychoanalytic Social Work* 6: 87–95.

Chused, J. F. (2007). Little Hans "analyzed" in the twenty-first century. *Journal of the American Psychoanalytic Association* 55: 767–778.

Cicerelli, V. J. (1995). *Sibling Relationships across the Life Span.* New York: Plenum.

Clemetson, L., and. Nixon, R. (2006) Breaking through adoption's racial barrier. *New York Times*, August 17, pp. A1, A22.

Coates, S. W. (2004). Bowlby and Mahler: Their lives and theories. *Journal of the American Psychoanalytic Association* 52: 571–601.

Cohen, R. (2005). The ethicist. *The New York Times Magazine,* November 27, p. 32.

Coles, P. (2003). *The Importance of Sibling Relationships in Psychoanalysis.* New York: Karnac.

———. (2007). Transgenerational conflicts between sisters. *British Journal of Psychotherapy*, 23: 562–574.

Colonna, A. B., and Newman, L. M. (1983). Psychoanalytic literature on siblings. *Psychoanalytic Study of the Child.* New Haven: Yale University Press. 38: 285–310.

Conley, D. (2004). *The Pecking Order.* New York: Pantheon.

Cooper, C. R., Denner, J., and Lopez, E. M. (1999). Cultural brokers: helping Latino children on pathways towards success. *The Future of Children When School Is Out* 9: 51–57. David and Lucille Packard Foundation.

Cooper, C. R., Jackson, E. J., Azmitia, M., Lopez, E. M., and Dunbar, N. (n.d.). *Bridging Students Multiple Worlds: African American and Latino Youth in Academic Outreach Programs.* http://www.bridgingworlds.org/pdfs/paper6.pdf (31 August 2010).

Cooper, S. L., and Glazer, E. S. (1998). *Choosing Assisted Reproduction.* Indianapolis: Perspective Press.

Dali, S. (1942). *The Secret Life of Salvador Dali.* Mineola, NY: Dover.

Dalsimer, K. (1979). From preadolescent tomboy to early adolescent girl: An analysis of Carson McCullers' *The Member of the Wedding. Psychoanalytic Study of the Child.* New Haven: Yale University Press. 34: 445–461.

Daly, M., and Wilson, M. (1998). *The Truth about Cinderella: A Darwinian View of Parental Love.* New Haven: Yale University Press.

Dawson, J. M., and Langan, P. A. (1994). *Murder in Families.* Special Report. U. S. Department of Justice. http://bjs.ojp.usdoj.gov/content/pub/pdf/mf.pdf (August 30, 2010).

Defoe, D. (1772). *The Fortunes and Misfortunes of the Famous Moll Flanders.* London: Constable, 1923.

De Groef, J., and Heineman, E. (1999). *Psychoanalysis and Mental Handicap.* London: Free Association Books.

DeSalvo, L. (1989). *Virginia Woolf: The Impact of Childhood Sexual Abuse on Her Life and Work.* Boston: Beacon.

De Vita-Raeburn, E. (2004). *The Empty Room.* New York: Scribner.

Disabled Online. (n.d.). Organizations for People with Disabilities. http://www.disabledonline.com/link-directory-organizations (August 15, 2010).

Doka, K. J., and Davidson, J. D. (1998). *Living with Grief: Who We Are, How We Grieve.* Philadelphia: Brunner/Mazel.

Doman, G. (2005). *What to Do about Your Brain-Injured Child.* Garden City Park, N.Y.: Square One.

Donor Sibling Registry. (n.d.).http://www.donorsiblingregistry.com (September 10, 2007).

Dunn, J., and Kendrick C. (1982) *Siblings: Love, Envy and Understanding.* Cambridge, Mass.: Harvard University Press.

Dunn, J., and McGuire, S. (1994). Young children's nonshared experiences. A summary of studies in Cambridge and Colorado. Pp. 111–28 in *Separate Social Worlds of Siblings: The Impact of Nonshared Environment on Development*, eds. Hetherington, E. M., Reiss, D., and Plomin, R. Hillsdale, NJ: Erbaum.

Dunn, J., and Plomin, R. (1990). *Separate Lives: Why Siblings Are So Different.* New York: Basic Books.

Dwyer, J., and Vig, E. (1995). *Rethinking Transplantation between Siblings.* Hastings Center Report 25, no. 6: 7–12.

Edward, J. (2003). The loving side of the sibling bond: A force for growth or conflict. *Issues in Psychoanalytic Psychology* 25: 27–43.

Eliade, M., ed. (1987). *The Encyclopedia of Religion.* New York: MacMullen.

Eliot, G. (1860). *The Mill on the Floss.* London: Pan Books, 1975.

Ellison, B., and Ellison, J. (2001). *Miracles Happen.* New York: Hyperion.

Erickson, E. (1963). *Childhood and Society*. New York: W. W. Norton and Company.

Feigelman, W. (2000). "Adjustments of transracially adopted young adults." *Clinical Social Work Journal* 17: 165–68.

Felberbaum, S. (2007). *Poetic License: Mourning, a Parallel Process Presentation*. National Membership Committee on Psychoanalysis in Social Work Conference, Chicago, March 9.

Finklehor, D. (1980). Sex among siblings. *Archives of Sexual Behavior* 9: 171–194.

Fliess. W. (1986) *The Complete Letters of Sigmund Freud to Wilhelm Fliess*. 1888–1904. Trans. J. Masson. Belknap: Harvard University Press.

Flomenhaft, D. (2006). *The Forgotten Ones: The Grief Experience of Adult Siblings of WTC Victims*. Ph.D. dissertation, New York University, December.

Fonagy, P. (1998). An attachment theory approach to treatment of the difficult patient. *Bulletin of the Menninger Clinic* 62(2): 147–169.

———. (2001). *Attachment Theory and Psychoanalysis*. New York: Other Press.

Fox, R. C., and Swazey, J. P. (1992). Leaving the field. *The Hasting Center Report*. 22 (5): 2–15. http://www.jstor.org/stable/3562136 (August 31, 2010).

Freedman, A. (1983). Psychoanalysis of a patient who received a kidney transplant. *Journal of the American Psychoanalytic Association* 31: 917–956.

Freud, A. (1961). *The Ego and Mechanisms of Defense*. London: Hogarth Press.

Freud, A., and Dann, S. (1951). An experiment in group upbringing. *Psychoanalytic Study of the Child*. New Haven: Yale University Press. 6: 127–168.

Freud, E. L., ed. (1960). *Letters of Sigmund Freud*, trans. T. Stern and J. Stern. New York: Basic Books.

Freud, S. (1887–1904). *The Complete Letters of Sigmund Freud to Wilhelm Fliess*, trans. J. M. Masson. Cambridge Mass.: Harvard University Press.

———. (1900a). The Interpretation of dreams. *Standard Edition*. London: Hogarth Press. 4:1–338.

———. (1900b). The Interpretation of dreams. *Standard Edition*. London: Hogarth Press. 5: 339–686.

———. (1909a). Notes upon a case of obsessional neurosis. *Standard Edition*: London Hogarth Press. 10: 153–249.

———. (1909b). Analysis of a phobia in a five-year-old boy. *Standard Edition*. London: Hogarth Press. 10: 1–149.

———. (1909c). Family romances. *Standard Edition*. London: Hogarth Press. 9: 236–241.

———. (1910a) The Origin and Development of Psychoanalysis. Chicago: Chicago Gateway Edition. 1965.

———. (1910b). A special type of choice of object made by men. *Standard Edition*. London: Hogarth Press. 11:163–175.

———. (1914). On narcissism: An introduction. *Standard Edition*. London: Hogarth Press. 14: 67–102.

———. (1915–1916). Introductory lectures on psycho-analysis: The archaic feature and infantilism of dreams. *Standard Edition*. London: Hogarth Press. 15: 3–239.

———. (1916). Some character-types met in psycho-analytic work. *Standard Edition*. London: Hogarth Press. 14: 311–333.

———. (1916–1917). Introductory lectures on psychoanalysis. The development of the libido. *Standard Edition*. London: Hogarth Press. 16: 243–463.

———. (1917a). General theory of the neuroses. *Standard Edition*. London: Hogarth Press. 16: 320–339.

———. (1917b). Mourning and melancholia. *Standard Edition*. London: Hogarth Press. 14: 239–258.

———. (1918). From the history of an infantile neurosis. *Standard Edition*. London: Hogarth Press. 17: 3–122.

———. (1920). Beyond the Pleasure Principle. *Standard Edition*. London: Hogarth Press. 18: 7–64.

———. (1921). Group psychology and the analysis of the ego. *Standard Edition*. London: Hogarth Press. 18: 67–143.

———. (1923). The ego and the id. *Standard Edition*. London: Hogarth Press. 19: 3–59.

———. (1925). An autobiographical study. *Standard Edition*. London: Hogarth Press. 20: 3–74.

———. (1926). Inhibitions, symptoms and anxiety. *Standard Edition*. London: Hogarth Press. 20: 77–174.

———. (1931). Female sexuality. *Standard Edition*. London: Hogarth Press. 21: 223–243.

———. (1940 [1938]). An outline of psycho-analysis. *Standard Edition*. London: Hogarth Press., 23: 141–207.

Gaddini, R. (2005). *Body Ego and Powerlessness and Aggression*. Paper delivered at the Clinical Social Work Conference, May.

Gartrell, N., Banks, A., and Reed, N. (2000). The National Lesbian Family Study: 3. Interviews with mothers of five year olds. *American Journal of Orthopsychiatry* 70 (4): 542–548.

Gergely, G. (2000). Reapproaching Mahler: New perspectives on normal autism, symbiosis, splitting and libidinal constancy from cognitive developmental theory. *Journal of the American Psychoanalytic Association* 48: 1198–1228.

Gibson, M. (2004). Melancholy objects. *Mortality* 9: 285–299.

Gold, D. T. (1987). Siblings in old age: Something special. *Canadian Journal of Aging* 6: 199–215.

Golombok, S., Brewaeys, A., Cook, R., et al. (1996). Children: The European study of assisted reproduction families: Family functioning and child development. *European Society of Human Reproduction and Embryology* 11: 2324–2331.

Golombok, S., Brewaeys, A., Giavazzi, M. T., Guerra, D., MacCallum, F., and Rust, J. (2002). The European study of assisted reproduction families: The transition to adolescence. *Human Reproduction* 17: 830–840.

Golombok, S., Cook, R., Bish, A., and Murray, C. (2008). Families created by the new reproductive technologies: Quality of parenting and social and emotional development of the children. *Child Development* 66: 285–298.

Golombok, S., Spencer, A., and Rutter, M. (1983). Children in lesbian and single–parent households: Psychosexual and psychiatric appraisal. *Journal of Child Psychology and Psychiatry* 24: 551–572.

Gombosi, P. G. (1998). Parents of autistic children. *Psychoanalytic Study of the Child* New Haven: Yale University Press. 53: 254–275.

Good, M. J. (1996). Suggestion and veridicality in the reconstruction of sexual trauma, or can a bait of suggestion catch a carp of falsehood. *Journal of the American Psychoanalytic Association* 44: 1189–1224.

Gottesfeld, M., and Pharis, M. (1977). *Profiles in Social Work.* New York: Human Sciences.

Green, A. (1999). *The Dead Mother: The Work of Andre Green,* trans. Gregorio Kohn. New York: Routledge.

Grosskurth, P. (1985). *Melanie Klein, Her World and Her Work.* London: Maresfield Library.

———. (1997). *Byron, the Flawed Angel.* New York: Houghton Mifflin

Hagman, G. (1996). The role of the other in mourning. *Psychoanalytic Quarterly* 65: 327–357.

Hardy, M. S. (2001). Physical aggression and sexual behavior among siblings: A retrospective study. *Journal of Family Violence* 16: 255–68.

Hartmann, H. (1939). *Ego Psychology and the Problem of Adaptation.* New York: International Universities Press. 1958.

Herman, J. (1992). *Trauma and Recovery.* New York: Basic Books.

Hetherington, E. M., and Clingenpeel, W. G.. (1992). Coping with marital transitions: A family system perspective. *Monographs of the Society of Research in Child Development* 57: 1–14.

Hetherington, E. M., Henderson, S. H., and Reiss, D. (1999). Adolescent siblings in stepfamilies: Family functioning and adolescent adjustment. *Monographs of the Society for Research in Child Development* 64: 222–247.

Hochman, G., Feathers-Acuna, E., and Huston. (1991) A National Adoption Center for the National Adoption Information Clearinghouse. http://naic/acf.hhsgov (March 17, 2006).

Hoffman, E. (1989). *Lost in Translation.* New York: Viking Penguin.

Hoffman, I. Z. (2009). Doublethinking our way to "scientific" legitimacy: The dessication of human experience. *Journal of the American Psychoanalytic Association* 57: 1043–1069.

Hoopes, J. (1982) *Prediction in Child Development: A Longitudinal Study of Adoptive and Nonadoptive Families.* New York: Child Welfare League of America.

Hotaling, G. T., Straus, M. A., and Lincoln, A. J. (1990). Intrafamily violence and crime and violence outside the family. Pp. 425–470 in *Physical Violence in American Families: Risk Factors and Adaptations to Violence in 8, 145 Families,* ed. M. S. Straus and R. J. Gelles. New Brunswick, N.J.: Transaction.

Hudson, G. A. (1999). *Sibling Love and Incest in Jane Austen's Fiction.* New York: St. Martin's Press.

Hushion, K. (2009). Observations on parental idealization of their adopted children and the vicissitudes of this phenomenon in families when adopted and biological children grow up together. Panel discussion presented at the 2009 American Association Conference for Psychoanalysis in Clinical Social, New York City, March 1.

Hushion, K., Sherman, S. B., and Siskind, D, eds. (2006). *Understanding Adoption.* New York: Jason Aronson.

Jacobs, T. J. (1988). On having an adopted sibling: Some psychoanalytic observations. *International Review of Psycho–Analysis.* 15: 25–35.

Jacobson, E. (1964). *The Self and the Object World.* New York: International Universities Press.

Jamison, K. R. (2004). *Exuberance.* New York: Knopf.

Jane Addams Hull House Association. (2001). Executive Summary. http://www.hull house.org/programsandcenters/program/neighbortoneighbor.html (July 8, 2007).

Johnson, G. (1998). *Invisible Writer: A Biography of Joyce Carol Oates.* New York: Penguin Press.

Jones, E. (1911). On "dying together." *Essays on Applied Psychoanalysis.* 2: 9–15. London: Hogarth, 1951.

Joseph, E., and Tabor, P. J. (1961). The simultaneous analysis of a pair of identical twins and the twinning reaction. *Psychoanalytic Study of the Child.* New York: International Universities Press 16: 275–299.

Kanter, J., ed. (2004). Face to face with children. *The Life and Work of Clare Winnicott.* London: H. Karnac.

Kellman, S. G. (2005). *Redemption: The Life of Henry Roth.* New York: Norton.

Kernberg, P. F., and Richards, A. K. (1988). Siblings of preadolescents: Their role in development. *Psychoanalytic Inquiry* 8: 51–65.

Kiell, N., ed. (1983). *Blood Brothers: Siblings as Writers.* New York: International Universities Press.

Klagsbrun, F. (1972). *Mixed Feelings: Love, Hate, Rivalry, and Recollection among Brothers and Sisters.* New York: Bantam Books.

Klein, M. (1937). *The Psycho-Analysis of Children.* London: Hogarth.

Kohut, H. (1971). *The Analysis of the Self.* New York: University of Chicago Press.

———. (1984) *How Does Analysis Cure?* Chicago, London: The University of Chicago Press.

Kottick, J. (2005). Therapists, anger, despair, cynicism. Pp. 84–102 in *Frozen Dreams,* ed. A. Rosen and J. Rosen. Hillsdale, N.J.: The Analytic Press.

Kraus, J. (Autumn, 1978). Family structure as a factor in the adjustment of adopted children. *British Journal of Social Work.* 8:327–337.

Krieder, R. M. (2008). *Living Arrangements of Children.* 2004. U. S. Department of Commerce, Economics and Statistics Administration, U. S. Census Bureau.

Kris, M., and Ritvo, S. (1983). Parents and siblings: Mutual influences. *Psychoanalytic Study of the Child* New Haven: Yale University Press. 38: 311–324.

Kulish, N. M. (1989), Mourning a lost childhood: The problem of Peter Pan. Pp. 82–100 in *The Problem of Loss and Mourning: Psychoanalytic Perspectives,* ed. D. R. Dietrich and P. C. Shabad. Madison, CT: International Universities Press.

Ladner, J. A. (1977). *Mixed Families Adopting across Racial Boundaries.* Garden City: Anchor.

Ledesma, R. (2003). Life on the border: Latinas and American-Indian women. Pp. 91–117 in *Therapies with Women in Transition,* ed. J. Sanville and E. B. Ruderman. Madison Conn.: International Universities Press.

Leichtman, M. (1985). Influence of older siblings on the separation–individuation process. *Psychoanalytic Study of the Child.* New Haven, Yale University Press. 40: 111–162.

Levick, S. E. (2004). *Clone Being: Exploring the Psychological and Social Dimensions.* New York: Rowman & Littlefield Publishers.

Levy, D. M. (1937). *Studies in Sibling Rivalry.* New York: American Orthopsychiatric Association.

Levy-Warren, M. H. (2001). A clinical look at knowing and telling. Pp. 251–275 in *Complex Adoption and Assisted Reproductive Technology,* eds. V. B. Shapiro, J. R. Shapiro, and I. H. Paret. New York: Guilford Press.

Lewin, V., and Sharp, B. eds. (2009). *Siblings in Development.* London: Karnac Books Ltd.

Lewontin, R. (1980). Honest Jim Watson's big thriller about DNA. *Chicago Sunday Times,* Book Week, 25, 1968. Pp. 1–2.

Live Organ Donor Consensus Group. (n.d.). http://www.kidney.org/transplantation/livingdonors/pdf/jama_article.pdf (April 21, 2010).

Mahler, M. (1977). *Psychoanalytic Movement.* Oral History Research Office. New York: Columbia University.

Mahler, M., Pine, F., and Bergman, A. (1975). *The Psychological Birth of the Human Infant: Symbiosis and Individuation.* New York: Basic Books.

Mann, T. (1912). The blood of the Walsungs. Pp. 255–284 in *Death in Venice and Other Tales,* trans. J. Neugroschel. New York: Penguin Putnam, 1998.

Marchand, L. A. (1973–1974). *Byron's Letters and Journals.* April 15, 1814. London: John Murray.

Marquardt, E., Glenn, N. D., and Clark, K. (2010). *My Daddy's Name Is Donor: A New Study of Young Adults Conceived through Sperm Donation.* New York: Institute for American Values.

McCullers, C. (1946). *The Member of the Wedding.* Boston: Houghton Mifflin.

Mehta, P. (1997). The emergence, conflicts and integration of the bi-cultural self: Psychoanalysis of an adolescent daughter of south Asian immigrant parents. Presentation at the Winter Conference of the American Psychoanalytic Association, New York City, December 20.

Merchlinsky. J. (2007). *One Sister's Story.* The Organization of Parents Through Surrogacy. http://www.opts. com/onestory.htm (August 4, 2010).

Meyer, D., ed. (2009). *Thicker Than Water.* Bethesda, Md.: Woodbine House.

Meyer, M. N. (n.d.). *States' Regulation of Assisted Reproductive Technologies.* The Nelson A. Rockfeller Institute of Government. http://www.rockinst.org/pdf/health care/2009-07-States Regulation_ART07.pdf (August 13, 2010).

Meyers, H. (2008). *Some Comments About Sisters Close in Age. Unbreakable closeness, Unavoidable Hostility.* Symposium. Sponsored by the Association for Psychoanalytic Medicine and the Society of the Columbia Center for Psychoanalytic Training and Research.

Miller, A. (1968). *The Price.* New York: Viking Books.

Miller, E. H. (1982). In Memoriam: Allie Caulfield in *The Catcher in the Rye. Mosaic* 15 (1): 129–140.

Minuchin, S. (1974). *Families and Family Therapy*. Cambridge, Mass.: Harvard University Press.

Mishne, J. (2002). *Multiculturalism and the Therapeutic Process*. New York: Guilford.

Mitchell, J. (2003). *Siblings*. Cambridge: Polity Press.

Mitchell, S. (1996). *Genesis*. New York: HarperCollins.

Modell, A. H. (1965) On having the right to a life: An aspect of the super-ego's development. *International Journal of Psychoanalysis* 46: 323–31.

Murdock, G. P. (1960). The universality of the nuclear family. Pp. 37–44 in *The Family*, ed. N. W. Bell and E. F. Vogel. Glencoe, Ill.: The Free Press.

Murray, C. (2003). Children raised in assisted human reproduction families: The evidence. Pp. 99–121 in *Assisted Human Reproduction*, ed. Philadelphia: Whurr.

Murray, J. S. (2000) Attachment theory and adjustment difficulties in siblings of children with cancer. *Issues in Mental Health Nursing* 21: 149–169.

Nachman, P., and Thompson, A. (1998). *You and Your Only Child: The Joys and Myths and Challenges*. New York: HarperCollins.

Nagera, H. (1967). *Vincent Van Gogh: A Psychological Study*. New York: International Universities Press.

Naipul, V. S. (2004). *Magic Seeds*. New York: Knopf.

National Autism Association. (n.d.). http://www/nationalautismassociation.org/familyfirst.php (November 12, 2009).

Nazario, S. (2006). *Enrique's Journey*. New York: Random House.

Neubauer, P. B. (1982). Rivalry, envy and jealousy. *Psychoanalytic Study of the Child* 37: 121–142.

———. (1983) The Importance of the Sibling Experience. *The Psychoanalytic Study of the Child*. New Haven: Yale University Press. 38: 325–336.

Neugeboren, J. (1997). *Imagining Robert*. Piscataway, N.J.: Rutgers University Press.

———. (1999). *Transforming Madness: New Lives for People Living with Mental Illness*. New York: William Morrow.

Newberger, J. (2001) *Growing Up Together*, published on Connect for Kids http://www.connectforkids.org/node/280/print (November 27, 2006).

New York Penal Law Section 255. 25 (n.d.). http://www.lectlaw.com/files/sex09.htm (August 8, 2010).

Neiderland, W. (1965). Narcissistic ego impairment in patients with early physical malformations. *Psychoanalytic Study of the Child*. 20: 518–534.

———. (1968). Clinical observations on the "survivor syndrome." *International Journal of Psychoanalysis*. 49: 313–315.

Northeast Ohio Adoption Services. (n.d.). http://www.noas.com/ (August 3, 2010).

Nuckolls, C. W. (1993). *Siblings in South Asia: Brothers and Sisters in Cultural Context*. New York: Guilford.

Nye, C. (2005). Conversations with Suwanrang: The treatment relationship in cultural context. *Clinical Social Work Journal* 33: 37–53.

Ōe, K. (1968). *A Personal Matter*. New York: Grove Press.

———. (1990). *A Quiet Life*. New York: Grove Press.

———. (1996) *A Healing Family*. Tokyo, New York: Kodansha International.

Olshansky, S. (1962). Chronic sorrow: A response to having a mentally defective child. *Social Casework* 43: 190–193.

Packman, W., Horsley, H., Davies, B., and Kramer, R. (2006). Continuing bonds and sibling bereavement. *Death Studies* 30 (9): 817–841.

Parens, H. (1988), Siblings in early childhood: Some direct observational findings. *Psychoanalytic Inquiry* 8: 31–50.

———. (1999). Twins and other siblings. Pp. 55–68 in *Brothers and Sisters*, ed. S. Akhtar and S. Kramer. Northvale, N.J.: Jason Aronson,

Parinaud, A. (1976). *The Unspeakable Confessions of Salvador Dali: As Told to Andre Parinaud.* New York: William Morrow.

Parmar, G., Wu, J. W. Y., and Chan, K. W. (2003). Bone marrow donation in childhood: One donor's perspective. *Psycho-Oncology* 12: 91–94.

Patterson, C. J. (1992). Children of lesbian and gay parents. *Child Development* 63: 1025–1042.

Pavoa, J. M. (2005). *The Family of Adoption.* Boston: Beacon Press.

Pelzer, R. B. (2005). *A Brother's Journey.* New York: Warner Books.

Perez Foster, R., Moskowitz, M., and Javier, R. A. (1996). *Reaching across Boundaries of Culture and Class.* Northvale, N.J.: Jason Aronson.

Phillips, R. S. C. (1999). Intervention with siblings of children with developmental disabilities from economically disadvantaged families. *Families in Society: The Journal of Contemporary Human Services* 80(6): 569–577.

Picoult, J. (2004). *My Sister's Keeper.* New York: Atria Books.

Pine, F. (2004). Mahler's concept of symbiosis and separation–individuation: Revisited, reevaluated, refined. *Journal of the American Psychoanalytic Association* 52: 511–533.

Pogrebin, R. (1998). A deep silence of 60 years and an even older secret. *New York Times*, May 16, pp. B9, B12.

Polit, D. F., and Falbo, T. (1987). Only children and personality development: A quantitative review. *Journal of Marriage and the Family* 49: 309–34.

Pollock, G. H. (1978). On siblings, childhood sibling loss, and creativity. *Annual Psychoanalysis* 6: 443–482.

Provence, S., and Solnit, A. J. (1983). Development-promoting aspects of the sibling experience. *The Psychoanalytic Study of the Child.* New Haven: Yale University Press. 38: 337–351.

Raible, J. (2005) *Sharing the spotlight: the non-adopted siblings of transracial adoptees.* Ph.D. dissertation, University of Massachusetts, Amherst.

———. (2006). The lifelong impact of transracial adoption: Learning from adoptees and their non-adoptive siblings. Keynote address, 4th Biennial Adoption Conference, St. John's University, New York City, October 14.

Rainbows. (2010). http://www.rainbows.org/statistics.html (April 13, 2010).

Rappaport, J. (1994). Sibling suicide: Its effects on the wish for a child and on the maternal transference/countertransference interaction. *Journal of Clinical Psychoanalysis* 3: 241–258.

Register, C. (1991). *"Are Those Kids Yours?" American Families with Children Adopted from Other Countries.* New York: The Free Press.

Reich, A. (1932). Analysis of a case of brother-sister incest. Pp. 1–22 in *Annie Reich: Psychoanalytic Contributions*. New York: International Universities Press, 1973.

Richards, A., and Kernberg, P. (1988). Siblings of preadolescents: Their role in development. *Psychoanalytic Inquiry* 8: 31–50.

Riggs, D. (1999). Sibling ties are worth preserving. *Adoptalk: New York State Citizens' Coalition for Children, Inc.* Reproduced with permission from Spring 1999 issue of Adoptalk, published by North American Council on Adoptable Children. http://www.nysccc.org/Siblings/sibties.htm (September 3, 2007).

Rosato, J. L. (2009). Regulating assisted reproductive technology: Avoiding extremes. Pp. 295–305 in *The Penn Center Guide to Bioethics*, ed. V. Ravitsky, A. Fiester, and A. L. Caplan. New York: Springer Publishing Co.

Rosen, L. S. (2002). The trauma of life-threatening illness: End-stage renal disease. *Dialysis and Transplantation* 31: 2950301.

Roskill, M., ed. (1986). *The Letters of Vincent Van Gogh*. New York: Atheneum

Rosner, S. (1985). On the place of siblings in psychoanalysis. *Psychoanalytic Review* 72: 457–477.

Ross, L. F. (1993). Moral grounding for the participation of children as organ donors. *The Journal of Law, Medicine and Ethics* 21: 251–257.

Roth, H. (1934). *Call It Sleep*. New York: Farrar, Straus and Giroux, 1991.

———. (1994) *Mercy of a Rude Stream* (1994). New York: St. Martins Press.

Rowe, D. (2007). *My Dearest Enemy: My Dangerous Friend*. London: Routledge.

Safer, J. (2002). *The Normal One*: New York: The Free Press.

Salinger, J. D. (1951). *The Catcher in the Rye*. Boston, New York: Little Brown and Company.

Sandler, J. (1960). The background of safety. *International Journal of Psychoanalysis*. 41: 352–356.

———. (1976). Countertransference and role-responsiveness. *International Review of Psycho-Analysis* 3: 43–47.

Schechter. R. A. (1999). The meaning and interpretation of sibling transference in the clinical situation. *Issues in Psychoanalytic Psychology* 21: 1–10.

Schooler, J. (2000) When siblings are separated. Adapted from a training curriculum entitled *Changing Hats: When Foster Parents Adopt*. Columbus, Ohio: Columbus Ohio Child Welfare Training Program/Institute for Human Services.

Schooler, J. (2002). When siblings are separated. Ithaca, NY. : New York State Citizens' Coalition for Children, Inc. http://www.nysccc.org/Siblings/adopfamsibs .htm (16 Dec. 2008).

Schore, A. N. (2003). *Affect Regulation and the Repair of the Self*. New York: Norton.

Seymour–Smith, M. (1989). *Rudyard Kipling*. London: Macdonald/Queen Anne Press.

Shakespeare, W. (between 1603–1607) *Macbeth*. New Haven, London: Yale University Press, 2005.

Shapiro, V. B., Shapiro, J. R., and Paret, I. H. (2001). *Complex Adoption and Assisted Reproductive Technology*. New York: Guilford Press.

Sharpe, S. A., and Rosenblatt, A. D. (1944). Oedipal siblings triangles. *Journal of the American Psychoanalytic Association* 42: 491–523.

Shengold, L. (1989). *Soul Murder*. New York. Ballantine Books.

Sherman, S. B. (2006). Identity and identification: being different and the quest to belong in an adopted young adult. Pp. 149–161 in *Understanding Adoption*, ed. K. Husion, S. B. Sherman, and D. Siskind. New York: Jason Aronson.

Sherwin–White, S. (2007). Freud on brothers and sisters: a neglected topic. *Journal of Child Psychotherapy* 33: 4020

Shlonsky, A. R., Elkins, Bellamy, J., et al (2005). The Other Kin: Setting the course for research, policy, and practice with siblings in foster care. *Children and Youth Service Review* 27:697–716

Sibs Place. http://www.sibsplace.org. Accessed February 7, 2009.

Sibling Support Project. http://www.siblingsupport.org. Accessed November 20, 2008.

Siegel, D. J. (1999). *The Developing Mind* New York: Guilford Press.

Simon, R. J., and Alsten, H. (2000). *Adoption across Borders*. Lanham, Md.: Rowman & Littlefield Publishers,

Simon, R. J., and Roorda, R. M. (2000). *In Their Own Voices: Transracial Adoptees Tell Their Stories*. New York: Columbia University Press.

Simpson, E. (1987). *Orphans: Real and Imaginary*. New York: Widenfeld and Nicholson.

Single Mothers by Choice. (n.d.). http://www.singlemothersbychoice.com/sibling.html (4 May 2010).

Siskind, D. (2006). The World of Adoption: An Introduction. Pp. 3–9 in *Understanding Adoption*, ed. K. Hushion, S. B. Sherman, and D. Siskind. New York: Jason Aronson.

Solnit, A. J. (1983). The sibling experience. *Psychoanalytic Study of the Child*. 8: 281–284. New Haven: Yale University Press.

Stepansky, P. (1988). *The Memoirs of Margaret S. Mahler*. New York: Free Press.

Stewart, R. B. (1983). Sibling attachment relationships: Child-infant interaction in the strange situation. *Developmental Psychology*. 19: 192–199.

Stocker, C. Dunn, J., and Plomin, R. (1989). Sibling relationships: Links with child temperament, maternal behavior, and family structure. *Child Development*. 60: 715–727.

Straus, M. S., and Gelles, R. J., eds. (1990) *Physical Violence in American Families: Risk Factors and Adaptation to Violence in 8,145 Families*. New Brunswick, NJ: Transaction.

Straus, M. A., Gelles, R. J., and Steinmetz, S. K. (1980). *Behind Closed Doors*. Garden City: Anchor Press/Doubleday.

Sullivan, P. M., and Knutson, J. F. (2000). Maltreatment and disabilities: A population based epidemiological study. *Child Abuse and Neglect* 24: 1257–1273.

Sulloway, F. (1996). *Born to Rebel Birth Order, Family Dynamics, and Creative Lives*. New York: Pantheon Books.

Thompson, C. L. (1996). The African-American patient in psychodynamic treatment. In *Reaching across Boundaries of Culture and Class*, ed. R. Perez Foster, M. Moskowitz, and R. A. Javier. Northvale, N.J.: Jason Aronson.

Twemlow, S., Fonagy, P., and Sacco, F. C. (2005). A developmental approach to mentalizing communities: I. A model for social change. *Bulletin of the Menninger Clinic* 69 (4): 265–281.

U.S. Census Bureau (2007). Single–parent households showed little variation since 1994, Census Bureau reports. http://www.census.gov/Press-Release/www/releases/archives/families_households/009742.html (October 1, 2009).

U.S. Department of Health and Human Services. Administration for Children and Families. Administration on Children, Youth and Families, Children's Bureau. AF-CARS Report, (2009) http://www.acf.hhs.gov/programs/cb/stats_research/afcars/tar/report16. htm (August 3, 2010).

U.S. Department of State. http://www.adoption.state.gov/news/totalchart.html (November 10, 2010).

Valenstein, A. F. (1973). On attachment to painful feelings and the negative therapeutic reaction. *Psychoanalytic Study of the Child* 28: 365–392.

Valone, K. (2005). Consilient psychoanalysis. *Psychoanalytic Psychology* 22(2): 189–206.

Van Gogh Bonger, J. (1913). Memoir of Vincent Van Gogh. Pp. 33–85 in *The Letters of Vincent Van Gogh*, ed. Mark Roskill. New York: Atheneum Press, 1986.

Van Sise, M. (2007). *The Effect of Sibling Interactions on the Social Skill Development of Children with PDD*. October 18, 2008. Stony Brook University, New York: The Cody Center for Autism and Developmental Disabilities.

Vivona, J. M. (2007). Sibling differentiation and identity development, and the lateral dimension of psychic life. *Journal of the American Psychoanalytic Association* 55: 1191–1215.

———. (2008). Transference and the lateral dimension of psychic life. Paper presented at Missing: Siblings in Psychoanalysis, Symposium sponsored by the Association for Psychoanalytic Medicine, New York, November 8.

———. (2010). Siblings, transference, and the lateral dimension of psychic life. *Psychoanalytic Psychology* 27: 8–26.

Volkan, V. D. (1972). The linking objects of pathological mourners. *Archives of General Psychiatry* 27 (2): 215–221.

Volkan, V. D., and Ast, G. (1997) *Siblings in the Unconscious and Psychopathology*. Madison, Conn.: International Universities Press.

Vonk, M. E. (2001). Cultural competence for transracial adoptive parents. *Social Work* 46: 246–255.

Waelder, R. (1936). The principle of multiple function. *Psychoanalytic Quarterly* 5: 45–62.

Waitman, A., and Conboy-Hill, S. eds., (1992). *Psychotherapy and Mental Handicap*. Newbury Park, Calif.: Sage Publications.

Wakefield, J. C. (2007). Attachment and sibling rivalry in Little Hans: The fantasy of the two giraffes revisited. *Journal of the American Psychoanalytic Association* 55: 821–849.

Wallerstein, J. S., and Kelly, J. B. (1980). *Surviving the Breakup: How Children and Parents Cope with Divorce*. New York: Basic Books.

Wallerstein, J. S., and Lewis, J. M. (2007). Sibling outcomes and disparate parenting and step parenting after divorce: Report from a 10-year longitudinal study. *Psychoanalytic Psychology* 24: 445–458.

Watson, M. M. (2003). Clinical issues with African-American women. Pp. 13–153 in *Therapies with Women in Transition,* ed. J. B. Sanville and E. B. Ruderman. Madison, Conn.: International Universities Press.

Weisner, T. S. (1982). Sibling interdependence and child caretaking: A cross-cultural view. Pp. 305–327 in *Sibling Relationships: Their Nature and Significance Across the Lifespan*, ed. M. E. Lamb. and B. Sutton-Smith. Hillsdale, N.J.: Lawrence Erlbaum.

White, L., and Riedman, A. (1992). When the Brady Bunch grows up: Step/half- and full sibling relationships in adulthood. *Journal of Marriage and Family* 54: 197–208.

Whitman-Raymond, L. (2005). Helpful and unhelpful interactions between professionals and parents of children with cognitive challenges: A developmental approach. Ph.D. dissertation, Simmons School for Social Work.

Wiehe, V. R. (1997). *Sibling Abuse Hidden Physical, Emotional, and Sexual Trauma.* Thousand Oaks, CA: Sage Publishing.

Wilcox, L., Kiely, J., and Melvin, C. (1996). Assisted reproductive technologies: Estimates of their contribution to multiple births and newborn hospital stays in the United States. *Fertility and Sterility* 65: 361–366.

Wilson, E. O. (1998). *Consilience: The Unity of Knowledge.* New York: Knopf.

Winnicott, C. (1955). Casework techniques: The child care services. *Case Conference* 1 (9): 3–15; *Social Casework,* 36(1): 3–13. Reprinted in C. Winnicott, *Child Care and Social Work* (7–27). Hitchin, Hertfordshire: Codicote Press, 1964.

Winnicott, D. W. (1953). Transitional objects and transitional phenomena: A study of the first not-me possession. *International Journal of Psychoanalysis* 34: 89–97.

———. (1960). Ego distortion in terms of the true and false self. In *The Maturational Processes and the Facilitating Environment* London: Hogarth Press; Toronto: Clarke, Irwin and Co. Ltd., 1965.

———. (1965). *The Maturational Processes and the Facilitating Environment.* London: Hogarth Press; Toronto: Clarke, Irwin and Co. Ltd.

Woolf, V. (1976). *Moments of Being: Unpublished Autobiographical Writings*, ed. K. Schulkind. New York: Harcourt Brace Jovanovich.

Wortman, C., and Silver, R. (1989). The myths of coping with loss. *Journal of Consulting and Clinical Psychology* 57: 349–357.

Wray, T. J. (2003). *Surviving the Death of a Sibling.* New York: Random House.

Wright, V. C., Schieve, L. A., Reynolds, M. A., Jeng, G., and Kissin, D. (2004). Assisted reproductive technology surveillance—United States, 2001. Division of Reproductive Health National Center for Chronic Disease Prevention and Health Promotion, CDC, USA. http://www/mcbinlmmm.nih.gov///pubmed/15123982?dopt=Abstract (November 11, 2008).

Zukow, P. G., ed. (1989). *Sibling Interaction across Cultures: Theoretical and Methodological Issues.* New York: Springer.

Index

About the Author

Joyce Edward, M.S.S.A., BCD, is a board certified diplomate in clinical social work and has served as a faculty member and training analyst at the New York School for Psychoanalytic Psychotherapy and Psychoanalysis in New York City. She has also been on the faculties of the Adelphi University School of Social Work, the Hunter College School of Social Work, and the Smith College School of Social Work. She has recently been appointed to serve as a mentor for the newly formed Psychoanalytic and Psychodynamic Teacher's Academy, developed by the American Association for Psychoanalysis in Clinical Social Work, the American Psychoanalytic Association, and the American Psychological Association.

Ms. Edward is the recipient of the National Coalition of Mental Health Professionals and Consumers First Annual Consumer Advocacy Award, the Lifetime Achievement Award of the American Association for Psychoanalysis In Clinical Social Work, and the Day-Garrett Award from Smith College School of Social Work. Her publications include *Separation Individuation: Theory and Application* which she co-authored with Nathene Ruskin and Patsy Turrini; *Fostering Healing and Growth A Psychoanalytic Social Work Approach,* which she co-edited with Jean Sanville and *the Social Work Psychoanalyst's Casebook Clinical Voices in Honor of Jean Sanville,* which she coedited with Elaine Rose.

CPSIA information can be obtained at www.ICGtesting.com
Printed in the USA
BVOW041112260412

288678BV00002BB/1/P